Other Books by Gary C. King

An Almost Perfect Murder

Love, Lies, and Murder

Rage

Other Books by Sheila Johnson

Blood Lust

Blood Highway

Blood Ambush

Blood Betrayal

DEAD OF NIGHT

GARY C. KING
WITH
SHEILA JOHNSON

PINNACLE BOOKS
Kensington Publishing Corp.
http://www.kensingtonbooks.com

PINNACLE BOOKS are published by

Kensington Publishing Corp.
119 West 40th Street
New York, NY 10018

All Kensington Titles, Imprints, and Distributed Lines are available at special quantity discounts for bulk purchases for sales promotions, premiums, fund-raising, and educational or institutional use. Special book excerpts or customized printings can also be created to fit specific needs. For details, write or phone the office of the Kensington special sales manager: Kensington Publishing Corp., 119 West 40th Street, New York, NY 10018, attn: Special Sales Department, Phone: 1-800-221-2647.

Pinnacle and the P logo Reg. U.S. Pat. & TM Off.

ISBN-13: 978-0-7860-2140-6
ISBN-10: 0-7860-2140-3
First Pinnacle Mass Market Edition: July 2014

eISBN-13: 978-0-7860-2916-7
eISBN-10: 0-7860-2916-1
First Kensington Electronic Edition: July 2014

10 9 8 7 6 5 4 3 2

Printed in the United States of America

This book is dedicated to the memory of Brianna Denison.

No place indeed should murder sanctuarize;
revenge should have no bounds.

—William Shakespeare

Experience has shown, and a true philosophy will
always show, that a vast, perhaps the larger portion
of the truth arises from the seemingly irrelevant.

—Edgar Allan Poe

Prologue

It was a cold night in Reno, but that hadn't kept the man from prowling through the neighborhoods near the university, looking for that one special girl he was hoping to find. She would be very petite, with long dark hair, and she would be vulnerable and unprotected, like the others had been. He was a very average-looking man, and he was being careful not to do anything to attract attention. He had done this before, and he didn't expect anyone to notice him as he searched for exactly the girl he wanted.

In the area that he was checking out, looking for unlocked doors and easy access, there were a lot of possibilities. It was past three in the morning, and most houses and apartments in the area, made up primarily of student residences, were dark. He was frustrated when the first place he tried to enter was too securely locked and he was unable to break in, even after damaging the door in an attempt to force the door open. He went farther down the street in the neighborhood and tried the door at another likely-looking house, but it was also locked. He could see a faint light inside and decided that there might be someone awake; so after twisting the doorknob a couple of times, he decided to move on. The people who lived in the area were mostly students, and many of them left their doors unlocked, but the ones he'd tried so far were secured. He had to find an unlocked door, or a girl who was outside, alone.

There were plenty of places for the man to hide while he waited for the perfect opportunity. Shrubbery, trees, sheds—all afforded shadowy concealment from the streets and sidewalks. Several times he had ducked back into the darkness when a vehicle would pull up to one of the houses and someone would get out and go inside, but it was never the exact, perfect girl that he was looking for. She had to be just right.

When a car stopped at the dark-colored house down the street from where he waited in the shrubbery and two girls got out, he immediately began watching closely. He edged closer to the house to get a better look as the car pulled away and drove down the street, but the girls had already gone inside. He slowly crept up nearer to the house, taking his time. If the right girl was there, there would be no hurry. He didn't like to rush.

There were several windows in the house, all without curtains. There was a glass door, also uncovered. He watched from outside while the girls got ready for bed. One of the girls went upstairs, but the other girl, who was getting settled in to sleep downstairs on the couch, was in full view from outside. The man's heart raced when he got a good look at her. She was exactly what he had watched and waited for: a tiny girl with long brown hair. She was beautiful. She was vulnerable. This was the one he would take.

The man watched and waited while the girl texted on her cell phone—it seemed like forever to him. Then, after she put the phone away, he gave her enough time to get to sleep before he made his move. It was too easy, he thought; there were no curtains or blinds, unlocked front and back doors, and the perfect girl, right there, waiting for him. She wasn't the first girl he had taken, but she would be the first he had grabbed from inside a house, the first he had taken while she slept. He reached into his pocket and gripped the thong panties he carried, fingering them while he thought about what he would soon be doing to her.

The girl had fallen asleep quickly; she was very tired and it was past four in the morning. She had been out for a long evening, and now all she wanted was to get some rest. She had just fallen sound asleep when something woke her; it was a noise or some kind of movement in the room. When she opened her eyes, all she could see was the pillow above her, coming down quickly onto her head. She opened her mouth to scream, but there wasn't time. The pillow was pushed down so very hard against her face that she couldn't breathe; it took only a few moments until everything went dark. Then, while she was unconscious, she was taken away, out of the house. She vanished without a trace into the dead of night. . . .

Chapter 1

Brianna Zunino Denison, nineteen, a beautiful and popular child psychology major who was in her sophomore year at Santa Barbara City College in Santa Barbara, California, had returned home to Reno, Nevada, for the 2007/2008 winter break. Brianna was so happy to be home for the holiday season, and she had been having a wonderful time, staying with her family at their Southwest Reno home. She had enjoyed spending time with her mother and brother, all her other family members, and visiting with her hometown friends from high school. Now she was making preparations to go back to California; she was due back at college in Santa Barbara on Monday, January 21. Brianna, who always made it a point to party responsibly, had made plans to go out for one last evening with her Reno friends on Saturday night, January 19, before heading back to school. They were going to attend some of the events associated with SWAT 72, an annual three-day college snowboarding event held at Squaw Valley USA, a popular ski resort located in California, forty-two miles from Reno, near North

Lake Tahoe. SWAT, which stands for "Summer Winter Action Tours," was a group that sponsored combined commercial snowboarding and concert events for college students by day, and concerts and parties by night in downtown Reno's casino district. It was Brianna's third year to attend the event, and she and several of her girlfriends had already gone to several of the activities associated with it that were being held in Reno. On that Saturday night, they were looking forward to going to a rap concert featuring Too $hort, which was also associated with the snowboarding group's events.

Brianna had always been very responsible and considerate of her family, and she had provided her mother, Bridgette Denison, a list of the parties that she and her friends would be attending. She also told her mother that since she would be out late and because there would be some drinking involved, she would be spending the night at the home of K.T. Hunter, nineteen, one of her girlfriends from high school. K.T. lived in a rental house that was located in the 1300 block of MacKay Court, near the University of Nevada, Reno (UNR), campus. Neither Brianna nor her mother had any reason to worry—they had known K.T. for several years, and the area of K.T.'s rental home, which she shared with three other girls her age, seemed to be in a safe-enough area of town.

Earlier that day, everything had seemed perfectly normal for Brianna and her family. The day began with her doing some chores and lounging around, wearing sweatpants, in her mother's house. Later that day, she and her mother went out to the movies and saw *27 Dresses*, a "chick flick," which they both liked. At times during the day, however, Brianna began having second thoughts about the evening of music and parties that she had planned to spend with her friends. She was nursing a cold and was not sure that she was really feeling up to going out for a long, late evening of partying. Finally, as she began to feel better later in the day, she decided that she might as well go ahead and go out to the concert, after all. Her mother had reminded Brianna how much she liked the act they were going to see, and jokingly told her daughter that she should go out that night. After all, Bridgette said, Brianna could be sick tomorrow. After gathering up the clothes, shoes, and cosmetics she would take along with her, she went into her mother's bedroom around 8:45 P.M. and said good-bye. She gave her mother a hug and then left.

After meeting up with her friend, K.T., the two girls got dressed and went to the rap concert at the Livestock Event Center together and reportedly had a really great time. Brianna wanted to get close to the stage, so the two girls pushed their way up to the front. They had a lot of fun at the concert, and they both believed it would be an evening to remember. Sometime before 1:00 A.M., the two girls met up with another friend, one of K.T.'s roommates, Jessica Deal. The trio left the rap concert together on a shuttle bus, which dropped them off near downtown, at the Sands Regency Casino and Hotel.

Downtown Reno has been known for some time as a place that is not very safe at night. There are a lot of drug problems, homeless people, panhandlers, and worse—meth addicts and others willing and eager to rob people to feed their habits. The girls were all drinking, but Brianna had reportedly only had a couple of drinks—she never, ever drank to get drunk, her friends said later. The girls stayed in the better areas of the casinos, carefully managing to steer clear of downtown Reno's safety issues. After Jessica left them to go back home to the house where she lived with K.T. and the other girls, Brianna and K.T. decided to have breakfast at Mel's Diner, part of the same Mel's Diner and Drive-in chain that was featured in the 1970s-era movie *American Graffiti*. The diner was located inside the Sands Regency, and they ate there before heading home to K.T.'s MacKay Court home, getting a ride with their friend Ian McMenemy. Brianna was tired and sleepy, and she knew that she would probably have to spend some time calling or texting her boyfriend, Cameron Wilson Done, before she could get some sleep. Cameron was angry that she had gone out with her girlfriends, and Brianna wanted to talk to him about what she considered his unreasonable attitude.

Brianna had spent the previous night at K.T.'s house, too. On that Friday night, she had slept in K.T.'s bedroom, on a crowded bed with K.T. and Jessica. But after returning home from Mel's Diner and not wanting to sleep again in that uncomfortable bed with her friends, Brianna had chosen to sleep on the living-room couch, instead. She had told her friends that she and her boyfriend had been fighting, and that she might want to call him or send him text messages. She felt it would be best if she slept on the couch so that she would not disturb them. It was a decision that would cost Brianna her life, some people later said as they reflected on the case.

Fear did not surface in anyone's mind until approximately nine o'clock the next morning, Sunday, January 20, when K.T. awoke and found that Brianna was not in the same place where she had last seen her at about four in the morning. Brianna had been on the living room's leather sofa, where she had intended to text and sleep. K.T. had provided her with two blankets, a pillow, and a two-foot-tall stuffed teddy bear, which had been given to her by a friend, before saying good night. Brianna had wanted to use the stuffed bear to help prop up her pillow. K.T. had then gone to bed in her own room, which adjoined the room where Brianna was sleeping on the couch, and had told Brianna that if she needed anything just "come in my room."

That morning K.T. and Jessica had gone into the kitchen and had begun making breakfast. At first, when K.T. failed to see Brianna on the couch, she just assumed that her friend had been unable to sleep and had probably gone to another bedroom upstairs. After all, Melissa Hamilton, the roommate who occupied the upstairs bedroom, was gone that weekend. A few minutes later, K.T. checked upstairs, knocked on the bedroom door, and said, "Hey, time to get up." She received no reply and found that the door to the room was locked. She then quickly checked throughout the rest of the house—Brianna was nowhere to be found.

Although K.T. was alarmed when she discovered that Brianna was not anywhere inside the house, she became even more distressed when she noticed that Brianna's belongings were still in the house right where she had left them when the girls came home at four o'clock. Then, when she noticed a stain that looked like blood on the pillow that Brianna had used—two reddish blotches and some spatter—K.T. became terrified. Something was terribly wrong, she knew. She began crying and decided that she should call Brianna's mother.

Frantic and fighting back the hysteria that threatened to overtake her, K.T. called Bridgette on Brianna's cell phone. She told her about Brianna's mysterious disappearance and what she believed to be bloodstains on the pillow. After a brief discussion, Bridgette Denison, whose first thought upon hearing about Brianna's disappearance was that things were "not good," told K.T. to call the police immediately. Bridgette told K.T. that she would be there right away.

The police arrived quickly at the two-story burnt orange house that morning. Perhaps they arrived swiftly because of Brianna's age, but more likely it was because there had been a number of sexual assaults that had occurred in recent months in the immediate neighborhood of the MacKay Court location. Officer Benjamin Rhodes, along with other officers from the Reno Police Department (RPD), was the first to arrive to take what initially had seemed like it would be a simple missing persons report about Brianna Denison. Rhodes quickly learned from questioning K.T. and the other girl that Brianna had gotten ready to go to sleep on the sofa in what the girls referred to as the "common area" of the house, only a few feet away from an unlocked glass-paneled front door. K.T. said that she and the other three girls who lived there often left that door unlocked because of all the coming and going of the residents. They locked their own individual bedroom doors, instead, when they went to bed for the night.

It was, after all, a house for college students, and K.T. said that she and the other girls basically led their own lives. None of them had seen the need to lock the common-area door, until now. Besides, she said, they treated the living room as a "hotel lobby" of sorts, and the door was left unlocked in case someone forgot their keys. Rhodes and other investigators, who became involved with the case later, quickly and easily saw that anyone looking inside from out on the street or sidewalk could have clearly seen Brianna through the glass-paneled front door as she slept, lying on the couch.

K.T. told the police that she, Brianna, and others, including roommate Jessica Deal, had gone out Saturday night, leaving the house sometime between 8:45 and 9:30 P.M. They had spent much of their time that evening at the rap concert and at the Sands Regency Hotel and Casino before going home separately. She told the officers how they had eaten an early-morning breakfast at Mel's Diner before four male friends dropped them off back home. K.T. said that they had watched the four male friends drive away as she and Brianna entered the house through the unlocked front door. She told the officers that they had changed into their sleeping clothes shortly after arriving home, and Brianna had seemed happy when she said good night to her. K.T. said that Brianna was sober at the time, and K.T. told the officers that she had then gone into her own room, taking her dog, a female Chihuahua named Chi-Chi, with her. She locked the bedroom door behind her, got into bed, and slept until around nine in the morning. K.T. told the officers that the dog typically barked a lot, even at her and her roommates. However, on that night, either the dog did not bark at all or, if she did, K.T. had not heard it. She said that she typically woke up whenever the dog barked. K.T.

concluded that if Brianna had, in fact, been abducted, then whoever had done it had been extremely quiet while they were inside the house and had not drawn the attention of the dog.

K.T. also said that she had not noticed any sign of forced entry to the house, confirming the belief that the common-area door had indeed been left unlocked that night. She also said that she had not seen any signs of a struggle having taken place. It looked like Brianna had just gotten up off the couch and left during the night, but that would not have been her style, K.T. said. She was too responsible to do something like that. Besides, she said, Brianna's car was in the shop for repairs, and she did not have any other transportation that would have been available to her, as far as K.T. knew.

There was also the fact that Brianna had left all of her clothes and her other belongings behind. When Brianna had gone to bed that night, K.T. told the officers, she had been wearing sweatpants and a white tank top with pink angel wings, rhinestones, and *Bindi* on the back. She had left behind her wallet, identification, cell phone, shoes, other clothing, and her jacket. It did not seem likely that she would have left the house, willingly or otherwise, without a jacket and shoes, especially at that time of the year. The morning that she disappeared, it was thirty-three degrees outside, far too cold to be walking around outdoors barefoot.

Strangely, however, the teddy bear that K.T. had given her to sleep with was also missing from the house. At first, K.T. said that she guessed that Brianna must have taken the teddy bear with her. It was described as a brown bear with a white belly, featuring a printed rainbow and multicolored balloons.

As the initial questioning continued, K.T. and Jessica told the police officers that they had noticed that one of the two blankets K.T. had given to Brianna hours earlier was still lying on the couch. Meanwhile, the other blanket was clearly out of place, lying on the floor of the kitchen, approximately six feet from the sofa and in line with the path leading toward the rear door of the house. Rhodes and the other cops became even more alarmed when they saw for themselves that the pillow Brianna had used was stained with a substance they believed to be blood.

Jessica confirmed that she and K.T., as well as other friends of theirs, had been with Brianna at the Sands Regency Casino and Hotel when Jessica had decided to call it a night at approximately 1:00 A.M. She explained that Brianna and the others had decided to stay behind for a while longer and that she, Jessica, had obtained a ride home with a man, a complete stranger, whom she had met at the Sands Regency. Jessica had not been able to find a taxi at that time of the morning and needed to be at work in a few hours. She said that she could have easily walked back to the house because it was not all that far away, but it was freezing outside that morning. That was why she opted to take the ride with the stranger, she said. Jessica told the officers that the man was white or possibly Hispanic, about forty-five years old, with a medium build, and was dressed well. She said that he drove a beige or light brown Chevrolet Suburban or GMC vehicle, and she did not know his name. Jessica admitted that she was somewhat naïve and had exhibited what might have proven to be a very serious "lapse of judgment" that morning when she flagged the man down in the parking lot at the Sands Regency. Her actions were particularly risky because there had been a number of sexual assaults either on UNR's campus or in the vicinity of the house she shared with the other girls. Jessica told the officers that since the MacKay Court house was fairly close to the Sands Regency, she had felt reasonably safe in riding with the man. Even though accepting the ride had been a "bad idea" on her part, she said, there had not been anything out of line done by the man, and he had not come into the house when he dropped her off out front at approximately 1:30 A.M. Jessica said that because he had not done anything inappropriate with her, she had no reason to suspect him of anything else. She told the officers that he appeared to be a normal person, not a shady character of any sort. Brianna and K.T., she said, had found a ride home later with some of their mutual friends.

Brianna's mother, Bridgette, gave the officers a detailed description of her daughter. She said that Brianna was five feet tall and weighed ninety-eight pounds, with long dark brown hair, blue eyes, a piercing on the right side of her nose, and a noticeable scar on her left knee. There was nothing to indicate that Brianna had been involved in any kind of disputes with anyone. As far as everyone knew, she did not have any enemies; there was no one who would have wished her any harm.

"Someone walked into my house and took my friend and did God knows what with her," a distraught K.T. said. "She is the nicest person, honest to God. She has such a good heart. It's so sad this happened."

At a loss to explain why the pretty blue-eyed brunette had disappeared, and terribly concerned that no one had heard from her, Brianna's friends and family found themselves now trying to sort things out so that they would be able to help the police as much as possible with their investigation.

Long before he was finished taking statements from everyone at the house, Rhodes realized that they were very likely dealing with much more than a simple missing persons report. Because Brianna's disappearance appeared especially suspicious, Lieutenant Robert McDonald, head of the Reno PD's Robbery/Homicide Unit, ordered detectives and crime scene technicians to report to the house. It was McDonald's day off; but because things did not sound at all good on this particular case from the start, he got dressed and went in to work.

Because of the serious implications, search dogs were brought in right away. However, they failed to pick up Brianna's scent outside, leaving the cops wondering if she had walked out of her own accord or, more likely, had been carried out of the house by someone. As everyone began to assume the worst, the police called in utility personnel from Reno's public works department. The men began removing manhole covers from nearby streets and checking to see if, by any chance, Brianna had been dropped down one of them and into a sewer. However, they failed to find any sign of her.

According to Commander Ron Holladay, of the Reno Police Department, investigators did not initially see any connections or "direct similarities" between Brianna's apparent abduction and the other sexual assaults—at least one of which had involved a kidnapping—but that each case would be carefully examined to determine if there were any common factors between them. Holladay confirmed that those cases were still actively being investigated, and that one immediate, obvious similarity was that they had also occurred during the early-morning hours between four and five o'clock. This had happened quite nearby, within two to three blocks of the MacKay Court address.

"If they are the same suspect, we would like to catch him, obviously," Holladay said.

Holladay also confirmed that a person on the street or sidewalk in front of the house would have had a clear view of the area where Brianna was sleeping, particularly while the lights were still on inside the house.

"Our hope is that Brianna will come home safely and walk through the door," Holladay said. "Our hearts go out to her family, and we hope we can solve this in a favorable way."

Chapter 2

Detective David Jenkins, a thirty-two-year veteran of the Reno Police Department who was nearing retirement and currently assigned to the Robbery/Homicide Unit, was assigned as the lead detective in the investigation of Brianna's disappearance. He arrived at the house soon after being notified of the unusual circumstances of the case. Almost immediately, Jenkins noted that the house was located in the immediate neighborhood where earlier sexual assaults against female UNR students had occurred. In fact, he noted, it was less than five hundred yards from where one of the young women, Virgie Chin, had been abducted by an unknown assailant and sexually assaulted after being driven to another location.

After being thoroughly briefed by Officer Rhodes and the other officers, and after conducting his own questioning of Brianna's mother and the residents of the house, Jenkins saw for himself that the pillow Brianna had used to sleep on was, indeed, stained with what he visually recognized and believed to be blood. Before he could call it blood conclusively, it had to be tested, but his gut instinct from his years of experience with homicide cases told him it was blood. He also saw that the pillow had what appeared to be smears of mascara on it, along with some orange staining and what looked like mucus or phlegm. In fact, he noted that there were three distinct stains on the same side of the pillow, positioned below the mascara stains. Each stain was irregularly shaped and was approximately one inch to three inches in diameter. One of the stains was about the size of a silver dollar. It would require DNA analysis by the crime lab to determine if the bloodlike stains were actually Brianna's, but it seemed likely to Jenkins that it was going to turn out to be hers. Jenkins also found a small bloodlike stain on the blanket that had been left lying on the floor in the kitchen.

After additional questioning, Jenkins learned that *both* the front and rear exterior doors to the house, not just the front door, were typically left unlocked by the girls who lived there.

So which door had the intruder entered the house through? Jenkins wondered. The front door or the back? It seemed likely that he would have used the same door for both entering and leaving the house, due to the comfort level he must have felt upon going inside.

As he walked through the house, Jenkins also noted that the curtains, shades, and other window coverings were limited or sparse. This provided anyone during the nighttime hours who might be outside looking in, from either the MacKay Court or College Drive sides of the house, with an unobstructed view of almost all of the downstairs interior. College Drive, just off North Virginia Street, runs east and west adjacent to MacKay Court. The only outlets from MacKay Court are Imperial Boulevard to the south and College Drive to the north. The house from which Brianna disappeared is nearest to College Drive, making that the most likely route that would have been used by whoever had snatched her—if it turned out that she had, in fact, been snatched. However, it was impossible at this point to say for certain which route had been used. Interviews with neighbors still had to be conducted to determine whether anyone had seen or heard anything suspicious during the hours in question.

Jenkins and the other officers who had reported to the scene believed that Brianna had to have disappeared sometime between 4:30 and 9:00 A.M. After briefly examining her cell phone, Jenkins determined that her last known contact with anyone most likely had occurred at 4:23 A.M., when she had sent and received multiple text messages from her phone as she communicated with someone in Oregon. Checking out the phone number that the text message had been sent to, Jenkins soon confirmed that the person Brianna had been texting in Oregon had been her boyfriend. He was in Oregon at the time of Brianna's disappearance and was immediately ruled out as being a suspect in any wrongdoing related to the case.

Detective Tom Broome, of the Reno Police Department, arrived at the house a short time later, accompanied by several members of the Washoe County Sheriff's Office (WCSO). Among the new arrivals were personnel from Forensic Investigative Services, including forensic investigator Candace Potts. They began carefully processing what they all believed would soon prove to be a crime scene. They looked painstakingly for any kind of clues that they hoped would give them an idea of what had happened there earlier that morning.

Potts photographed the house thoroughly, inside and out, and ran her flashlight along the doors in an attempt to illuminate any fingerprints that might be there. Her efforts paid off; a total of fourteen readable prints were found and retrieved. The latent lift fingerprint cards were sent to the crime lab for analysis. Potts and the forensic team also collected a number of swabs from eight sites in the house in hopes of locating and identifying potential DNA evidence.

Potts saw that there was an unidentified substance on the outside rear doorknob. She collected swabs from that location to analyze later at the Washoe County Crime Laboratory. The blankets and pillow that Brianna used were also photographed, bagged and tagged as evidence, and were taken to the crime lab, along with the other potential evidence that had been gathered at the house.

Before the day was over, officers canvassed the area and began interviewing the neighbors to see if any of them had heard or seen anything unusual on the night of January 19 and in the following early-morning hours. Unfortunately, only one man reported noticing anything that could potentially be a clue.

The man, Daniel Pitman, lived next door to the house from which Brianna disappeared. He told the officers that he had been sitting in his living room, at approximately four-thirty or five on the morning of January 20, using his laptop computer to check out eBay, when he saw a shadowy figure outside his house as it passed by a window, going in the direction of the MacKay Court address. Daniel said that the lights inside his house were off at the time, and it may have appeared to someone outside that no one was awake inside his house at that time of the morning. He also said that he had heard a noise, like someone was turning the door handle or pushing on the door itself. He said that he did not get up to investigate and had dismissed the incident as being nothing to worry about.

"I used to live in a fraternity," the neighbor said. "I thought it was a drunk kid trying to find his way home and had the wrong house."

During the time of the neighborhood canvass, police officers went through garbage cans and, with the help of search-and-rescue officers, also began looking through the bushes in the area to see if perhaps Brianna's clothing, personal property, or even her body could have been lying hidden out there somewhere.

In the meantime, Reno police stepped up efforts to find the man who purportedly gave Jessica a ride home in his Suburban SUV early Sunday morning. They issued a description of the man and his vehicle, asking him to come forward for questioning. The police insisted that he was not a person of interest but merely a potential witness who, they hoped, might have seen something in the neighborhood while dropping off Jessica. It was also possible, the cops reasoned among themselves, that the man could have returned to the house later that early morning and abducted Brianna.

As their efforts to do whatever was necessary to find Brianna were under way, additional plans were put into place to begin a major search effort using dogs, search-and-rescue teams, and volunteers in the days that lay ahead. The Regional Sex Offender Unit, which is comprised of officers from the Reno PD and Sparks Police Department (SPD) and the Washoe County Sheriff's Office, geared up to begin interviewing all of the registered sex offenders living within a mile of the MacKay Court residence. There were at least a hundred sex offenders living within that relatively small area, but there were hundreds more living outside that boundary who would also have to be looked at if their initial efforts failed to turn up a potential suspect, according to RPD spokesman Steve Frady.

"It's something that's done in cases like this," Frady said. "Police detectives are covering every aspect of the disappearance to try to obtain any new leads that can help bring Brianna safely home to her family. . . . We are continuing to talk to people."

There were more than seventeen hundred registered sex offenders living at that time in Washoe County, including in and around Reno, whom the detectives planned to contact as part of their investigation. First, however, they would focus on the hundred or so sex offenders who had been identified as the ones who were living in the immediate area of UNR and MacKay Court, which was considered a low number when compared to the rest who were living in the county. The offenders being looked at had been convicted of all levels of sex crimes and were regularly monitored by the police.

Detectives were told that Brianna was always security conscious and responsible. Why, then, many people wondered, had she gone to sleep in a house with unlocked doors in plain view from the street through a glass-paned door and windows that were uncovered? It just did not make sense, given her reputation for being mindful about her safety and security. Even though she was very tired when she went to bed on the couch, and distracted by the disturbing series of text messages to and from her boyfriend, surely she should have noticed she was in full view of anyone outside.

On Monday, January 21, 2008, K.T. moved herself and her belongings out of the house on MacKay Court and into her parents' home because she no longer felt safe after Brianna disappeared. Not only did she feel unsafe after what had happened at the house, she felt horrible not knowing what had happened to her friend whom she called "Bri." She had, after all, gone to Reno High School with Brianna, and the two had remained close friends after graduation.

"I feel like I'm in a nightmare," K.T. said. "I think this can't be happening, but the more time that goes by, the more it sinks in. I just want Bri to come back home."

Meanwhile, John Walsh, host of *America's Most Wanted* (*AMW*), sent a television film crew to Reno to begin gathering information about Brianna's case. He wanted to get as many details as possible for his next show, Saturday, January 26, 2008, in the hope that putting out the information about her disappearance as soon as possible might yield results. It would be only the first of several *AMW* shows that would be devoted to the case.

Chapter 3

By Tuesday, January 22, 2008, the Reno Police Department announced that the FBI had joined the investigation into the mysterious disappearance of Brianna Denison, according to spokesman Steve Frady. Reno police detectives had been in contact with the FBI's local office since Brianna's disappearance, and the FBI had officially opened its own case and assigned a special agent to work with the Reno police detectives. In the meantime, Frady said that the RPD investigators were continuing to talk to people, getting information and following leads, much of which they could not yet talk about publicly.

"It's all very suspicious at this point," Lieutenant McDonald said. "She hasn't attempted to make contact with any of her family members or friends."

In the two days since Brianna vanished, Reno officers continued to canvass the neighborhood of the MacKay Court residence and the adjacent areas, and continued to conduct searches of the vicinity. One area, that of nearby Rancho San Rafael Regional Park and its perimeter, was also searched extensively, and the effort included the use of helicopters and canine units. A day earlier, on Monday, the Reno Police Department had established a twenty-four-hour tip line in an attempt to generate new leads, which detectives followed up on as quickly as possible, almost as soon as they came in. The authorities also continued looking for the man who drove Jessica home in his SUV to determine if he had seen anything unusual when he dropped her off. So far, despite having obtained security camera surveillance photos that had been taken as the vehicle left the Sands Regency Casino and Hotel on its Arlington Street driveway, their efforts had failed to locate the man. They continued to emphasize that the man was not a suspect in the case, but only a person of interest.

The entire Reno community quickly rallied around the search effort for Brianna. Her photo was featured on casino marquees, and flyers with her pictures were circulated all over town and placed in many of the city's businesses. The Denison family also offered a $100,000 reward in the case, and the local Secret Witness Program offered an additional $2,500.

On Thursday evening, January 24, 2008, a candle-light vigil was held for Brianna at Reno High School. More than three hundred people were there that evening, with most gathered in front of the school in a display aimed at showing that the community, family, and friends of Brianna had not given up hope for her safe return. In addition to holding candles, many wore blue ribbons and chanted, "Come home, Brianna." Posters and signs were handed out to many of those in attendance. These featured her picture, along with text that read, *Please come home, Brianna!*

"Brianna's favorite color is blue," said Nicole Bridges, a close friend of the missing girl. "Another friend of Brianna's came up with the idea of making blue ribbons."

During the following night, another vigil was held at the Lawlor Events Center on the UNR campus. It, too, had a large turnout in support of the missing teen. Family and friends were all wearing blue campaign buttons, sometimes referred to as metal or plastic pins, circular and often with images and text, like those sometimes used by politicians; T-shirts with Brianna's picture were handed out to many people in the crowd.

"Now, with these T-shirts, we can really keep her image alive," said Brianna's aunt Lauren Denison. "Our rallying cry is, if the abductor sees this, open your heart and give her back to us. We want this god-awful person to be aware that he is not only putting a great deal of hurt on Brianna, her family, and friends, but also the people who know him. Please just give her back and run off if you need to. Bring Brianna back to us."

The next evening, Saturday, January 26, 2008, *America's Most Wanted* aired its first of many episodes about the case. Host John Walsh and others provided a detailed narrative of what was known so far by the police. Photos of Brianna were shown several times, and a plea for information was made. Although the airing produced a number of phone calls, none of them, unfortunately, provided any clues whatsoever to Brianna's whereabouts.

Before the first week of the investigation into Brianna's disappearance was over, the man who had driven Jessica home on the morning Brianna had disappeared—the motorist whom the police were actively seeking—finally came forward and identified himself after learning that law enforcement was looking for him. After being questioned, he was ultimately cleared of having had any part in the disappearance.

"We have eliminated him as having any involvement in the case," Frady said. Apparently, Jessica had gotten very lucky that night. Fortunately for her, engaging in such risky behavior as flagging down a perfect stranger for a ride had not resulted in disaster.

Reno police continued their search for Brianna over the next several days, using search crews, dogs, and additional helicopters to comb the vast areas near UNR, the surrounding snowy foothills, and other isolated areas in the region. Police feared that their search dogs, which had failed to produce any results, might completely lose Brianna's scent because of some approaching heavy snowstorm activity. Uniformed officers also continued going door-to-door through the neighborhood in a dedicated effort, ultimately hoping to find someone who may have seen or heard anything suspicious around the time that Brianna was believed to have been abducted. They gave it their very best effort, but they failed to turn up anything significant.

Officers and volunteers also searched other areas around Reno, including along the Truckee River, which runs through the center of town, and along the Union Pacific railroad tracks, with no results.

With no suspects and very few clues, Brianna's family and friends, who wanted very much to believe their loved one was still alive, were frightened beyond description. They desperately hoped that

Brianna was being held captive somewhere, and that her abductor would eventually let her go so that she could return home. Everyone, including the police, had come to believe that Brianna had been taken by a stranger. It was a case that had Reno investigators baffled.

"We're hoping we get the one big clue that comes in and is really critical," Frady said. "We're going wherever we can go with this case."

A little more than a week into the investigation, the local and national news media began to question whether Brianna's disappearance might somehow be related to the earlier UNR sexual assaults against female students. Detectives, however, through Reno Police Department spokesman Frady, said that at that time, there did not appear to be such a connection. At least, there was not one that they had identified as of yet, other than the close proximity to the MacKay Court residence.

However, the police assured reporters that investigators were continuing to examine the earlier incidents, just in case the attacks and Brianna's disappearance were, after all, connected. Detectives also told reporters that they were waiting for results of the crime lab analysis that was being conducted on the suspected blood spots on the pillow and blanket that Brianna had been using on the morning she disappeared.

Meanwhile, Brianna was described in media reports as being a good, responsible, considerate girl, who had maintained a very close relationship with her mother. In her family's own words, she was known for possessing a "tremendous, outgoing nature" and "compassion" for others, as well as for her "million-dollar smile and sparkling blue eyes." Born on March 29, 1988, Brianna was affectionately called "Breezy" by her mother, because she reminded her of a "breath of fresh air on a cool summer day."

Brianna had spent much of her childhood in Reno, Nevada, as well as in Mendocino, California, where her mother was originally from. The family had moved to Mendocino after the sudden, tragic death of Brianna's father, Jeff, who had committed suicide when Brianna was only six years old. The family moved back to Reno in 2002, when Brianna was in middle school, and she graduated from Reno High School in 2006. According to Lauren Denison, her aunt, and a Reno resident, Brianna was strong-willed and feisty as a child. She easily convinced her cousins and friends, no matter their gender, to dress up in girl's clothing to attend her tea parties. Although the boys hated it, they still loved Brianna so much that they always went along with her wishes.

Following graduation from high school, Brianna left home to attend Santa Barbara City College, where she was a sophomore at the time of her disappearance. According to her aunt, she became motivated to study child psychology after undergoing art therapy following the death of her father. Family members described her as spiritual, and they said that she was respectful and trusting. She also loved children and animals, and was especially fond of her dog, Ozzy, a sheltie. She always thought of others, and was always concerned about the well-being of family members and friends.

"She never forgot a birthday or anniversary," Lauren said. "Even when she went away to college, she really kept in touch."

She also loved the beach and the sun, and family members said it was doubtful that she would have ever moved back to Reno on a permanent basis after college. She hated to be cold, her aunt said.

According to her family, Brianna loved to travel and had visited a number of places in the United States and Europe, including Hawaii, New York, Mexico, Jamaica, Japan, Egypt, Hungary, Austria, and France. She had also studied abroad for a year in Rome, Italy, while in high school. However, her friends and family did not believe that Brianna had gone traveling again; they feared something far worse had happened to their little girl. Utilizing local media sources, including the *Reno Gazette-Journal,* Brianna Denison's family pleaded for the public's help in finding her.

"You never know who could have caught a glimpse of something," Lauren said. "This is a person's worst nightmare. If anyone has seen or heard anything, call the police or the Secret Witness hotline. Call even if you just think you saw her. . . . This gives us fear, knowing the type of person she is. She would contact us if she could. We adore her and want her back."

Brianna's maternal grandfather, Bob Zunino, expressed similar feelings.

"From day one, it was love at first sight," Bob said of his granddaughter. "If she's with someone now, we want her back. We want her back."

Fear for Brianna's well-being naturally increased for her family with each passing hour following her disappearance. Despite the best efforts of everyone involved in the search for Brianna, detectives knew only too well that time would soon be working against them, if it wasn't already. Nonetheless, her family was determined to keep Brianna and any information about her in the public eye and maintain a strong public face.

"We have completely decided to keep this alive for Brianna," Lauren said. "We are real people with real emotions. . . . We have put them on the back burner to be strong to do what it takes to get her back. But we are hurting."

Chapter 4

As the investigation into Brianna Denison's disappearance continued, extensive searches of the neighborhood where the MacKay Court home was located, as well as searches of adjacent neighborhoods, utilizing search dogs, consistently failed to turn up any sign of the missing young coed. As Jenkins and his colleagues continued working around the clock in their efforts to find out what had become of Brianna, the earlier nonlethal attacks against young college girls rose to the surface once again. Some investigators, including Jenkins, now began to believe that they could very possibly be linked to one another, either by physical evidence or the suspect's modus operandi, or both.

It was along that line of thinking that prompted the substance that had been found on the rear door of the searched house—which investigators would not publicly identify—to be analyzed swiftly at the Washoe County Crime Lab. An unidentified male DNA profile was quickly developed from a swab of the doorknob's exterior surface. The sample contained a foreign (meaning not specific to the residents of the house) Y, or male, chromosome that matched a foreign Y chromosome DNA profile that had been collected from the rape kit of one of the earlier sexual-assault victims. It matched the rape kit of Virgie Chin, twenty-two, an exchange student from Taiwan who had been attacked by an unknown male a month earlier.

Had the rear door, then, been the suspect's entrance to the house? Or had it been his exit with Brianna? Or both? Jenkins continued to consider the possibility of the intruder's choices at this point, but the evidence was beginning to suggest that he had used the rear door for both entry and exit. The rear door also provided a little more privacy, lessening the chances that the suspect might be seen by someone in the neighborhood.

Delighted that progress had been made so quickly and that the cops now knew that they were almost certainly dealing with the same perpetrator, Jenkins decided to review the Chin case once again to see if he could pinpoint any similarities that might exist between that case and the disappearance of Brianna Denison.

Virgie had been assaulted during the very early-morning hours of December 16, 2007, Jenkins read from the earlier case file. Officer Andrew Hickman, along with several other Reno police officers, had been sent to an address in the 1400 block of North Virginia Street to meet with the young coed who had reported that she had been kidnapped and sexually assaulted. When Hickman and the other officers arrived, Virgie told them that she lived in an apartment at the address where they took her statement.

Virgie had told the officers that she had arrived in her car in the parking lot outside her apartment at approximately two in the morning. She had just gotten out of the car when she was suddenly assaulted by a man she did not know, who knocked her to the ground and violently forced her into a nearby vehicle. He also attempted to choke her with her right arm, by pressing it down across her throat. When he failed in that effort, he placed his hand over her nose and mouth, causing her to pass out. She said that the assailant had covered her face with a hooded sweatshirt. He drove her a short distance, perhaps only three or four minutes away, to a dark and secluded area, where he stopped and threatened her with continued physical violence if she did not cooperate with him.

"If you see my face, if you tell the police, I will kill you," he purportedly had said. He then forced her to commit oral sex, and he penetrated her vaginally with his fingers. Virgie said that when the sexual assault was over, her assailant kept the panties she had been wearing and drove her back to her residence. He also told her that he "might be back."

Virgie was subsequently examined on the evening of the attack for evidence of the sexual assault. Several swabs were collected from her and submitted to the Washoe County Crime Laboratory for analysis and comparison of potential genetic, or DNA, evidence from the unidentified suspect. That was how the match was obtained by Washoe County Crime Lab analyst Lisa Smyth-Roam.

At one point, Reno police placed information on their website for the public concerning DNA testing and comparisons. The site explained that DNA is an acronym for "deoxyribonucleic acid," which is the chemical inside the nucleus of cells that carries the genetic instructions for making living organisms. It is one of two types of molecules that encode genetic information. To the layperson, DNA can seem complicated when, in fact, it can be looked at simply as a blueprint of sorts for a person's body and how everything inside the body works. A person's DNA is unique, unless a person has an identical twin. DNA can be extracted from nearly any tissue, including hair, fingernails, bones, teeth, and bodily fluids. When DNA is left at the scene of a crime, such as what was left at the house from which Brianna Denison was believed to have been abducted, and where there is no known suspect for the investigators to focus on, it can be compared to databases of DNA profiles. Such a data bank is the Combined DNA Index System (CODIS) of criminals or suspected criminals who have been arrested. Often a match to a suspect is obtained, which is what Jenkins and his colleagues were hoping for in this case. CODIS, it should be noted, is maintained by the FBI. It is one of the most frequently used databases by law enforcement personnel. However, Jenkins and his fellow officers were disappointed when the comparisons did not yield any hits in any law enforcement databases, including CODIS. This was a strong indication to the investigators that the suspect was not a known registered sex offender. Registered sex offenders are required to provide a sample of their DNA, which is kept on file indefinitely. All that law enforcement knew at this point was that the person who had assaulted Virgie Chin was the same person who had left his DNA on the outside rear doorknob of the MacKay Court crime scene.

Jenkins noted that Smyth-Roam had also examined clothing that had been worn by Virgie at the time of her abduction and assault. The crime analyst also had collected gray-colored fiber evidence that was consistent with carpet upholstery inside motor vehicles. Like the DNA, the fiber evidence held great potential if it could be conclusively matched up to a suspect's vehicle.

Jenkins conducted a number of follow-up interviews with Virgie in an effort to obtain additional information. As a result, Jenkins learned from Virgie that her assailant was a white male, most likely between the ages of twenty and thirty years old. In her description of him, she said that he was taller than five-nine and shorter than six-three. He was a large man, with a somewhat heavy build. He had brown hair, and she described him as having a long face with a square chin. She said that he spoke English and did not have a noticeable accent or regional dialect. His hands were comprised of "thick, meaty" fingers, she said, and the skin of his abdomen, groin, and upper legs was noticeably lighter than that of his hands and forearms. Virgie said that he wore a mustache and a goatee, with a gap where there was no hair between the ends of the mustache and the top of the goatee. The hair below his chin was about a quarter to a half-inch long and was soft, not prickly like beard stubble normally is. His genital and groin area was without hair, she said, with smooth skin as if hair removal cream or some similar process of hair removal had been used. He also had an "innie" belly button; and his stomach was not excessively firm, but it was not flabby. The hair on his arms was described as light. She said that her assailant did not smell of alcohol, smoke, or cologne.

At one point, Virgie remembered that her assailant

had been wearing a red short-sleeved shirt, with a medium blue neckline. Its finish was slick, like it was made of silk or polyester. It might have had a word embroidered on the upper left breast area. He wore pants that reminded her of sports pants, made out of a soft material with an elastic waistband, but no zipper. She also said that she had seen a baby's shoe on the front seat's floorboard.

Virgie also was able to provide Jenkins with specific details about her assailant's vehicle. She told him that it was a late-model pickup truck, with an extended crew cab, and that it had reclining bucket seats. She described the upholstery as either gray or black, and the vehicle had a raised center console, with a hinged lid, between the bucket seats. It was also equipped with adjustable headrests, which extended up and down on metal posts on both seats, and it had an automatic transmission, she said. She said that there were interior cab lights mounted forward on the roof of the cab above the rearview mirror. The passenger seat height was approximately thirty inches from ground level, and it required a big step up to get inside the cab, she recounted. Virgie's recall in describing the suspect, his clothing, and his vehicle was remarkable, especially considering the terrifying ordeal she had gone through at his hands.

She also told Jenkins that she had been at home when someone attempted to break into the back door of her apartment on the same morning that Brianna had disappeared. Whoever had attempted the break-in had nearly broken the door, as it had begun to buckle inward before the burglar had given up. The doorknob had been broken off in the process. She said that she had called 911, but the would-be intruder had fled prior to police arriving.

When Jenkins read the report of that incident, he realized that it had occurred only a few hours before Brianna disappeared. Because Virgie's apartment was located in the vicinity of the MacKay Court residence, Jenkins could not help but wonder if the same perpetrator had been involved in both instances.

Jenkins later took the vehicle's description provided by Virgie and consulted with a number of local automotive collision and repair businesses. He discovered that a number of Toyota Tacoma four-wheel-drive pickups made between 2001 and 2006 matched the description she had provided of her assailant's truck.

As with any investigation of great intensity, many lines of inquiry were being pursued simultaneously as each respective investigator did his or her part to help solve the case. It was no different in the investigation to solve the mystery of what had happened to Brianna Denison. As Reno investigators already were aware, the December 16, 2007, assault on Virgie Chin had not been the only such crime that had been committed against a female UNR student.

At approximately 5:00 P.M. on November 13, 2007, a twenty-one-year-old female UNR student was walking through a parking lot at an apartment complex in the 400 block of College Drive, not far from where Brianna Denison had vanished, when an unknown male came up to her from behind and placed her in a choke hold. The suspect dragged the victim between two parked cars; at one point, he pushed her to the ground and groped her. She fought her attacker, and she yelled and screamed despite the suspect's warnings to stop making noise and to be quiet. Apparently fearing that all the commotion would draw attention to what he was trying to do to her, the attacker stopped after kicking the victim in the head and arm. He then ran away, leaving behind a few packages of unopened Trojan condoms, which bore an expiration date of 5/2012 and a lot number of TT7135WZ908. Investigators believed that the condoms were possibly placed into circulation in October or November 2007. Jenkins believed that the would-be rapist had accidentally dropped the condoms as he fled from the scene.

As Jenkins had expected, the DNA evidence from the November 13 assault was ultimately linked to the December 16 sexual-assault case, which had already been linked to Brianna's disappearance. The authorities now knew that they were looking for the same perpetrator in all three cases.

Another earlier attack against a female student in her twenties took place around 10:00 P.M. on October 22, 2007, in a UNR parking garage, where campus security parked their vehicles. That incident was also looked at by Jenkins as possibly being linked to the other assaults. In that case, the UNR student reported that she had been raped on the first floor of the parking garage between two parked cars, as in the November incident. Astonishingly, the location where the crime occurred was within one hundred yards of a campus police station. It was clear to Jenkins that the circumstances of the assault and the attacker's method of operation were similar to the other cases. However, the October case was not conclusively connected to the others by way of DNA or other evidence.

Nonetheless, according to Commander Holladay, the detectives were "not discounting the possibility these cases may be connected all together. Some of the characteristics are similar that she has given."

Holladay added, "However, I wouldn't go as far as to say they are an exact match by any means." He said that "not consistent" would be a more accurate way to describe the October incident with the other incidents.

After analyzing the various cases, Jenkins and the other Reno investigators now believed that their unknown suspect might have been acting out, using dominance and power against his victims, and had evidently been escalating in the severity of his attacks. It was also noted at this early point in the investigation that all of the attacker's female victims were all petite with long, straight hair. Even more chilling was the fact that the attacks against the UNR students, as well as Brianna's abduction, had all occurred within a four-block radius. At the very least, everyone agreed that they had a predatory serial rapist on their hands, one who knew this neighborhood.

Because of the UNR students, it was an environment rich with potential victims. Aware that a large number of pretty young coeds were often out at night, coming and going at all hours, the rapist might very well have figured that he had hit the mother lode. If he had it in his mind that he was looking for a particular type of victim with regard to size and general appearance, as many serial predators do, all he would need to do to find one that fit his preferences was to troll the streets around UNR. Then he would eventually find a victim who was an exact match for the type that he desired. Many involved in the case also believed that their suspect was not necessarily new at this; he might have been victimizing young women, perhaps in a different locale, for some time. If he had a criminal record, which seemed likely, the information would eventually surge to the forefront, once they identified the person responsible for the crimes. And the authorities were determined that they would, eventually, find the man they were looking for. As the case geared up to become the biggest manhunt in Reno's history, everyone involved in it also hoped that the suspect had not escalated his aberrant behavior to include murder in the case of Brianna Denison.

By this time, the detectives had worked up a composite drawing or sketch of the suspect, largely from the descriptions provided by Virgie Chin and by Amanda Collins, the alleged October 2007 parking garage victim, and released it to news media outlets. The sketch was also posted in strategic locations around town, including the UNR campus, with the hope that someone might recognize the man in the drawing and call in a tip. The composite sketch was completed by Detective Paul Villa, who worked in the fraud division of the Reno Police Department.

Villa had been doing the double duty for eleven years, sometimes providing as many as thirty sketches of suspects annually. He was the only police sketch artist in Washoe County at that time. As he interviewed a crime victim, Villa focused on the descriptions provided by the victim of the suspect's eyes, nose, and mouth. These were features, he said, that were difficult to change without major reconstructive surgery. In this case, Villa had been helped in compiling the sketch by Amanda Collins, who had been able to see parts of the face of the man who had raped her.

Not long after the sketch was released and circulated throughout the community, Villa, who was also at times running the Brianna Denison tip line, received a call from a man who complained about the composite drawing.

"It's awful," the caller told Villa. "How dare you circulate that! I could do a better job."

Villa told the man that he thought the sketch was a "pretty good" one. "Not the best," he said. "But it's the image the women saw."

Villa thanked the caller and assured him that the tip would be forwarded through the proper channel. Some would later wonder whether the caller had been the person the cops sought.

Lieutenant McDonald said that he placed considerable value on Villa's sketches, which he said were quite accurate.

"As we get more high tech and advancements are made in DNA, we still know there are no replacements for things like sketches," McDonald said. "It's how good the detective is who is interviewing victims and witnesses, and using that talent to put the images on paper."

The description accompanying Villa's sketch, which varied slightly from the earlier descriptions, now indicated that the suspect was a five-eight to five-ten white man in his twenties or thirties, with light brown or dirty blond hair. He had a slender to a medium build and was wearing a dark hooded pullover sweatshirt, athletic-type nylon sweatpants, with black stripes, and white tennis shoes. The victims of the other attacks had described their assailant's age as twenty-eight to forty.

McDonald cautioned the public not to take Villa's sketch of their suspect, or any other artist's sketch, for that matter, as being carved in stone. Rather, they should use it as a guide, something that might spark a memory or remind them of someone they knew.

"Sketches are not a photograph," McDonald said. "They usually have some sort of resemblance to a number of people. The danger in using sketches is that some people may use it as gospel and we may lose a suspect. . . . Detective Villa is very good. He's an asset to the department."

According to Villa, most victims do not forget what their assailant looked like, even when they wait for a considerable period to report the crime. It is often the questions from the person completing the sketch that draws out the details that result in the suspect's image going down on paper. Detectives decide on a case-by-case basis whether to use a sketch artist based on how serious the crime is, whether or not a victim feels like providing the details needed to make the sketch, available lighting where the crime occurred, how close the victim was to a suspect and, perhaps most important, how close a look the victim got at the suspect. Problems can arise, however, when a victim or witness, who understandably has gone through a traumatic and stressful ordeal, focuses only on a specific aspect of the crime—as opposed to focusing on many details— and whether or not multiple witnesses and/or victims remember things differently.

* * *

Investigators also publicly revealed at that time that the suspect had flashed a silver-and-black handgun when he attacked the parking garage victim from behind. He had held the gun to her head as he sexually assaulted her between two parked cars. It was so far the only known instance in which their suspect had shown a weapon to a victim.

"It is hugely important to solve a case like this in the first twenty-four to thirty-six hours," Commander Ron Holladay said, referring to Brianna's disappearance. "Every bit after that reduces our chances of finding her alive."

"Every day that goes by, it's worse," agreed McDonald.

But that was not all that was worse. The stains on the pillow and blanket that Brianna had used had been confirmed as being human blood—Brianna's.

Chapter 5

When it was made public that DNA had linked Brianna Denison's abductor to the same male offender who had kidnapped and sexually assaulted Virgie Chin just before Christmas, along with a description of the still-unknown suspect and the type of vehicle he was believed to have been driving, nothing short of fear combined with outrage could adequately describe the public's reaction. The news even brought in volunteers from two well-known national missing children's organizations: the Laura Recovery Center for Missing Children, out of Friendswood, Texas, and the Polly Klaas Foundation, which was based in Petaluma, California. The crews made plans not to search only in and around Reno—they would also search, on foot, several state parks, lakes, and reservoirs. Their plans also included walking along highways in the area, including U.S. 395 through Carson City and Interstate 80 to the east, all the way to Fernley. Although the assistance from the two groups was welcomed, their involvement caused it to become almost a certainty to the interested public, and to Brianna's family, that the searchers were now very likely looking for a body.

"We are hopeful still that Brianna is alive and hope this new development will help facilitate her release if she is being held against her will," Lieutenant Robert McDonald said about the DNA link between Brianna's disappearance and the rape cases. "We have his DNA, and we are going to find him, if not today or next week or next year, then ten years from now. We will find him. We won't ever give up. . . . There is no statute of limitation on this."

It was also publicly revealed at that time that someone had attempted to break into Virgie Chin's locked apartment only hours before Brianna went missing, a fact that they had only talked about among themselves until now. The police naturally suspected that the culprit was the same man they were already looking for, who they now believed might be someone who frequented, lived, or worked in the area. The attacks had occurred in close proximity to each other, during similar times of the day, with the assailant using similar attack methods. The unknown suspect's DNA had already been entered into the CODIS database, but it had not matched any of the DNA profiles in the system at that time. It was said that there were very large backlogs, however, of DNA profiles waiting to be entered into the system—a possible explanation of why there was no match. Of course, it was also possible, even most likely, that the suspect had not yet been arrested for an offense of the type that would require his DNA to be entered into the system.

The authorities continued to regularly update the public about the details of the case, releasing as much information as they felt was safe to release without risking the integrity of their investigation. The detectives now said they believed that Brianna's abductor had entered and exited through the house's rear door after prowling the university area neighborhoods during the early-morning hours. He may or may not have seen Brianna through the windows as she slept on the couch, though it seemed very likely that he had. But the investigators had to also consider the possibility that he had simply stumbled upon her after entering the house. Detectives said that he was almost certainly looking for a victim when he found Brianna—regardless of how he had found her—and that he had very likely been fantasizing about attacking a woman beforehand.

While many volunteers searched the highways and other outdoor locations, Reno police officers returned to the area of the UNR campus, including the neighborhood surrounding MacKay Court, and posted updated flyers about Brianna's abduction. Commander Ron Holladay also urged members of the public to come forward with any information they might have about the case, no matter how unimportant or trivial it might seem to them. He asked that people be alert about anyone who might have drastically changed his behavior or appearance, moved out of the area suddenly, or may have had items relating to a small child inside his vehicle.

Meanwhile, in the aftermath of Brianna's disappearance, a Brianna Search Operations Center was set up inside Circus Circus Hotel and Casino, located near downtown, where volunteers were recruited and urged to join the search effort. Hundreds of volunteers showed up and registered for what would become daily searches. Flyers, along with blue ribbons that said, *Got Bri,* were distributed by the local and national support and search operations. The dedicated corps of volunteers braved the harsh, cold weather of the northwestern Nevada winter each day to conduct grid searches in designated areas.

It was at this time that Governor Jim Gibbons issued a statement praising the overwhelming community support in the search for Brianna. He urged fellow Nevadans to make themselves available for a large organized search that was set for Saturday, February 2, 2008, in which his wife, First Lady Dawn Gibbons, was planning to participate.

Gibbons's statement read:

This very tragic case has prompted local residents to rally behind ongoing search efforts with overwhelming support. I commend the volunteers and law enforcement personnel who are working around the clock to find this young woman. You can always count on Nevadans to answer the call of those in need, and it gives me great pride to see the community joining together to reunite Brianna with her loving family.

The disappearance of this young woman reminds us that so many children and adults remain missing across this country. My thoughts and prayers remain with all families whose loved ones have not been found.

I thank all those who have given their time to this

cause and I encourage anyone interested in participating in the search efforts to join their fellow Nevadans this Saturday, February 2 at 8:30 a.m., at the Brianna Search Center located in the Circus Circus Hotel and Casino convention center.

The search efforts were not only to look for Brianna, but also for any clues that might be found, such as clothing or other evidence. They were hunting for anything that might shed light on what had happened to her.

"As a mother of a child nearly the same age as Brianna," Dawn Gibbons said, "my heart goes out to the entire Denison family. I continue to be impressed by the overwhelming community support and the many volunteers dedicated to the ongoing search efforts. This tragic case has touched the hearts of so many across the state."

Gibbons's son had attended Reno High School with Brianna.

"Every woman is in danger, every day," as long as Brianna's kidnapper remained at large, said Denison family friend Jennifer Bushman, responsible for spearheading the Bring Back Bri campaign.

Meanwhile, news that the UNR attacks had been linked with the disappearance of Brianna had another impact on the community. According to UNR police chief Adam Garcia, "Brianna has disappeared. She has fallen off the face of the earth. . . . From our perspective, we don't have any credible leads in which to follow up at this point." He said that Brianna's vanishing without a trace appeared to have had an effect on the students' awareness regarding their safety, particularly the female students.

"This young woman was of college age, hanging out with other college kids, and in the eyes of our students, they see a lot of themselves in this situation," Garcia said. "But they really need to be concerned with their safety whether this happened today, last week, or tomorrow."

According to Todd Renwick, associate director of police services at UNR, students had become fearful and were "losing sleep" because of their worry that anyone could become the attacker's next victim.

"We have to try to calm down the campus," Renwick said.

Renwick said his office was receiving more calls than usual from students concerned about their safety. He said that the increase in calls was an indication that the students were now being more aware of their safety, but it also indicated that they were clearly very frightened.

"When you look at the overall scheme," he said, "you can still say the campus is safe. But we have thousands of people who are frightened to go from point A to point B."

"It's unnerving," student Kristin McCarthy, a UNR senior, said. "The flyers serve as a reminder that it's not safe to be alone at night because this is not something that's happened once. It's happened too much in Reno."

Some students who never before had carried pepper spray were now buying it. In fact, area retailers began having difficulty keeping it stocked.

"Who's to say that person [the offender] isn't sitting by the business building right now, you know, just chilling at midnight, waiting to snatch someone up coming from the gym?" asked Sherleta Gambrell, twenty, a sophomore. "It's ridiculous. It's not cool."

Other students chose to focus on self-defense classes.

"With all the events that have happened on campus, it's a good skill to have," said a female student.

DeWayne Manning, a UNR self-defense instructor who also taught boxing classes, was asked to offer a special session of his self-defense class after Brianna's abduction. He explained that the classes were "packed" with students wanting to learn how to protect themselves. In addition to the regular class offering, he provided female students with a booklet called, "Through a Rapist's Eyes," which explained what rapists look for in a potential victim. He also provided the students with a list of "dos and don'ts" to follow if they were ever faced with being raped or otherwise sexually assaulted.

"The more information you have, the better off you're going to be," he told a class. "I want to make you guys aware so when you walk out on the street, you're not going to be a victim or a target."

In light of the fear and concern being expressed in the entire community, and particularly among the student population, Garcia began e-mailing students and university staff to keep everyone updated on the status of the case. UNR police also hosted a safety presentation on campus, and they included a community briefing with Reno police to help address the safety concerns being expressed.

"I find any crime of this nature despicable regardless if it is connected to the campus or not," Garcia said. "In our mind, the close proximity of the events hit home when we first heard of the November assault, and we have followed it closely since then. . . . We are asking that people take their safety into account. I still feel the campus is safe. People should be concerned for their safety, but that should not be translated into being frightened. They should take appropriate actions to protect themselves."

One student, Argituxu Camus, twenty-seven, from Europe, said that she had begun to wonder when the attacks against women in Reno were going to end.

"If someone really wanted to come into our house, they could," Argituxu said. "I don't feel safe here at all. . . . I'm just very scared and have decided with my friends to organize ourselves that if we need to be walking around after five P.M., we coordinate our schedules and all walk together. If we can't do that, we are definitely calling for a campus escort."

Argituxu said that it was frustrating for the female students to have to worry on a daily basis about finding an escort. She said that she often walked to class from her apartment on College Drive, located just across the street from where Brianna had been abducted.

Another foreign student, Mariann Vaczi, thirty, from France, was concerned because she said that someone had attempted to break into the home she shared with Argituxu Camus. She said a man ran away after a resident of the house peered at him through the window blinds after he attempted to open their sliding glass door. She said the incident was not reported to the police.

"It's just shocking," Mariann said. "I've been to another college in America and there was nothing like this happening there."

Yet another female student, Chelsea Utick, nineteen,

said that she had been so affected by Brianna Denison's abduction that she dropped an evening class and added one during the day so that she would not have to walk outside during nighttime hours.

"'Scary' is the right word," Chelsea said. "When I heard that she was my age, I thought, 'Oh, my goodness.' This is really terrifying."

Chelsea said that she remained cautious and always locked her doors and windows.

"It's silly to leave your door open," she said.

As police patrolled UNR's campus in early February, more than one hundred students assembled in the Joe Crowley Student Union building to hear Officer Eric James provide a safety presentation on how a person could help prevent herself from becoming a victim.

"Personal safety cannot be guaranteed, but good personal practices minimize the risks," James told the crowd. "These little tips are what keep people alive."

James explained that most criminals commit their acts from opportunity. He said that when opportunities are decreased by people being aware of their surroundings, keeping their property—such as home and vehicles—secure with doors and windows locked, and just generally being alert, especially when outdoors, people can effectively diminish their chances of becoming crime victims.

Among the tips James offered was to fight for your life if accosted, and to make a scene to try and attract attention from other people, such as screaming and fighting off the attacker. He also advised that wildly flailing one's arms in a move he called "the windmill" can be effective in preventing an attacker from grabbing his potential victim's arms.

"Your first response should be to flee," James said. "Do the windmill and run. It's going to work."

He also advised that using a cell phone, as if taking a picture of a suspect with it, could be "very effective" in thwarting an attack. He also recommended calling the police immediately any time that any sort of suspicious activity was witnessed. To avoid becoming a victim, James said that it was unwise to hitchhike, to avoid taking shortcuts through darkened alleys or behind buildings, and if followed, to make every effort to get to a public place as quickly as possible. He advised that a person should use every means available to defend herself.

"If you are being attacked, kick, scratch, punch, and stab," he said. "Do anything to get away. Aim for sensitive spots. Nothing is off limits."

In the meantime, with hopeful anticipation, Brianna's mother, Bridgette, held out that her daughter would be returned to her, unharmed. At the same time, though, she began bracing herself for the worst.

"I told Bridgette that I am amazed at how she is managing," longtime friend Catherine Farahi told a reporter for *People* magazine. "And she said, 'Wait until they tell me they have Bri's body, and we'll see how strong I am.'" Nonetheless, Catherine said that the family had not given up hope for Brianna's safe return.

In reality, Bridgette Denison, a skin care expert

who worked with a plastic surgeon, was heartbroken, as any parent would be, over the failure of the countless number of searches to turn up any sign of her daughter.

"I am scared and empty and lonely," she said. "In nineteen years, I have never gone twenty-four hours without talking to her—it's just killing me."

Interestingly, Brianna Denison was characterized by so many of those who knew her as a selfless person who, had someone else been missing, would have been out there herself, volunteering, braving the harsh weather, and taking part in the search effort, trying her best to help in any way.

Chapter 6

As the search for Brianna continued, it was pointed out by the Reno Police Department that recent legislation with regard to DNA had made the collection of DNA from suspects of certain crimes mandatory. Nevada was one of the states affected by the legislation, and the sudden surge of DNA samples had caused a serious backlog in the entering of the DNA profiles into databases for most labs, including the Washoe County Sheriff's Office Crime Lab.

Washoe County had fallen way behind in processing DNA samples in October 2007, when the Nevada State Legislature required that all convicted felons provide DNA for the FBI's CODIS database. Naturally unhappy that their suspect's DNA profile had not matched any that had already been entered in the system, the police and local business leaders, along with the Denison family, appealed to the public to raise funds so that approximately three thousand DNA samples of known offenders in Washoe County could be analyzed and entered into the system in a timely manner. After it became clear that the backlog could mean a delay of six months or more before the possibility of a match could be made of their suspect, local residents and casino owners quickly raised $181,000 to help clear the backlog. This could give them results in a matter of weeks instead of months, *if* their suspect had a felonious criminal record and had been required to provide his DNA sample. It was, admittedly, a big *if,* but the swift fund-raising was amazing to law enforcement.

"It was really unbelievable," said Deputy Brooke Keast, Public Information Officer for the Washoe County Sheriff's Office. "The community and business leaders are the heart and soul of this fundraising effort. An elderly woman from Georgia on a fixed income called and was very emotional because Brianna reminded her of her two granddaughters. She wanted to send us a donation to do something for Brianna."

Meanwhile, as police continued to remind Reno residents that they were looking for a violent serial rapist who may have turned to murder, sporting-goods stores and gun shops reported that sales of pepper spray and Taser devices—stun guns—had been selling faster than they were able to keep the items stocked. Reno's young women seemed to be looking for anything they could find to help defend themselves in the event that they were victimized. Some stores even reported having people on lengthy waiting lists for the self-defense items they sold.

"We probably sell thirty to forty of them a day," said Robert Currier, of Scotland Yard Spy Shop, located on Virginia Street, regarding sales of pepper spray. "We have a list of thirty people who have already paid and are waiting for us to stock it again."

David Currier, Scotland Yard Spy Shop's owner, said that he traveled to Sacramento, California, to purchase 160 additional canisters of the pepper spray after selling more than four hundred cans in his shop.

Other stores, such as REI, reported that they were having to turn away customers.

Yet another store, Sports Authority, which had two outlets in Reno, reported that their stock of pepper spray had been depleted for days; and ABC Lock and Glass, in nearby Sparks, Nevada, depleted its stock of more than one thousand cans on the weekend following Brianna's disappearance.

"One friend who couldn't find any [pepper spray] in the stores is walking around with a pocketknife," said K.T. Hunter. "We are all terrified."

Firearms sales were also way up. One gun shop reported that they had two to three times as many people as usual looking at guns because of the sexual assaults and Brianna's disappearance. A five-shot .38-caliber revolver that sold for more than $600 was the most popular gun being purchased by their customers.

As word of the near-panic buying of defense items got out, Reno police issued advice that the purchasers of the weapons and pepper spray needed to be sure to learn how to use them.

"I was talking to a young woman the other day who purchased pepper spray and said she had no idea how you were supposed to use it," said Kellie Fox, a Reno police officer. "If you don't know how to use something, or you're not comfortable with it, it's not going to help."

* * *

By the third week of the search effort for Brianna, Reno police investigators continued to follow up on more than a thousand tips and leads that they had received from a variety of sources, including the Secret Witness Program tip line. Volunteers continued to go out nearly every day, and they were searching again in areas where the snow had begun to melt. At any given time, there were as many as twenty searchers on horseback and countless others on foot using more than seventy trained search dogs in the organized efforts to find Brianna. Local restaurants also donated meals on a daily basis to the search command center.

Meanwhile, efforts were under way through business donations and citizen contributions to set up the Bring Bri Back Foundation. This was an organization designed not only to help find Brianna Denison, but also to help educate people looking for other lost loved ones in how to set up search command centers, conduct the searches, and do the many other things that can help in search efforts for missing persons.

Even though the days had turned into weeks since Brianna disappeared, the community was nowhere near ready to give up the search efforts. Her mother had effectively used the many media opportunities that had been made available to her in order to keep the public informed about her daughter. She also hoped perhaps to appeal to the sympathy of Brianna's abductor to let her go, if he was still holding her. In fact, on Thursday, February 14, 2008— Valentine's Day—Bridgette Denison went on television to speak to her daughter in the hope that she might see and hear her heartfelt message.

"I just want to say to my daughter, Brianna, that I love you and I miss you," Bridgette had said. "Nobody's ever giving up. There are thousands of people looking for you, and I don't want you to give up. I know you're hurt, honey, but I really need you to hang in there."

Chapter 7

The next day, Friday, February 15, 2008, Alberto Jimenez stepped out to grab a sandwich for lunch at a nearby Subway restaurant located near where he worked as a senior manufacturing engineer. His workplace, EE Technologies, was located on Double R Boulevard in South Reno, near a brush-covered field. It was a cool, clear day and on his way back to work he took a shortcut through the field, located on the southwest corner of Double R Boulevard and Sandhill Road, which had, until recently, been covered with snow from a recent storm. As he walked back through the field to return to work, Alberto noticed an evergreen tree that was lying out of place in a field of sagebrush. He could see two bright-colored orange objects, "neon-like," beneath the tree. At first, he could not make out what they were. He thought they looked like fabric material of some sort and wondered what they were. These items, too, seemed out of place lying in the middle of a sagebrush field. As he came closer, he saw that they were brightly colored orange socks with yellow flowers, on a human-like form. At first, he thought he had stumbled upon a discarded department store mannequin, but he was horrified when he realized that the socks were being worn on someone's feet—actual human feet. Curiosity, however, overcame his horror and caused him to move even closer to get a better look at what he had found. He soon was able to tell that he was looking at a dead female body, nude except for the bright orange socks, lying underneath a discarded Christmas tree. There appeared to be a wound of some type on her right arm, and the right half of her face was almost devoid of flesh, leaving two rows of teeth showing. There were no weapons of any kind that Alberto could see. It was at about that moment that he realized he needed to get some help quickly. Although he had heard about the Brianna Denison case, he had not made the connection in his mind at that point that the body might actually be hers. Alberto was unnerved by his macabre discovery and headed quickly back to work to tell his boss, EE Technologies manager Scott Ferris, about what he had found. Retracing Alberto's footsteps, the two men returned to where the body lay in the field, ten feet or so from the road.

They saw that the body, lying faceup, was in a shallow ditch or gully, and they could tell that it appeared to be a young white female. They noted that there was no flesh on the corpse's face, as if animals had gotten to it. They could distinctly see the teeth, and they saw that they looked as though they were very white. The woman's left arm was raised above her head, and her right arm was bent, exposing the open wound that Alberto had noticed. Except for the obvious decomposition in the area of the face, the rest of the body appeared normal—"like a body," the men said. Scott Ferris took out his cell phone and called 911 at 12:13 P.M. to report the gruesome discovery.

The police sprang into action immediately, and only six minutes later, Officer Victor Ruvalcaba, of the Reno Police Department, was among the first of several officers to arrive. He looked closely at the body and confirmed that there was decomposition on the head and face, and there was some deterioration of the skin tissues. He could tell that the body appeared to have been there in the field for some time, but he could not say for how long with any degree of certainty because of the cold weather, which might have served to preserve it for a time. He began photographing the corpse in the position where it had been found. Suspecting a likely homicide, officers utilized yellow crime-scene tape to cordon off 2.5 acres surrounding the area where the body lay. Many of those present already had a gut feeling that the body was that of Brianna Denison. However, because of the corpse's condition and the fact that there was no means of identification present, no one could say so with absolute certainty. According to Steve Frady, they did not have an ID, "not even a tentative ID."

Frady told an Associated Press reporter who had shown up at the site, "I'm not going to speculate, because we don't know who the person is. We're processing this as a crime scene. We do that with death investigations. They are gathering information and evidence and photographing the area. . . . We don't know how long the body has been out there. It's definitely a female. We don't know the age."

* * *

It was not long before Detective David Jenkins was notified of the female body found in the field, and he arrived at the scene shortly after being told about it, feeling that the worst had happened and Brianna Denison was no longer lost. He was followed by District Attorney (DA) Richard Gammick and Deputy District Attorney (DDA) Elliott Sattler, who had been carrying the Washoe County District Attorney's Office "homicide cell phone" at the time. The DA's office has a system in which the DDAs each take turns carrying this cell phone. After receiving a hit, the DDA passes the phone on to another deputy district attorney, who keeps it until that DDA receives a so-called hit.

Investigators on the ground were also supported by a helicopter from the Washoe County Sheriff's Office, which was used by the pilot for aerial observation and photography of the site, in part to help map out the area for law enforcement from the air and to examine the scene from a bird's-eye view to determine whether there were any other bodies or other potential evidence in the area. As it turned out, after taking a thorough look, the helicopter crew could see that there were no other bodies or additional evidence. When the area was mapped, it was noted that the location where the body was found was approximately eight miles from the house where Brianna disappeared.

Jenkins and the others saw that a large gray rock lay on the right side of her body, the significance of which, if any, was not immediately apparent. The investigators also found two pairs of women's thong underwear beneath the corpse's right thigh. These were a petite size, and they were intertwined. One pair was pink and white and made of lace, and was decorated with hearts. The other pair was darker in color and had a Pink Panther design on it; this was the character that appears in movies and cartoons. Appearing to be somewhat stained, the thong panties were bagged as evidence and would later be examined for a DNA profile. The discovery would soon receive nationwide attention as investigators attempted to identify the persons who owned the underwear. For now, the authorities were keeping the information about the panties to themselves.

The news media had also shown up at the site soon afterword about the body had gotten out via the police scanners that they always monitored. Reporters and cameramen were keeping a vigil of sorts just outside the perimeter of the designated crime scene. At times during that long afternoon, an occasional passerby would walk up and ask if Brianna had been found, saying that they had volunteered for some of the search teams and had spent time looking for the young woman. They expressed their feelings of dread and dismay, saying that they hoped the body that had been found did not turn out to be Brianna's.

The remainder of the day was spent photographing the entire area, being sure that there were plenty of images of the body from many different angles. Detectives from the Reno Police Department, as well as the Washoe County Sheriff's Office, crime scene technicians from the Washoe County Crime Lab, and investigators from the FBI worked in the field throughout much of the afternoon. They combed the area where the body was found for clues, gradually working their way outward to include much, if not all, of the field that had been cordoned off.

Nearby open fields were also searched by police officers.

By 5:00 P.M., the body in the field still had not been positively identified. It had been partitioned off and shielded from the public's view with black draperies as the authorities prepared for its removal and transport to the Washoe County Morgue, located only a few miles away. By the end of the day, investigators speculated that the body had been at the location where it was found for at least a week, possibly a great deal longer. It was difficult for anyone at the scene to tell for certain, partly because the area had previously been covered in snow. If not for the recent snow, the investigators believed that the body, in all likelihood, would have been discovered sooner.

Dr. Ellen Clark, a forensic pathologist and chief medical examiner (ME) for Washoe County, had first viewed the body at the site of its discovery. When she arrived, the scene had been cordoned off. She was taken to the side of the field where the body had been discovered. The body was lying in a culvert or ravine, and there were several sticks and evergreen tree debris fragments over the top of the body, which was nude except for the orange socks. Dr. Clark noted the two pairs of panties under Brianna's right thigh, and she saw there had been fairly conspicuous scavenger or carnivore activity to the face and upper right side of the shoulder.

Some animals had consumed part of the fleshy portions of the face and the front of the body, Dr. Clark reported.

After Brianna's body was transported to the coroner's office, Dr. Clark performed her initial examination. The body was described in her report as that of a petite, young Caucasian woman, approx-imately five-two in height and weighing 107 pounds. Several evidence swabs were taken from the body and were given to Marci Magritier, a WCSO forensic investigator. According to Dr. Clark, there was an obvious neck injury in the form of a ligature groove or furrow encircling or extending over the front of the neck.

Lieutenant Robert McDonald also showed up at the crime scene that afternoon, and he could see in Jenkins's face and in the faces of the other investigators that the hope everyone had held out for so long was finally beginning to fade away. After looking over the crime scene, McDonald was now almost certain that the body that had been found in the field spelled bad news for Brianna's family. He and another detective drove to the home of Brianna's mother and, as gently as they could, brought her up to speed on everything that was occurring. This was an attempt not only to inform her of the events, but also possibly to prepare her for the worst news that she would likely ever receive.

McDonald told Bridgette that the body was most likely going to prove to be Brianna's. She asked them about Brianna's nose piercing and the small stone it held, and whether the ears on the body they found were pierced or not—Brianna's ears were not pierced—and whether they had observed the scar on her ankle. McDonald could only tell her that they were unable to determine those identifying distinctions because of the elements and that they would have to wait until the autopsy and DNA analysis to determine whether the body was Brianna's.

Meanwhile, detectives noted that the area where the body was dumped was within a minute or two of the freeway, causing them to wonder whether the location was familiar to her killer because it was on his way either to or from home to work. They also considered that it might have been familiar to him because of having to drop off a child at school or day care, or perhaps picking up a child before going home. There probably had to be some element of familiarity that brought him to that area to dispose of the body, the cops reasoned.

The detectives also had to consider whether their suspect was even still in town. It had, after all, been nearly a month since Brianna had disappeared, if the body proved to be hers. If he was single, it would have probably been a good idea if he had left town. On the other hand, if he was married or otherwise attached, perhaps with a child, his sudden departure might raise flags when it was coupled with the public descriptions that had been released of the suspect and his vehicle. If that was the case, it seemed reasonable that he would want to stick around for a while, let things cool off a bit, and then leave. But there was also the question of whether he could control himself during such an interim, and not offend again. He had, after all, been fairly brazen at first, as if he was trying to challenge the authorities to find him and stop him. But after Brianna's disappearance, the attacks seemed to stop, which returned the investigators to the question of whether the attacks had stopped because the killer had left town or because he was controlling himself to allow things to cool off? No one knew, of course, at that point, but nearly everyone close to the case agreed that the assailant was obviously being careful not to raise any flags that could point to his identity.

The next morning, Saturday, February 16, 2008, officers took search dogs through many of the other open fields in the area near the crime scene, along with members of the Washoe County Sheriff's Search and Rescue Team. It did not appear that anything else of significance was found during the searches subsequent to the discovery of the body— if there had been, the police were not talking about it yet.

In the meantime, later that day, a definitive autopsy was performed on the body. Like everyone had expected, but dreaded, Dr. Ellen Clark determined through DNA analysis that the remains found in the field were those of Brianna Denison. Ligature injuries and sexual-assault injuries were identified, with no defensive wounds being noted. Dr. Clark also concluded that Brianna had been the victim of a homicide and that she had died as a result of asphyxia by strangulation. The ME also concluded that the elastic strap or band of the pink thong underwear fit the configuration and size of the ligature mark around Brianna's neck.

The two pairs of panties found beneath Brianna's right thigh were examined at the crime lab by Lisa Smyth-Roam and found to contain both male and female DNA profiles foreign to Brianna's known DNA profile. Smyth-Roam also analyzed swabs that Dr. Clark had collected from the exterior surfaces of Brianna's genitalia from which she identified a sperm fraction—further analysis by Smyth-Roam resulted in the identification of a complete male DNA profile. Not surprisingly, one of the thong panties found with Brianna's body also contained the same unidentified suspect's DNA profile, which had been established from two of the victims of the earlier attacks of UNR students and which also had been found on the outside rear doorknob of the house from which Brianna had been taken. For all that detectives knew at this point, their suspect's DNA could very well be sitting in the Washoe County Crime Lab's backlog of samples waiting to be entered into the system. It was, at the very least, frustrating that they could not get a hit on the suspect's DNA. Investigators continued working under the theory that Reno had a serial rapist on its hands, and that he had now graduated to murder.

The black Pink Panther panties were not Brianna's, and the detectives wondered to whom they had belonged. They also actively tried to determine to whom the unknown female DNA on them belonged, but there were no immediate hits. It was possible, they reasoned, that it belonged to yet another woman who might have been assaulted. Investigators also considered that the underwear could possibly have been stolen in a burglary. Police later placed photos of the thongs on a website about the case. They asked the owner to come forward because she might have information that could lead police to the man who killed Brianna. They emphasized that they really needed the woman's help in finding their suspect.

"I would say this is a serial rapist," Deputy Police Chief Jim Johns said at a news conference held shortly after the body found in the field had been positively identified as Brianna Denison. "We have two, probably three cases linked through DNA. The totality of the information in this case leads us to believe it is a sexually motivated crime. I'm worried this guy is still out there, and I'm worried somebody else is going to get hurt."

Johns told reporters that investigators believed that their suspect lived somewhere near the UNR campus, located just north of Reno's downtown casino district, and that because of his familiarity with the city, they were all but certain that he lived somewhere in Reno, if not near the campus. Johns also said that it was possible that the suspect's workplace might be closer to the city's southeast side, near where Brianna's body was found. He said that publicity surrounding the case could result in the suspect stopping his attacks, but Johns added that investigators feared that he might strike again.

"Somewhere in our community there is a wife, a mom, a girlfriend, a sister who recognizes this suspect," Johns said. "Likely, he looks like somebody you would least suspect, but that is the person who is responsible for this crime."

Johns also said that investigators were still working under the presumption that the same person was responsible for the UNR attack in which he boldly raped a woman at gunpoint in the same parking garage where the campus police parked their cruisers. Johns said that he believed the "chances are very good" that police would catch the perpetrator.

"It could be tomorrow, next month, or next year," he said. "We are going to find this suspect."

Johns told the public that the community could be of great help in the identification and arrest of the suspect in the case. He asked that the community remain observant and, in particular, to look for changes in behavior of people they might know who matched the general description of the suspect, even if they did not believe the person being observed could be capable of such heinous crimes as had been committed in Reno. He said the signs that people should be looking for in potential suspects could be a change, such as if the person had suddenly become overly anxious or nervous, or someone who had suddenly quit his job or moved away from the area without explanation, or someone who had unexpectedly sold a vehicle that resembled or matched the description of the truck previously provided by Virgie Chin.

Meanwhile, investigators began talking publicly about offender profiles. Although they had been working with the FBI's Behavioral Science Unit (BSU) on producing a profile of the Reno serial sexual predator, who had now turned to murder, Reno police detectives and officials were also in contact with New Jersey psychotherapist and forensic social worker John Kelly.

Kelly described himself as a behavioral profiler whose firm, System to Apprehend Lethal Killers (S.T.A.L.K., Inc.), was in the process of preparing a profile report about Brianna's killer for the detectives. Their motto, appropriately, was "Solving murders is our business." Lieutenant Robert McDonald, however, was quick to point out that Kelly's reports and opinions had not been solicited by Reno detectives.

Nonetheless, Kelly said that his concern focused on the fact that many serial killers were serial rapists before they began killing. Kelly said Brianna's killer was likely a narcissistic egomaniac with a God complex, and that he was likely enjoying the attention he was getting on television and in newspapers, particularly since murdering Brianna. He likely also enjoyed the fear he had created within the community.

Kelly said that not only did the suspect have power sexually over someone, but now he had experienced power over life and death. Once he crossed that line, it was hard to go back. The suspect was definitely a budding serial killer, Kelly stated, and he said he didn't think he was going to stop.

Kelly believed the killer likely participated in some sort of athletic activity, given the type of clothing he was described as wearing during his attacks. Rapists and sexual killers fantasized a lot about wielding power and control over their victims, Kelly said, and often became addicted to those fantasies. Stressful situations, such as a divorce or the loss of employment, often caused such individuals to cross the line. The way they dealt with stress was to stay in the fantasy all the time, Kelly said, adding that was very soothing for them and helped to take them out of the reality of what they were doing.

Such people, Kelly said, often began their aberrant behavior as voyeurs, often peeking into windows of unsuspecting victims. The victims in Reno's cases, Kelly noted, were similar in appearance, and it seemed likely that their attacker had been watching them before striking. He also said that the killer was probably familiar with the area where he dumped Brianna's body. That was the point at which they were most vulnerable, since they tended to go somewhere they believed was totally safe and familiar. They also had to have the ability to make sure no one was coming in either direction, Kelly added.

Kelly said that Brianna's killer might be shorter than the average male. Since he was driving a truck with some height, Kelly said the killer might feel like he is a king sitting on a throne as he looked down on others. It could also explain why he chose victims who were not tall. Since the suspect was going after short women, Kelly said, that told him that the man wanted to make sure he had complete control. Kelly said that he didn't believe the killer was very tall, or didn't feel like he could control a taller victim.

Former New Orleans detective Larry Williams, who was working at the time of Brianna's murder as a forensic security consultant, told the Reno cops that it was his opinion that the killer would likely continue raping women, perhaps without a desire to kill his victims. However, Williams said, that assailant might resort to murder if he lost control or otherwise believed he had no choice. If he believed he did not have a choice, Williams said, that rapist would not think twice about taking another life. Williams also believed the killer might be taking advantage of the naivete of younger college students.

"These students don't think about all of the horrible things that can happen," Williams said. "They are living in an area where things are positive, and they drop their guard. They are normally not concerned with the dark side of life."

Reno police officials, however, emphasized that despite the profiles that others were doing of their killer, the FBI BSU profilers said that it was much too early to be calling Brianna's murderer a serial killer or to speculate that he might become one. Lieutenant McDonald went a step further by stating that he did not necessarily agree with Kelly's opinion, which was based largely on media reports, that their suspect was becoming a serial killer.

"There is no illusion that the suspect is a serial rapist, and he is clearly a murderer, but is he a serial killer?" McDonald asked. "We don't know. . . . We've been calling him a serial rapist. It is what it is. You've got a guy here in four instances and all he's trying to do is rape young women, all of them in good shape with long hair. . . . He certainly has a target group in mind."

McDonald added that there had been a considerable amount of guessing about what happened in the sexual attacks and Brianna's murder, and that much of the guessing had not been accurate and was mostly speculation.

"These speculations are creating a sense of a different individual than the one who we might be looking for," McDonald said. "Although this person is a deviant, he probably wouldn't appear as a monster in the community walking down the street. You wouldn't recognize him as a deviant."

Bridgette Denison later said that the detectives had told her that it was now their opinion that Brianna had not been abducted from the MacKay Court residence, as they had originally thought. She said that they now believed that Brianna was killed inside the house, and her body removed after death.

"They think he strangled her right then and there," she said. "And it was a matter of seconds. That's all I know. I did not want any more details."

She issued a statement in which she thanked the community and the police for their help during the search for Brianna: *On March 29, 1988, Bridgette and Jeffrey*

*Denison were given the incredible gift of their daughter Brianna.
On January 20, 2008, she became the daughter of our entire
community. . . . We ask once again that if there is anyone out
there with information, we beg you to come forward. Now is
the time.*

Governor Jim Gibbons issued a statement of sympathy to the Denison family, asking the community to
continue helping the police in their efforts to find the
killer of Brianna Denison: *Brianna's story has clearly
captured the hearts of our entire community and state.*

Even though the search for Brianna was now officially over, the Reno community continued to do
its part in remembering the slain young woman by
wearing blue ribbons and placing them on trees and
other locations, as requested by her family. It was not
long before the local Walmart stores, craft shops,
and other retail outlets sold out of the royal blue
ribbon, Brianna's favorite color, which many people
began referring to as "Bri Blue." Now that her body
had been found, the search for Brianna's killer had
quickly become the focus of the community.

"Now we're on a manhunt," Brianna's mother said.

There were still a lot of questions that the detectives hoped they would soon be able to answer. If Brianna was killed in the MacKay Court house, did her
killer rape her there before killing her? If so, why
had no one in the adjacent bedroom heard anything? Or did he kill her and then rape her corpse,
perhaps at a different location? At what point did
the killer remove her clothing? She was reported to
have been wearing sweatpants and a light top when
she went to bed on the couch. Where were her
clothes? Had he kept the clothing items as souvenirs
or as a trophy of his kill? Or had he disposed of
them at a still-undetermined location? And what

happened to the teddy bear that Brianna was using to prop up her pillow? It was nowhere to be found. It had, after all, been reported by Virgie Chin that a child's shoe was on the floorboard of his truck. Had he given the teddy bear to a child, perhaps his own? As Jenkins and his colleagues prepared to continue moving forward in their search for Brianna's killer, it became obvious that the answers to many of their questions might be difficult to obtain—if they could ever hope to obtain them at all.

Chapter 8

On Friday night, February 22, 2008, a week after Brianna Denison's body was found, an outdoor candlelight vigil was held at the industrial area location where her body had been found. A white cross had been placed in the field near the spot where Alberto Jimenez had stumbled upon the then-unidentified corpse, and mourners piled dozens of floral bouquets at the location. More than five hundred teddy bears had also been placed there, along with other stuffed animals and hundreds of blue ribbons as the large crowd of candle-bearing mourners paid their respects to the slain young woman. The mayor of Reno, Bob Cashell, along with a great number of the people that had been involved in the search effort, showed up.

"This is a great showing that this community is not going to cower to a monster like this," Mayor Cashell told the crowd at one point.

Lauren Denison was there, along with other family

members and friends. She said that they were all overwhelmed by the show of support.

"Here you have this horrible person who is still on the loose, and you just pray to God he won't hurt or kill anyone else," Lauren said. "On the other hand, you have this phenomenal outpouring from people. How wonderful. . . . It's just so overwhelming."

Schoolchildren placed a sign at the memorial that read: *You changed a community. You changed a nation. We will never forget you.*

The following night, a celebration-of-life ceremony for Brianna called "Live, Love and Unite" was held at the Reno-Sparks Convention Center in honor of the slain coed. More than three thousand mourners attended to pay their respects to Brianna and her family; many of her loved ones vowed they would never forget her. More than twenty of her friends went onstage in front of the crowd, many of them crying, to pay homage to the girl they had loved.

"She was always an angel that protected us," said Brianna's best friend, Danielle DeTomaso. The two young women had been friends since they were in nursery school together. "Now she's with her father watching over us, guiding us as we grow. Even though she's not on earth, her spirit will live in our hearts forever."

"Brianna is a strong and glorious masterpiece who touched lives the world over," said a family friend, Jain Lemos, between tears.

Another good friend, Daneh Farahi, walked up to the microphone and tearfully said, "God needed an angel to watch over the rest of us, and he chose the best angel. While we cry because we miss her, we all now have an angel watching from above."

Others spoke about Brianna's kind heart.

"She always was concerned about others, giving and sacrificing what would be good for herself," her cousin Ashley Zunino said.

Brianna's aunt Lauren asked the group of mourners to keep Brianna in their hearts and minds as police searched for her killer. Lauren stated that "we have a job to do to bring this person to justice."

Marc Klaas, who lost his daughter, Polly, to a murderer, was also there to pay his respects, having traveled to Reno from out of state. Klaas founded KlaasKids Foundation after his daughter, at the age of twelve, was abducted at knifepoint from her mother's Petaluma, California, home during a slumber party on October 1, 1993, and was later strangled by Richard Allen Davis. Klaas obviously felt the need to be there because of the common bond he shared with the Denison family.

"Bri's family has joined a fraternal legacy, but the price of admission is the loss of a child," Marc Klaas said. He also told the crowd that they should be proud for coming together as a community. "You came out to take a stand against injustice and look evil in the face. Everyone across the country is watching how Reno has reacted to this."

Appallingly, the Westboro Baptist Church staged one of its notorious protests at the memorial service. They garnered little attention and even less publicity for its efforts.

* * *

Toward the end of February 2008, the Reno detectives, working with the information they had so far put together about their suspect, decided to contact a legal brothel called the Moonlite Bunny Ranch, located about thirty miles south of Reno. They wanted to see if they could turn up any new leads. Everyone realized it was a long shot, but they took what descriptive information they had and contacted the brothel's owner, Dennis Hof, to see if any of the girls who worked there had encountered anyone as a client who might fit the suspect's general profile and description. Hof agreed to help the cops, and the Reno detectives went to the ranch and talked with the girls.

It turned out that one of the women told detectives about a regular client who appeared to fit the killer's general profile, at least as police then knew it. The man in question had tried to choke the woman a few times during their sexual sessions, and it had frightened her terribly, although she had walked away basically unharmed afterward.

The woman agreed to lure the man back to the ranch, and investigators went undercover so they would be nearby in the event that the man became violent again. Little out of the ordinary occurred, but the woman retained the condom they had used, as well as a glass that the man used for a drink. She turned both over to the police. Detectives immediately sent the items off to the crime lab for DNA analysis but, unfortunately, no cigar—the DNA did not match that of their suspect. They had hit another dead end, despite making their best efforts.

* * *

Meanwhile, on Monday, March 3, 2008, Lieutenant Robert McDonald told reporters for the *Reno Gazette-Journal* and the Associated Press that there had been a mix-up of sorts on a pair of thong underwear that had been found with Brianna's body. When her body was discovered, Reno police initially reported that the DNA of an unknown woman was found on the Pink Panther thong underwear, along with the DNA of the serial rapist they were hunting. But, according to McDonald, the DNA belonged to both an unknown female and an unknown male—not their suspect—and that the mix-up, due to somebody being "misinformed," was "really not that big of a deal." It had occurred when investigators made a misstatement to the media. He said that a forensic connection by DNA to Brianna and two previous attacks still existed and included "the abduction scene and the scene where Brianna was found. . . . From the beginning, the lab had stated the offender's DNA was not on there. It was never an error made by the lab."

"We are still certain he left the underwear," McDonald added. "We are one hundred percent convinced the offender left the underwear there. . . . They weren't left lying in the field by somebody else. Why it was left there? We don't know. We don't know if it was taunting. We don't believe it was. They may have been left there by accident. . . ." McDonald urged citizens to come forward and identify the panties.

The lieutenant said that the investigators were attempting to determine if the unknown DNA belonged to another victim of an assault. He said that their suspect took a pair of women's panties with him in at least one of the other attacks.

The officer also clarified that the serial rapist was linked by DNA to the sexual attacks of November 13 and December 16, 2007, and to the murder of Brianna Denison. He said that the rape by gunpoint of a student inside a UNR parking garage on October 22, 2007, did not have a forensic link to their suspect. Investigators, however, still believed it was connected to the other incidents. He added that DNA also linked the suspect to the attempted burglary of the December victim's apartment a few hours before Brianna disappeared from the MacKay Court residence.

McDonald also said that investigators had received a preliminary profile from the FBI's Behavioral Science Unit that described their suspect as very likely being a younger, inconspicuous man who would blend well into the community. He would probably have little or no criminal history. He could be characterized as an introvert who liked to remain in the background. He would likely not be the type who would be seen by anyone as a monster.

Reno police officials added that their suspect seemed to be attacking petite young women with straight, long hair. The severity and violence associated with the attacks had escalated with each subsequent attack.

"He is someone's boyfriend or husband, or the coworker you have coffee with," McDonald said in describing the profile.

In the meantime, Washoe County Crime Laboratory director Renee Romero told the community that progress was being made in processing the backlog of more than three thousand DNA samples. She expected the backlog processing to be complete by mid-March. However, by Tuesday, March 4, 2008, there were no hits or positive DNA links to Brianna's case or to the sexual attack cases from the samples that had already been entered into state and national databases. Investigators, however, remained hopeful that such a link would soon be found so that they could identify their suspect.

Two days later, on Thursday, March 6, 2008, Reno police had more to say about the panties found with Brianna's body. According to Commander Leigha Struffert, the second pair of panties—not the dark-colored Pink Panther panties, but rather the pink ones—belonged to one of the UNR students who lived at the MacKay Court residence. Struffert said that tests showed that DNA on those panties belonged to their owner, whom police did not identify at that time, and to Brianna Denison and her killer. Struffert said that one of the girls who lived in the house had come forward and identified the thong panties as belonging to her. She said that investigators did not yet know how the panties came into the suspect's possession, and that there was no evidence indicating that any of the roommates' rooms had been burglarized.

Struffert also said that investigators were convinced that the killer had a panty fetish, a penchant for collecting some of his victims' underwear. She said that he had taken a pair of underwear from a previous victim, although she would not disclose that victim's identity, citing the fact that some information known only to the police and the perpetrator needed to be withheld. She said that investigators

still needed the owner of the Pink Panther underwear to come forward, because she might have
information that could be critical to the solving of
the case. She asked that people who had been
burglarized, but had not reported the burglary,
come forward with their information. She asked
that people who had lost underwear after doing
their laundry at a Laundromat notify the police
as well.

"The drive is to get the owner of the Pink Panther
underwear to come forward," she said.

Like McDonald had done, Struffert said that it
was likely the suspect was known in the community
and that he probably still lived in the area.

"It could be your father, brother, your boyfriend,"
Struffert said in driving home her point. "There is
something about this person that someone knows
about that just isn't right. We ask you to come forward."

One thing seemed certain about the underwear—
the rapist-turned-killer was collecting women's thong
panties. But why? Was he attempting to preserve souvenirs of what he was doing?

So far, Struffert said, investigators had received
more than twenty-five hundred calls through the tip
line and through regional and federal law enforcement sources. She also indicated that the heightened awareness that was experienced throughout
the community had proven helpful to detectives. It
was just a matter of time before a suspect was identified and apprehended. In the meantime, the city remained on high alert.

* * *

On Tuesday, March 11, 2008, John Walsh, civilian crime fighter and host of *America's Most Wanted,* after having aired three episodes about the case on his television show, expressed his disappointment to a reporter for the *Reno Gazette-Journal* that the suspect in Brianna's case had not yet been caught.

"It's a horrible fact that innocent women on the streets of this college town are vulnerable," Walsh said. "Brianna was taken right out of a living room. This could be your beautiful daughter in college, and you have the hopes someday she will contribute to society, and her life is ended by some sicko nightmare."

Walsh said that in his twenty years of doing *AMW,* experience had shown that many serial rapists escalated their level of violence and sometimes turned into serial killers. He said that he thought that this particular suspect would have been easier to identify and apprehend, particularly with the intricate descriptions such as a "shaved pubic area" having been made public.

"I've caught guys on *America's Most Wanted* with less information," Walsh said. "This is a dangerous guy who is preying on women. We have to catch him."

Walsh explained that over the years that *AMW* had been on the air, the show had been responsible for catching nearly one thousand fugitives. A large number of such cases were solved simply by people calling in tips.

"This guy crossed the line from serial rapist to horrible coward murderer," Walsh added. "He's nothing but a coward. Someone needs to come forward, because someone knows him."

Walsh said that female citizens in the community

would continue living in fear until the suspect was identified and arrested.

"I'm sure when you go to your car at night when you're leaving work, you're going to be looking over your shoulder to make sure he's not in the parking lot," Walsh said to the female reporter and to the women in the community. "When these guys are out there, as cunning as they are, as lucky as this guy is, you are at risk."

Chapter 9

On Thursday, March 13, 2008, Washoe County Crime Lab director Renee Romero revealed that their DNA backlog had finally been processed at an approximate cost of $150 for each sample. Much of the cost was covered from the appeal for public funding when, after all was said and done, approximately $292,000 was collected, leaving a shortfall of nearly $160,000. Unfortunately, the DNA from the serial rapist who murdered Brianna Denison was not among the more than three thousand samples that had been input into CODIS, as well as local systems. During the time frame in which police had been searching for the serial rapist and murder suspect, more than five hundred oral swabs had been collected from male subjects to analyze their DNA and these, too, had been included with the samples that had been processed.

"To have a DNA hit on the attacker would have been a long shot, since the backlog wasn't that old," said Brooke Keast, public information officer for the Washoe County Sheriff's Office. "At the same time, it was worth the attempt to rule out the possibility.

We did have thirty hits (not related to their murder suspect), and that's thirty crimes that can be solved."

Keast added that the thirty hits were for crimes that ranged from robbery and burglary to a very violent sexual assault. The perpetrator for the latter crime was already in jail for a different crime at the time the DNA hit was made for the violent sexual assault he had committed.

It is interesting to note that "touch DNA" technology, which is what linked two of the UNR sexual assaults to Brianna's case, provides a suspect's genetic makeup simply by testing of clothing items, weapons, and so forth, which often reveal skin cells that have been left behind and are invisible to the unaided eye. It is particularly useful when the suspect does not leave behind forensic evidence such as blood, saliva, or semen. The technology was fairly new, and had been in use for about three years at the time of Brianna's disappearance. In 2008, it was used to gain the freedom of a Colorado man who had been falsely imprisoned in that state for more than nine years for a 1987 slaying that he did not commit. It also helped Reno police catch a suspected serial rapist in early 2008, a man who had been breaking into women's homes in 2006 and 2007. According to Lieutenant McDonald, it's difficult not to leave behind any DNA unless "you're in a full hazmat bodysuit."

It is not often, however, that touch DNA provides major breaks in cases, because the technology is dependent on the quantity of skin cells left on an item by a suspect, according to Renee Romero.

"People don't leave a ton of DNA behind just by touching something," said Romero. "But every now and then, you get more, depending on whether the person naturally sheds more cells, or if they had a longer period of contact. You can't tell why one case received better results than the other."

In the earlier Reno serial-rapist case, the suspect was arrested after crime lab analysts found his DNA in scratches that a middle-aged woman sustained during a robbery and assault. The suspect's DNA was also found in his victim's bathrobe, and investigators were able to link the suspect's DNA in that attack to a 2006 assault, despite the fact that the assailant tried very hard to remove as much forensic evidence as possible from his crime scenes. He forced his victims to wash themselves, and he took away any clothing articles and bedding items that he touched. He also used cleaning products to wipe down the areas with which he had come into contact and had shaved his body. He had also worn a stocking cap. The rapist had previously spent twenty years in prison for raping and stabbing a girl from Douglas County, Nevada, but was paroled in 2002. Fortunately, his DNA was included in a database for convicted offenders. Reno investigators were also very pleased that touch DNA had provided the link between Brianna's death and the other sexual assaults.

Still reeling over the death of her daughter, Bridgette Denison told the *Reno Gazette-Journal* on Wednesday, March 19, 2008, that her worst fear had been realized when she learned of Brianna's murder.

"It's a parent's worst nightmare," she said. "What's the hardest for me, more than thinking about my daughter being murdered or what he did to her, is that I miss her. . . . I just miss her. I still don't know how I'm going to . . . finish my life . . . without her."

She recounted how her husband, Jeff, had committed suicide after ten years of marriage, when

Brianna was six and her son, Brighton, was only fifteen months old. Brianna's untimely death sent her into mourning a loved one again—this time her own flesh and blood.

"With what I went through with my husband and now this, I really blew it," she said. "When I lost him, I thought that I had paid my dues and thought that I was home free. I know now it's not good to think like that."

Bridgette said that her husband's suicide had brought her family even closer, that the kids all had to help out, and that they'd had to become more of a team. She said that Brianna had become very protective of her after her father's death, and that their bond had become strong. Other people said that they had noticed that strengthened bond, too, and said it was like Brianna and her mother had become best friends—they did everything together. Even as she grew older, she remained close to her mother and always followed and respected her mother's rules.

Bridgette recalled that when Brianna was in high school, the teenager seemed more like a roommate to her mom than a daughter. Brianna was occasionally more responsible than her mother, despite her young age. She said that when Brianna left for Santa Barbara to go to college, that first year she'd had to spend without her daughter living at home was horrible for her. She said she had felt sad because it was as though she had lost her *roommate*. Bridgette said that she cried often, even though she and Brianna talked and sent text messages to each other daily. Even though they had remained in close contact while Brianna was away at college, her mother had worried about her, as any mother would worry about her child that she could not see every day. As 2008 began, Bridgette said that she and her son, Brighton, who was fifteen, had been planning Brianna's twentieth birthday party as they both tried to get accustomed to her not being at home as often.

"She was full of life, excited, and passionate about becoming a child psychologist," Bridgette said. "She loved where she lived, and she just had it together more than other kids."

Now that Brianna was never coming home again, she said, the only choice she had was to take things as they came, one day at a time. Bridgette also said that she planned to keep herself busy with her efforts to find Brianna's killer, and to bring into being her idea about a Bring Bri Justice Foundation (BBJF), designed to provide support and assistance to other families of crime victims.

Bridgette said that she intended to make something positive come from her daughter's murder by fighting for tougher laws to keep repeat sex offenders behind bars, and also to work for changes so that crime labs would receive adequate funding for processing DNA from offenders. Some of that work would be accomplished through the BBJF, of which she would become president. The foundation was a goal that she needed to keep alive.

Bridgette's top priority, however, was catching the perpetrator who murdered Brianna.

"We are limited in what we can do to catch this guy," she said. "But I am not going to stop until I find him. I can't imagine one more family going through this situation. I am putting my heart and soul into finding and catching him. . . . If he's not here near our campus, I can tell you he's at another one. . . . He is a really twisted, crazy man, who is still out there. I . . . do not believe he is in control of himself and won't do this again. I am amazed he hasn't done this again already. . . . We are going to bring Bri justice, so maybe she can rest."

Bridgette expressed her appreciation to the community for their support during such a difficult time, but she admitted that it was often difficult for her every time she saw someone wearing a blue ribbon. Despite that emotional difficulty, she said, she hoped that the community would keep remembering Brianna and would continue to support law enforcement until the killer was identified and apprehended.

"It feels really good," she said of the community support. "I feel like I'm not alone. It really feels like she became Reno's daughter. At least ninety percent of the people in this town have children and probably feel like it could have happened to them. And it could happen to another girl, if he's not caught soon."

For the moment, however, Bridgette was making plans to bury Brianna next to her father on March 29, Brianna's birthday. She would have been twenty.

Chapter 10

By the third week in April 2008, investigators returned to the subject of the pair of black Pink Panther thong underwear that had been found with Brianna's body, containing the DNA of an unknown man and an unknown woman. The authorities again made a public appeal during a press conference for the owner of the thongs to come forward and help them with their case.

Lieutenant Robert McDonald said that the investigators believed that the intertwined panties had not been "posed" by the suspect, which would likely have been the case if he had wanted investigators to find them. Instead, McDonald said, the detectives believed that he might have dropped them out of his pocket accidentally as he moved Brianna's body. This theory would fit with the police contention that their man was a panty fetishist, who liked to collect his victims' underwear. If he had left them there on purpose, the authorities believed, he would have used them to leave the investigators a message—if for no other reason than to taunt them.

"Those panties came from somewhere," the lieutenant said. "They obviously belong to someone. Some woman is missing those. We've been hoping the person would come forward. . . . Did they come from another of the man's victims of an unreported assault? Did he steal them in a burglary or from someone at a Laundromat? Did the owner once date this guy? Somehow, this woman came into contact with the killer. If she comes forward, it may be the break we need."

McDonald said that there were a number of possible scenarios of how their suspect could have gotten hold of the Pink Panther panties. He added that detectives would have no way of knowing how he had gotten them until their owner came forward and identified them.

"We don't care what her story is," McDonald said. "We'd just like for that woman to come forward. She may know something that can help us, even if she doesn't realize it. It could be the key to catching the killer."

McDonald returned to the subject of the other pair of panties found with Brianna's body and how the owner, who had lived at the MacKay Court residence, had come forward and said that she did not know how her panties had been stolen. McDonald hinted at the possibility that the killer could have stolen them at any time, since the residents of the house always left the doors unlocked. Was it possible that Brianna's killer had entered that house earlier, before she was killed? If so, that meant that her killer had been watching the house. It was a chilling thought, but it was also possible that he had found the panties on the morning that he killed Brianna.

McDonald said that the detectives were interested in

learning more about men who collected women's underwear. He said that the team already had received a number of tips about the so-called underwear fetishists, but the information they developed from those tips had not provided anything to lead them to the man for whom they were looking.

Meanwhile, as one day followed another, and soon turned into weeks, and then months, the search for Brianna's killer yielded few clues, leaving many of Reno's younger women, especially those who were UNR students, wary about their safety. By June 2008, security was still high at UNR, even though the regular academic year had given way to summer sessions. UNR's typical enrollment of about 16,500 students diminished dramatically when the spring semester ended in mid-May, but the summer session had approximately sixty-five hundred students enrolled for classes. Another five thousand or so middle-school and high-school students were also expected on campus during the summer months when they would be attending programs in "Kids University" or some of the other summer academic and sports programs held on campus. According to UNR police chief Adam Garcia, the UNR campus never closed, requiring the campus police to maintain normal staffing levels of twenty-eight sworn positions, as well as patrol officers and supervisory personnel.

"Our operations continue as always," Garcia said. "We run as all police departments do, twenty-four/seven, and we don't take into account whether or not school is in regular session. We still have a lot of properties that we are responsible for.

"We (the police) can never let our guard down and must always remain vigilant," Garcia added, saying that it is human nature to become complacent as time passed after a tragedy. "I would hope (non–law enforcement) people would do the same. With or without the specter of the unfortunate death of Brianna, we still encourage people to be aware of their surroundings, whether it's dark or during the daytime. People need to take stock of their own safety and travel in groups and report any suspicious activity to the police."

Some female students reported feeling safe on campus during daytime hours, but they admitted that fear usually began to set in come nightfall. Jung Eun Lee, a clinical psychology student, was one such student. Jung, who lived in a neighborhood near the university, said that she tried to avoid being on campus at night, or even anywhere near the campus outdoors during the evening hours. However, she sometimes had to do clinical work in the evenings at UNR.

"I still feel a little afraid," Jung said, even though months had passed since Brianna was killed and the other attacks occurred. "Even though it's still light now at seven-thirty or eight at night, I ask my cohorts to give me a ride home."

A number of UNR's administrative employees were also on guard about their safety after Brianna's murder. Kathy King, fifty-seven, who worked in the cashier's office of student services, told a reporter for the *Reno Gazette-Journal* that she typically walked across campus to the downtown area after work to catch a bus. Due to her safety concerns after the UNR attacks and Brianna's murder, she said she began taking Virginia Street as an alternate route, instead. Virginia Street is a major thoroughfare between the campus and downtown and is heavily traveled. After a while, however, feeling a little safer, she reverted to her old route of walking across campus.

"I felt it was a random act," Kathy said. "And I always see the campus police patrolling everywhere, so I feel safe."

She said that she still felt concerned for her safety at times. When she had those moments of insecurity, she simply used the campus-escort service—which was not being offered during the summer months because it was operated by students and required student participation. King said that she also carried a police whistle with her, which had the police telephone number printed on it. The whistles were blue in color and distributed earlier in the year as part of the campaign to find Brianna.

Journalism student Denise Parker, who worked at the Joe Crowley Student Union, told a reporter that when she worked late she would make sure that she could get a ride home with a friend or coworker. She said that she felt "pretty safe on campus," but she tried not to think much about what had happened to Brianna.

In the meantime, the search for Reno's elusive rapist-turned-murderer continued.

Chapter 11

By the time mid-July 2008 rolled around, the police were still just as actively trying to identify Brianna's killer as they had been from the outset of the case, but what had seemed at first to be the most promising leads had all but dried up. Members of law enforcement, as well as the citizens of the community, were left wondering who and where the killer was and whether or not he would strike again. Many people began to lose faith in the investigation; some began questioning whether or not Brianna's murderer would ever be caught.

According to Lieutenant Robert McDonald, the investigators now believed that their suspect had gone underground and was keeping a low profile. They theorized that he had even moved to another community, since none of the sex crimes that had been committed in Reno after Brianna's murder had been linked to the DNA of the unknown suspect.

"It's frustrating to have this guy's genetic name, but not their given name," McDonald said. "It's frustrating we haven't had the right lead to develop the right suspect. Yet. For [Brianna's] family and the community, we want to bring some resolution and catch this person so everyone will feel safer [when] he's behind bars. . . . Eventually this person will return to their pattern. . . . We don't want to displace the problem elsewhere and have more women raped, because we know that other communities do not have the same sense of heightened awareness. We know he was stalking and targeting his victims, who were opportunities, but not at random."

Many people, however, such as UNR employee Kathy King, still mistakenly believed that the attacks had been random.

McDonald said that investigators believed the man they were looking for was not a ladies' man. They speculated that he would be "comfortable standing in the back of a room, unassuming." He stressed that when the perpetrator got caught, this man's family, friends, and coworkers would be surprised and would likely say that they could not believe he was capable of committing sex crimes and murder.

During the months since Brianna's murder, investigators had focused on leads about a number of suspects, with detectives thinking that several of them had been *the one* that might crack their difficult case. However, once a suspect's DNA was compared to that of the DNA collected during the investigation— and there would prove to be no match—the detectives would move on to another potential suspect. This was a process that had occurred several times so far.

"We've been down that road before, where we have thought a certain lead was 'the one,' and then the bubble burst," McDonald said. "But we have not lost our focus or our enthusiasm."

* * *

Although leads seemed to be getting more and more scarce with the passage of time, they were still coming in steadily; each day there were tips for the detectives to follow up on.

According to Sergeant Chuck Lovitt, of the Robbery/Homicide Unit, more than six thousand tips had come in by the end of July 2008—two thousand more than they had in April. He said that he reviewed the tips each and every day, and did not discount any of them, no matter how insignificant they might seem, until they had been thoroughly checked out. Even though the leads had become scarcer, Lovitt said those that were more vague in nature, such as calls about a man having a goatee or about a man who drove a particular type of truck, had declined. This, then, usually resulted in the tips that came in later in the case sometimes being of potentially greater value to investigators. In other words, he said, the later tips most often indicated *why* a particular person was suspicious as opposed to someone simply calling in a matching general physical description. And even though leads had slowed to a trickle when compared to the numbers they were getting during the first few months of the investigation, they were still coming in. The key seemed to be to keep the case alive and in front of the public. Every time new information was released or older details repeated, an influx of new tips would come in. Lovitt suggested that area residents should consider the descriptions of the suspect and his truck carefully. If either seemed familiar to them, residents should try and remember whether the person they were thinking of had gone through any changes in behavior or appearance around the time that Brianna disappeared.

"Every day I wish it would be the day we catch him," Lovitt said. "This has been a significant part of my life, and everyone's life who has been involved. We are deeply invested in this case and will be working hard until we catch this guy."

Even seasoned detective David Jenkins admitted the difficulty that he and other investigators were having with the case.

"Sexually motivated crimes committed by strangers are difficult to solve," Jenkins said. "There's no association with the victims, and they are solved at much lower rates. We're really left at the mercy of tips."

Jenkins recalled a similar case from September 3, 1977, regarding the abduction, rape, and slaying of six-year-old Lisa Bonham, who had been kidnapped from Reno's Idlewild Park, located a short distance southwest from downtown. She had been taken by a convicted child molester, who had been paroled from prison in 1976 for previously molesting two young girls. The similarities between the Lisa Bonham case and that of Brianna Denison were obvious: Both involved an innocent young person—girls in each case—who had been kidnapped and killed by a serial predator. In both instances, the perpetrators were not immediately caught, and there was DNA evidence involved in each case. In the Bonham case, however, DNA had not been developed to the point where it could be useful to detectives at the time of the girl's murder. Instead, Jenkins had to wait more than twenty years to solve the case.

In recapping Lisa's case, Jenkins explained that Lisa's family had been vacationing in Reno, visiting relatives, after a long driving trip that had taken them to Mississippi and Georgia, where they had visited other relatives. Lisa and her brother had been playing at the park, where there were amusement rides at the time, when they ran out of money. Lisa left her brother and ran three blocks to her uncle's house to get another dollar from her mother, who was busy preparing their motor home for the family's departure.

"In that three-block distance, she disappeared," said Jenkins, who had joined the Reno Police Department a year earlier. He said that the case stunned Reno residents, like Brianna's case had.

After Lisa failed to return to her uncle's house, her family and Reno police mounted a massive search effort, much like Brianna's family had done. They went over virtually every inch of the park where she had been playing. The first clue of foul play was received the next day when a couple, who had been out picking up aluminum cans, called police. Upon hearing of Lisa's disappearance, they reported that they had found a little girl's short-sleeved shirt, red-and-white-checkered shorts, white socks, and red sandals in a trash can at a rest area outside Reno, in Toiyabe National Forest. The little girl's brokenhearted parents identified the clothing as belonging to Lisa. Fearing the worst, everyone then geared up to begin looking for a body.

"Reno was an even smaller community back then, and that crime really rocked the community. There were thousands of volunteers that participated in the search for Lisa," Jenkins said.

Approximately two months later, two teenage

boys hiking northwest of Reno, near Verdi, Nevada, found a human jawbone and reported it to the police. Investigators searched the area and found the rest of the remains, which were eventually identified as Lisa's.

Despite a massive effort by Jenkins and the Reno Police Department, the case soon went dormant and remained so until 1993. Jenkins was reviewing the department's unsolved murders at that time when it suddenly dawned on him that advances in forensic science and DNA technology might be able to shed new light on Lisa's case, specifically on the identity of her killer. At the time of Lisa's disappearance, forensic technology had been more useful in eliminating potential suspects as opposed to identifying them.

"It was never sufficient to identify a specific individual," Jenkins said of 1977 forensic technology.

Jenkins sent Lisa's clothing to the crime lab, where a DNA sample was taken from semen stains on her shirt and sock. Analysts first began checking the DNA sample against a list of possible suspects, and then against lists of known sex offenders from Nevada, Northern California, and the Pacific Northwest. In each instance, there were no hits, and it took until May 2000 before a match was found, in part because of backlogs in processing DNA in the crime lab.

"It just takes time to process all the samples," said Renee Romero, who was DNA technology leader at the Washoe County Crime Lab at that time. "I don't think there's a state that doesn't have a backlog."

Back at that time, the backlog was created, in part, by efforts of DNA testing laboratories to keep pace with advancing scientific technology, Romero said.

When the hit in Lisa's case occurred, which still

would have to wait for confirmation, it had led Jenkins to child molester Stephen Robert Smith, fifty-seven, who had been working all those years as a card dealer at a Reno casino. As Jenkins waited for the DNA confirmation he needed in order to make the arrest, officers closely watched Smith's comings and goings. While waiting, Jenkins showed Smith's photo to Lisa's parents, who did not know him—he was a stranger to them and to their family.

Smith was arrested at his Sparks, Nevada, home and charged with Lisa's murder. Jenkins subsequently learned that Smith had been convicted in 1969 of abducting and sexually molesting two young girls in Sparks, a Reno suburb, after being arrested in Reno for the attempted abduction and molestation of another young girl. He had been sentenced to two life prison terms with the possibility of parole. Unfortunately, he had indeed made parole seven years later. He had never been seen as a suspect in Lisa's murder, and might not have ever been identified as her killer if his parole officer had not convinced him to provide a DNA sample to authorities in 1997.

"It's the oldest DNA hit we've ever had at this agency," Jenkins said. "And I'm led to believe that it may be the oldest in the country [in 2000]."

"It was very covert," Jenkins said later as he recalled being notified of the DNA hit in 2000 by the commander of the Washoe County Crime Lab. "He said to call him back from a landline. Right away, I knew this wasn't a garden-variety thing. He said, 'You're not going to believe it. We got a match.'"

"It was euphoria," Lisa's mother, Doris Bonham, said about receiving Jenkins's phone call to tell her that Lisa's killer had been found. She made her comments to a reporter for the *Reno Gazette-Journal* by telephone from her home in California. "Finally we had the answer we've been waiting for. I was imagining the people in the crime lab as windows were popping up on their computers saying they had a match. That must have been very exciting.

"Anger wasn't my first emotion," she added, speaking of the emotions that she had experienced when she had learned that her daughter had been murdered. "It was the realization I would never see her again and that our lives would be turned even more upside down."

On October 3, 2000, Stephen Robert Smith pleaded guilty to Lisa's murder after agreeing to accept a punishment of life in prison without parole, which would have allowed him to avoid a sentencing hearing in which many, if not all, of the details of his crimes would be presented.

Jenkins learned from Smith that he had taken Lisa to the little-used Dog Valley Campground, located near Verdi, Nevada, near the Northern Sierra Nevada Mountain Range in the Toiyabe National Forest, where he attempted to smother her to death. Lisa, however, managed to get loose from her restraints, after which Smith "twisted her neck" until she remained still. Washoe County DA Richard Gammick later said that Smith had "made a deal with the Devil," and called Smith a "hard-core pedophile."

Smith's guilty plea in open court had been the first time that Lisa's mother had seen her daughter's killer, enabling her to finally put a face to the demon that had taunted her for more than twenty-three years. Bonham, who did not believe in closure, said that the details she heard about the crime were painful, but it had been nothing that she had not already imagined. She said that she had awakened at two-thirty every morning since her daughter's murder and wondered whether Lisa's death had been quick, or whether Lisa had suffered for a long time.

"It's never gone," she said. "It's always lingering back there somewhere. . . . It's still very hard every time I hear about one of these awful cases, because you just relive that day. You get that anxious feeling again that won't go away."

Doris Bonham said that she had always remained confident that her daughter's killer would eventually be found and brought to justice, especially after she had read an article about DNA technology and the crime lab. Doris felt that DNA would provide the answer. She believed that sooner or later, it would provide the answer in Brianna's case as well.

"If it hadn't been for DNA, we would go to the grave wondering," she said.

"It was great to be able to play a role in letting the family know who did this terrible thing to their beautiful little girl," Jenkins said about his call to Doris Bonham. "They could finally have a face to put to the person who did this."

According to Jenkins's partner on the Smith case, Detective Jim Duncan, now retired, Smith was a predator who hunted for his victims by placing himself at locations where he would be close at hand to his victim type.

"I don't think he picked his victims," Duncan said. "He picked his places."

One of those places was, of course, Idlewild Park, and Smith's method of operation was similar to how Brianna's killer had lurked around the neighborhoods near UNR.

"This guy [Brianna's killer] was actively hunting for an opportunity, not an individual," Jenkins said. "He has a predator mentality, like Smith."

Jenkins stressed that crimes such as the ones that had involved Lisa and Brianna are proof that any female could become a victim. Although the much-needed DNA match in Brianna's case had not occurred yet, and despite the fact that leads were gradually beginning to slow down, Jenkins remained confident that they would find their suspect in Brianna's case and bring him to justice, too, when they got the right lead and combined it with the right evidence.

"The big break in the case will be an innocuous, garden-variety lead," Jenkins said. "I don't think it's going to be an, 'Oh, my God, this is the break we're looking for,' but a low priority tip we work that turns out to be the guy. I would love very much, if I'm retired or not, and I'm still kicking and drawing breath, to be there when someone tells Brianna's family who he is. . . . If it takes twenty-three years—God, I hope not—eventually we will get him."

As with the fewer leads, by midsummer there were also noticeably fewer blue ribbons around town. Earlier the ribbons could easily be spotted on car antennas, pinned to people's clothing, and attached to trees and fences in the city. There were fewer sales of guns, Tasers, and pepper spray, too; area women seemed less interested in taking self-defense classes. However, Lauren Denison, among others, was concerned that women were beginning to let their guard down while the killer still remained at large somewhere out there, possibly in Reno.

"Every time some weirdo is arrested, I hope against hope that it's him, and that he wasn't arrested for murder," Lauren said. "My biggest fear is waking up and he will have murdered someone else. This is why we still have to be on top of our game. Brianna was one of the most cautious girls, and safety was always in the front of her mind. If it can happen to a girl who was knowledgeable and well-versed in safety, it can happen to anyone."

"It's easy for people to grow tired and bored with the story when it doesn't involve someone you love," Jenkins said. "He may not murder again, but he will offend again."

It was possible, everyone conceded, that Brianna's killer had already offended again—but in a different locale. If he had committed sexual assaults elsewhere, the link to his DNA would eventually show up—it was just too bad that his DNA had not already given the detectives a name. Everyone associated with the case, with the likely exception of the killer, was a supporter of DNA technology.

John Walsh had talked about it often, and he was one of the main leaders on the bandwagon when many in law enforcement were trying to establish a national DNA database years before CODIS became a reality. Even with CODIS in place—which was intended, initially, to be used to index sex offenders, but was later expanded to include all felony offenders—there was still much work that remained to be done. Walsh, along with countless others, believed that DNA processing needed to be a major law enforcement priority.

"Wouldn't you want to know if the person who raped you was a serial rapist or criminal on the loose?" Walsh asked rhetorically. "We need to enter evidence from rape kits into the national database. . . . We are also working so that every person accused of a felony would have to submit their DNA. It's something that should have been done years ago. . . . We are . . . finding that due to staffing shortages or lack of funding, that parolees are out there committing murders and no one made the link because their DNA was not yet in the system. It really needs to be a state and federal priority."

When Walsh's son, Adam, was murdered in 1981, "there was no DNA [technology]," he said. Walsh said that the main suspect was in prison, and the FBI had said that they would gladly test a piece of bloody carpeting found in his car. However, the Hollywood, Florida, police had lost the evidence, according to Walsh.

"It was a terrible travesty," he said. The suspect in the Adam Walsh case recanted his confession at one point, but Walsh and the authorities would have known if he was actually the person who had murdered Adam if DNA technology could have been used at that time.

"We've never gotten justice," Walsh said. "We had worked to get all states to collect the DNA of every felon. When we first did it in Florida, within six months, eighty cases were solved and eleven people were freed. DNA convicts the guilty and frees the innocent."

Brianna's family agreed; and although they did not know it yet, they would later find themselves working with legislators to change and broaden DNA legislation nationally in order to create a more consistent and complete database that could better serve the needs of law enforcement.

Chapter 12

Once again, time began to pass quickly for many people in the community, but not for Brianna's family or for the investigators who were trying to identify her killer and bring him to justice. The remainder of July and most of August 2008 passed uneventfully as the citizens of Reno, Nevada, went about their business and tried to move on without constantly looking over their shoulders. They no longer cowered in fear that the serial-rapist-turned-murderer was lurking somewhere nearby, waiting for his next victim of opportunity. A new school year had begun at UNR a week before Labor Day, and many of the returning students were reminded of the Reno attacker and Brianna's murderer. However, many of the incoming new students, particularly those from out of town, did not have the same sense of trepidation as the returning students, who had been enrolled at the time Brianna had been kidnapped.

After everything that had occurred during the previous school year, UNR officials decided to approve a nearly twenty-one-minute video, "Take Back the Night," which demonstrated self-defense for females and showed them that they had the power to defend themselves and avoid becoming a victim. Produced by Jack Sutton, a Reno optometrist and Emmy-winning producer, the video was filmed on the UNR campus and in local apartments. It featured students and members of student government, many of whom demonstrated safety tips. The student actors also showed how they could easily become involved in a dangerous situation and be attacked simply because they were not paying attention to their surroundings. University police and self-defense instructors also played a large part in the making of the DVD, demonstrating how being prepared can often serve as the best defense against an attacker. Such preparations, they said, included carrying a whistle, staying alert, and looking around often. Eliminating or limiting the use of distracting elements, such as iPods and cell phones, while out and about, was also recommended. The video served to remind nearly everyone in Reno of the potential danger that existed from the still-at-large perpetrator and others like him—criminals who might be out there, waiting for an opportunity to attack. It was received well by the UNR students. They and the other residents in the UNR neighborhoods tried to remain cautious while they did their best to make it business as usual as the new academic year began.

On Labor Day, September 1, 2008, Brianna's family launched another blue ribbon campaign, "Tie a Ribbon for Bri Day." The effort was, of course, aimed at keeping Brianna's murder in the forefront of the minds of area citizens, and served as a reminder that her killer was still out there. Two months later, on Saturday, November 1, 2008, Brianna's mother, family, and friends opened the Bring Bri Justice Foundation, bringing Bridgette Denison's goal to support crime victims to realization. The plan was to use their energy to help others avoid facing the same sort of horrifying tragedy they had experienced.

Barbara Zunino, Brianna's maternal grand-mother, said that the family was very outgoing, and that was what had kept them motivated and made them stronger.

"You just have to do it," she said. "You can cry the whole time or you can get mad. I got mad."

"We'll be working hard to save other people," Lauren Denison said.

The mission statement of the foundation read: *The Bring Bri Justice Foundation will use all available resources to help our community and their families by rais-ing awareness about violent crimes, personal safety, and en-suring justice is served.*

The foundation's new website stated that the or-ganization's current focus was on DNA legislation by assisting in finding funding for the currently *un*-funded DNA laws in Nevada, to aid in broadening the sampling of DNA to include all those *arrested* for felonies—not just those who were convicted—and to assist in funding the backlog of samples already taken in the state of Nevada. Also listed was the foun-dation's strong interest in changing and broadening DNA legislation nationally in order to create a con-sistent database to aid law enforcement.

Valerie Van Antwerp said that the foundation wanted to "do everything in our power to make sure this doesn't happen to another family, and one really good way to stop that from happening is to have as much DNA in the database as possible."

Another project of the foundation were their Brianna Guides, which were kits designed to help people who were faced with the tragedy of having to search for missing loved ones. The packages of material included directions for setting up a recovery center, a media guide, instructions for the most effective law enforcement communication, and community contacts for both volunteers and aid. Thanks to the Brianna Guides, the experience garnered by the foundation members would be an invaluable aid to others who found themselves in the same position as Brianna's family and friends.

The foundation also had a strong commitment to community personal safety. It planned to produce safety-awareness kits, to hold community-safety events, and to promote campus-escort services and the use of student-courtesy vans.

Board members of the foundation included Brianna's mother, Bridgette, who served as president, and her aunt Lauren Denison, center coordinator, plus five other friends and family members, all dedicated to creating a meaningful and lasting memorial to Brianna through the work of the foundation. The outpouring of love from the community would be in their hearts forever, Lauren Denison said, quoting from a Maya Angelou poem, "'If you find it in your heart to care for someone else, you will have succeeded.'

"The community has succeeded," Lauren said.

A touching statement from the Zunino-Denison family was included on the website that was set up for the foundation. Saying that on January 20, 2008, she had become not only their own beloved daughter, but the daughter of the entire community, the statement read:

> *We want to thank the Reno Police Department for all their support, the community of Reno, the devoted volunteers, the searchers, the media, and everyone involved in the search for Bri.*
>
> *This is a difficult time. We ask first that every woman be diligent about their own safety and that each and every one of you protect the women and children in your community. We ask once again that if there is anyone out there with information, we beg you to come forward. Now is the time.*
>
> *And finally, we want to say that we are grateful for many things. Grateful for all of your actions, thoughts and prayers. Grateful for the gift of Brianna in all of our lives. Grateful for the joy she brought us and for the cherished memories of her that are a source of comfort. Memories that give us strength to see beyond our sorrow, sustaining us in spite of our grief.*
>
> *Please don't forget Brianna. . . .*

When the foundation held its grand opening and appreciation celebration, it was planned as both an introduction of the organization to the community and a demonstration of the family's thanks to the people of northern Nevada for all that so many had done in the search for Brianna. The celebration was an all-out, family-friendly event, which included games and giveaways, raffles, face painting, balloons, a bounce house, live music, food, and drink. Neatly tucked away among the activities that were strictly for fun was a fingerprinting stand. Scores of parents took advantage of the opportunity to have their children fingerprinted as an identification aid. The focus of the day was on safety awareness, and it was free and open to the public. The friends and family who made up the foundation were determined to remain highly positive and proactive about preventing other cases like Brianna's. Because of their attitude, and also because of the enormous community support the case had generated, the day was hailed as a great success.

It would seem later that the foundation's well-received grand opening was not the only thing that would be instrumental in getting justice for Brianna Denison. As fate would have it, on that very same day when the BBJF was holding its grand opening, the Reno Police Department received a tip on their Secret Witness line from an anonymous caller who claimed to have information that might prove useful to the investigation into Brianna's murder. The caller said that a man named James Michael Biela had been exhibiting some strange behavior. The caller claimed that Biela fit some of the suspect criteria that police had developed in the various cases over the past year and had made public about the man they were looking for. According to information that was later made public, the Secret Witness caller was a friend of the woman who was Biela's girlfriend at the time, Carleen Harmon.

Carleen, the caller said, had supposedly mentioned to her friend that she had found women's thong underwear in Biela's truck sometime in the past year during the time frame in which the detectives were interested. After all, they believed that their suspect harbored a fetish for women's underwear, and anyone matching such a profile would naturally become a primary suspect, "a number one priority," in their investigation.

The investigators, of course, had no idea at this point whether the tipster had become somehow emotionally moved to call the tip line because of publicity surrounding the opening of the Bring Bri Justice Foundation, or whether the tipster had been planning the call for some time and that the timing had merely been a coincidence. In retrospect, however, the cops were very grateful for the tip because it turned out to be their big break in the case. Finally here was the break that they had long been waiting and hoping for—and might have still been a long time coming if it had not been for the Secret Witness Program call.

On beginning to check out the tip, Detective Adam Wygnanski learned that James Biela had received training in plumbing and pipe fitting and was employed by J.W. McClenahan Co., a commercial-plumbing company. In February 2008, he had been working on a project at Charles River Laboratories. On February 15, the day Brianna's body was found, he asked for a voluntary layoff from that employment, allegedly so that he could move up to Washington for employment on a project known as the Moses Lake Power Plant. His friend and coworker, John Latham, said Biela seemed frustrated and antsy. Around ten or eleven that morning, John said, Biela had demanded a layoff.

Because the news, at that time, had just begun

reporting that Brianna's body had been found, the two men talked about it for a bit. At that time, Biela said, "The bitch probably had it coming."

John Latham, who was the company's foreman, said he didn't think much about the odd comment; he said he thought it was probably a joke. He gave Biela his check and didn't see or hear from him for several months. In the fall, Biela returned to the area and began to work again for J.W. McClenahan at the Ritz-Carlton at Northstar ski resort.

Detective Wygnanski went to Biela's home in Sparks and found no one there, so he left a business card asking Biela to contact him. Biela did call him a short time later.

"My suspicion began with that phone call," Wygnanski later told a reporter. "I told him we were conducting an investigation and I needed a few minutes of his time." They agreed to get together after Biela left work, arranging to meet at a Wendy's parking lot, since Biela didn't want to have the meeting at his home. "I didn't tell him what it was about, and he hung up. I thought it was strange that he never asked me what the investigation was about. If the police come to your house and leave a card that says they're from the Robbery/Homicide Unit, wouldn't you want to know what it was about?"

When they met, Wygnanski explained to Biela that he was working the Brianna Denison case, and Biela's name had come up, along with a number of other male subjects. They talked about the Secret Witness tip and Wygnanski confirmed that Biela was white, twenty-seven years old, and matched the general physical characteristics of the suspect who had been described by Virgie Chin. It was almost uncanny how much Biela resembled the sketch drawn by Detective Villa in January, shortly after Brianna disappeared. At one point, Wygnanski asked Biela for a voluntary saliva swab that could be used as a DNA reference sample to be compared to the suspect DNA profile developed during the investigation so that he could eliminate him as a suspect. Not surprisingly, Biela refused to provide the swab, saying that he had no faith in the accuracy of DNA testing.

"He said he had no involvement and refused to give me a DNA sample," Wygnanski said. "He said he didn't trust it. I told him it was a quick way to eliminate himself, and that we had a lot to do and would like to move on with the investigation."

Wygnanski wrote in his report that Biela had appeared to be very nervous during their meeting. Biela would not make eye contact with him. He also noted that the suspect was sweating and was fidgety. Before concluding the preliminary interview with his subject, Wygnanski confronted him with the fact that he had learned that Biela had worked as a pipe fitter on a construction project on the UNR campus, which Biela had promptly denied.

Wygnanski also had learned that Biela was the registered owner and frequent driver of a 2006 four-wheel-drive Toyota Tacoma pickup truck, with an extended cab, with a gray interior, during the time frame of the sexual assaults and Brianna's disappearance. Biela, however, continued to deny that he had anything to do with Brianna's murder. Wygnanski had no choice at that time but to let him go. Biela also told the detective that his girlfriend, Carleen, could provide him with an alibi for his whereabouts on the day that Brianna had disappeared.

"After my meeting with him, I was convinced he was the guy," Wygnanski said.

* * *

Five days later, on Wednesday, November 12, 2008, Jenkins and Wygnanski both met with and interviewed Carleen Harmon. During the interview, Carleen stated that she had been involved in a romantic relationship with Biela for about six years, and that she and Biela had a four-year-old child together, a boy. When delicately pressed for assurances that Biela was the boy's father, Carleen told the detectives that she had no doubt whatsoever that Biela was the child's father.

Surprisingly, Carleen did not provide Biela with an alibi. She said that she was not able to account for his whereabouts during the early-morning hours of either December 16, 2007, the morning that Virgie Chin was attacked, or on January 20, 2008, when Brianna Denison had disappeared. She explained that she and Biela, despite their six years together, had what had often been a tumultuous romantic relationship. She told the officers that the relationship had been especially difficult in October 2007, with them fighting almost every day. By December 2007, they were sleeping apart. She said that during the winter months of 2007 and into 2008, Biela would just up and leave their residence for days at a time, with no explanation. During those absences, she said, when she asked where he had been, he would tell her that he had been sleeping in his truck.

Carleen also told the detectives that Biela had left the Reno area between March 2008 and September 2008 to work as a pipe fitter somewhere in the state of Washington. While he was gone from Reno, Carleen said, Biela sold his Toyota Tacoma pickup truck and purchased another truck.

When Biela decided to move back to the Reno area, Carleen explained, she had gone to Washington in September 2008 to help him make the move. While there with him, she said, she had found some petite-sized women's thong panties inside his vehicle. She suspected that he had been cheating on her. When she confronted him about the underwear, she said, he had gotten angry at first; then he finally told her that he had stolen them from a woman at a Laundromat in Washington.

During their interview with Carleen, Detective Jenkins and Detective Wygnanski asked her if she would voluntarily provide a DNA reference sample from her son that they could compare to the suspect's DNA sample. Because she was confident of Biela's innocence, she agreed. Both detectives witnessed the DNA reference sample as it was collected from the child. Afterward, they personally delivered the sample to the Washoe County Crime Laboratory.

Following the interview with Carleen, Jenkins and Wygnanski, along with several of their colleagues, began putting together additional background on James Biela. To the investigators, it began to look like he very likely might be the man they had been hoping for so long to find.

James Michael Biela had been born on June 29, 1981, in Chicago, Illinois. He was nine years old when his family moved to Reno. Later in life, he would be known as the life of the party or a barroom gathering, a funny guy who also took martial arts classes. Friends and acquaintances said that he had a quick temper, and some people described him as a bully. He joined the Marine Corps right after high school. After completing basic training in San Diego in autumn 1999, he was promoted to the rank of lance corporal and stationed at Fort Lejeune, North Carolina. He was discharged from the Marine Corps in 2001 for drug use.

On July 12, 2002, during the early-morning hours, a short time after his return to the Reno area, Biela caught the attention of authorities when he drunkenly threatened a former girlfriend's neighbor with a knife and was arrested. At that time, he lived in the Truckee Meadows area. Angi Carlomagno, the former girlfriend, filed a restraining order against him because of his violent tendencies. He pleaded guilty in April 2003 to a misdemeanor charge involving the knife incident.

In that incident, Biela had shown up at Angi Carlomagno's home after the two had split up a month earlier. He was drunk, and he ran over her mailbox and the mailbox of a neighbor. Angi told police that she was awakened early that morning by the sounds of her dogs barking. When she got out of bed, she found that Biela had entered her house and was standing there, confronting her with a beer in his hand. Angi ordered him to leave her house and took his beer away from him; then she followed him outside.

"He had a knife and came into my house without consent," she said. "He kicked my dog and grabbed me. The police came and a report was made."

While she argued with Biela as they stood along the side of the house, a neighbor, Sukhjit Singh, tried to assist her by trying to pull her into his house through a sliding glass door.

Biela pulled a knife from a sheath on his belt on his right side and made a swinging motion toward Singh with his knife, the police complaint said. *Singh said he was going to call the police.* Afterward, Biela left the Carlomagno residence and drove away. A third person witnessed the incident from inside a neighboring house.

However, according to police, Biela's harassment of Angi did not end at that time, despite the temporary protection order (TPO) she had filed against him. On August 22, 2002, he purportedly called her at work three times, "wanting to talk." She told him during the first call that she did not want to talk to him and hung up. During the second call, the receptionist told Biela that Angi was out and unavailable. When he called back a third time, he pretended to be from Wells Fargo. However, when Angi recognized his voice, she promptly hung up once again.

At one point, on September 6, 2002, Biela allegedly made contact with her at the Silver Peak Brewing Company while she was in the company of her boyfriend. He tapped her on the shoulder and told her he wanted to talk to her. The encounter ended up as more than just a conversation. Biela began yelling obscenities at her and trying to fight with her boyfriend in front of the restaurant/brewery, ultimately ending with him being kicked out by the establishment's staff. That same night, Biela called and left seven lengthy voice mail messages of approximately fifteen minutes each on Angi's telephone, saying that he was going to "get" her. Angi stated that all of the calls had been "explicit and of a threatening nature." She said that Biela also sent her "various explicit and threatening e-mails." Angi's TPO was, of course, granted, but the efforts of the police to serve

the restraining order on James Biela were not successful.

Biela was originally charged with felony assault
for the knife threat, and the charge was reduced to
simple assault—a misdemeanor—according to
court records. Biela pleaded guilty to the lesser
charge, according to court documents, and was sentenced to "driving under the influence" (DUI)
school and ordered to have no contact with Angi
Carlomagno for a year. In short, he got off easy and
did not serve any jail time. Furthermore, no DNA
samples were collected at that time, because the
charge had been reduced to a misdemeanor.

Detective Jenkins made a note to himself to check
out Biela's prior criminal record more thoroughly,
just to determine whether anything else existed that
might have slipped through the cracks.

On Tuesday, November 25, 2008, Jenkins received a call from Jeff Riolo, a DNA analyst at the
Washoe County Crime Laboratory. The call reminded Jenkins of the one he had received more
than eight years earlier from the commander of the
crime lab—the call that a match had been hit regarding Lisa Bonham's killer. On this occasion,
Riolo told Jenkins that he needed to meet with him
about the case.

When Jenkins arrived at the crime lab, Riolo told
him that he personally had developed the DNA profile that Jenkins and Wygnanski had collected from
James Biela and Carleen Harmon's son nearly two
weeks earlier. He had compared the boy's DNA profile to that of the suspect's DNA profile, which had
been kept at the crime lab, he said. Riolo also told

Jenkins that he had determined that the biological father of the submitted child's DNA reference sample "could not be excluded as the source of the suspect DNA profile." In simpler terms, Riolo had said that he had concluded that the DNA reference sample from James Biela's son indicated that the boy was related to the suspect in the Brianna Denison murder. The boy was also related to the suspect in two of the sexual assaults from which they had developed the suspect's DNA profile.

Riolo also told Jenkins that the probability of excluding a random individual as the source of the suspect DNA profile was 99.98 percent in the Caucasian population, 99.99 percent in the African-American population, and 99.97 percent in the Hispanic population. It looked like a near certainty that James Biela was their man. However, before they could be absolutely positive, they would have to take him into custody, charge him, and obtain a court order for a sample of his own DNA.

Being the lead detective in the case, Jenkins wrote up his affidavit for an arrest warrant, presented it to a judge for his signature and, once the warrant had been signed, he made plans with his colleagues to take Biela into custody that same day.

Knowing that an arrest was imminent, the investigators had been surreptitiously watching Biela for most of the day. They had been keeping close tabs on him since he had been identified as a person of interest from the Secret Witness telephone call. Also to be considered were the strong gut feelings that both Jenkins and Wygnanski held that he was their guy. Toward the end of the day, the officers followed Biela to the Stepping Stones Children's Center, a day care facility in South Reno, when he showed up there to pick up his son. He was taken into custody without incident by the detectives who came to the center to arrest him, effectively putting an end to the ten-month manhunt for Brianna's killer.

"He seemed surprised," Wygnanski said later. "We wanted to arrest him before he got to the day care, but we arrested him when we did because we didn't want to take a chance on anything going wrong."

After his arrest, Biela was taken to the Reno Police Department and placed in an interview room. Detective Jenkins gave him his Miranda warning, then questioned him briefly.

When Jenkins asked him, "Had you intended to kill this girl?"

Biela said, "I don't want to answer that."

Jenkins also asked him "about the girl who lived on North Virginia Street."

Biela said, "What girl?"

When he was asked about the thong underwear that Carleen Harmon had found in his truck, he said, "I don't want to talk about that. That's bad news."

At one point, Biela also said that he didn't believe in DNA evidence, saying, "I told you, I don't believe in that shit."

The interview was interrupted by Carleen Harmon's arrival and the videotaped meeting that then followed between her and Biela.

Following Biela's arrest, Jenkins called Bridgette Denison to inform her that Brianna's alleged killer had been arrested. It reminded him, he said, of the time he had called Doris Bonham in 2000 to inform her that the death of her daughter, Lisa, had been solved after DNA linked the girl's killer to a convicted sex offender.

"As Mrs. Denison succinctly pointed out, the arrest was good, but it wasn't going to bring Brianna back," Jenkins said. "I hate the word 'closure,' but I hope her family has some comfort. . . . Absolutely, we believe this individual is responsible for these crimes. The greatest benefit to this arrest is that in these cases, there is a likelihood these crimes will continue. Now he's off the streets. . . . But I recognize this is the beginning, not the end. This is a long way from over."

Jenkins also pointed out that this had not been the first time during the investigation that he and his colleagues had gotten excited over a possible suspect.

"A lot of us were reluctant to get excited about this one, Biela, because a lot of other leads had not panned out," Jenkins said of the investigation.

Jenkins recounted how he had been the lead detective over the past several years in a number of high-profile cases, including that of the murder of Nevada's state controller Kathy Augustine, as well as the murder of Charla Mack by her husband, Darren Mack. Jenkins pointed out, however, that the Brianna Denison case was different from those other cases, and much more difficult to solve, because the suspect in her death and the other sexual assaults had chosen his victims at random.

"I hope anyone else who is privy to any information about Mr. Biela will come forward," Jenkins said.

The cops continued to investigate their suspect and learned that Biela had been laid off from his job as a pipe fitter the previous week. This made his arrest even timelier, since because of his being out of work, he would have had more time on his hands. This, in their view, would have considerably raised the potential for him to commit additional crimes.

Biela was subsequently transported to the Washoe County Jail, where he was booked on charges of murder, kidnapping in the first degree, and sexual assault. The six-foot-tall, 190-pound prisoner seemed stunned at times; at other times, his face seemed blank or expressionless, aside from an occasional slightly worried look. At those times, it was as if he somehow knew what was coming at him next. Jenkins had also obtained the court order for a DNA sample, which was taken from Biela that evening. It normally takes approximately twelve hours to process, meaning that Jenkins and the other investigators would not know until the following day with absolute certainty that Biela was their man.

Early the next morning, there was no longer any doubt—crime lab personnel had put in overtime hours to process the sample as quickly as possible. Their work confirmed that Biela's DNA matched the DNA left on Brianna's body, as well as on the body of the December 2007 victim, Virgie Chin, the forensic evidence he left on the back doorknob of the MacKay Court residence, and on a condom packet found near the location where the November 2007 victim had been attacked. Biela's DNA also matched DNA found on one of the pairs of thong panties found lying beneath Brianna's legs at the site where her body had been discarded. The crime lab also soon matched Biela's DNA to that of yet another rape victim, in addition to Virgie Chin.

With the DNA evidence against him, particularly that which was left on Brianna Denison's body and that which was left on the back doorknob of the

MacKay Court address, it appeared that the detectives had successfully built a rock-solid case against their suspect. There were also the gray fibers that had been recovered from the December victim's clothing. That victim, who had been sexually assaulted inside a pickup truck, had provided significant details about the crime and her attacker, in addition to the fiber evidence. Police knew that the truck Biela had owned at the time of the December attack—but had subsequently sold—had gray upholstery.

Washoe County DA Richard Gammick called a press conference at the Reno Police Department, near the downtown Reno area, to tell the community about the events of Biela's arrest. A large crowd, which included several members of Brianna's family, showed up to hear what the officials would have to say about the arrest. Gammick told the crowd that he and Deputy District Attorney Elliott Sattler would be prosecuting Biela, but the DA said that he would determine later whether or not he would seek the death penalty in the case.

"We're going to prosecute this case to the maximum," Gammick said. "He held the community at bay way too long, and is what I call a 'hometown terrorist.' There's no question about it."

"He was the unassuming monster we had been saying he would be, the whole time," Lieutenant Robert McDonald said. "He is a dangerous individual who was stalking women by stealth and escalating in his violence. He was a local terrorist and frightened the community for nearly a year. We'll all sleep a little better tonight, but there's always another monster hanging around. We got him, but let's not put our guard down. . . . What a great Thanksgiving gift for the community. It's something to celebrate."

Lauren Denison told reporters that she and her family were pleased that Biela was in police custody, where he "can't hurt anyone else."

"Can you believe it?" Lauren said. "The police said the DNA came back, and it's him. . . . That's huge for us—that we're not waking up every day wondering, 'Has he struck again?' This is what we have been waiting for."

Crying, Lauren read a statement at the public gathering on behalf of Brianna's mother and brother: "'On behalf of Bridgette and Brighton, and the whole Zunino-Denison family and the Bring Bri Justice Foundation, we are pleased this person is off the streets and can't hurt anyone else. I want to thank law enforcement, the media, and the community for working together as a team and not ever giving up and making it happen so we can get this guy.'"

"I'm proud of our unit for sticking together and not giving up," Wygnanski told reporters. "My condolences to the family and thanks to our own families for putting up with us for all the long hours we worked. It's just very rewarding for us to finally get this person. We did everything we could to eliminate him [from suspicion as the person responsible] and we couldn't. All we had was evidence to say that he was responsible. I'm happy for the Denison family, and it brings a form of closure, but it will never bring Brianna back."

Chapter 13

The news of Biela's arrest traveled quickly through the community. Residents living in the area where Brianna was snatched expressed their relief that Biela was in custody, and UNR students were particularly elated that a suspect in the murder and community rapes had been identified and jailed. Although students expressed a sense of relief, there was also a strong sense that they would continue to remain on their guard and continue traveling in groups, particularly when they were out late. Many said that they planned to continue to avoid walking alone on the streets, whenever possible. University police were also relieved, but they approved and supported the caution that was still being exhibited by the students.

"He can't hurt any more teenagers . . . like I am," said an eighteen-year-old female UNR student.

"A lot of us around here were still scared something might happen," said a male sophomore student who, just before the start of the new school year, had moved into the house from where Brianna was abducted. "It's good to know they got him."

K.T. Hunter was understandably one of the many students expressing relief on learning that Biela had been arrested. K.T. said that she was "crying with happiness" over the arrest, and was at the same time "excited." She also experienced revulsion, she said, at the sight of his photo, which had begun appearing all over the media outlets by that time.

"I was so grossed out and I wanted to throw up and yell at him," K.T. said of seeing Biela's photograph. "I had just as much emotion when I saw his picture as I did when they said they found her body. I am relieved. I am happy he was found and that he's not going to get away with what he did, and now girls on campus can finally feel safe."

K.T. said that she was actually surprised at what Biela looked like, and she found it repulsive that he was the father of a small child.

"I am really disgusted because I know what he did," she said. "But I thought he would look creepier and would be younger."

"We would remind the community that the arrest of this one suspect should not give people a false sense of security, or reduce their desire to be vigilant in practicing personal safety on a daily basis," UNR police director Adam Garcia told a gathering at a press conference after news of Biela's arrest was made public. "University police will continue to provide information and services, and will continue to urge students to exercise caution and practice sound safety measures both on and off campus.

"We congratulate the Reno Police Department and all law enforcement agencies involved in the ongoing effort to solve this case, which had a huge impact on the university community," Garcia added. "Even though the arrest cannot make up for the loss of Brianna, it is extremely satisfying to know that the suspect in this terrible crime may now face the consequences of his actions. We hope the arrest will bring some peace to Brianna's family."

At his arraignment the morning after his arrest—the same day that his DNA sample had been matched to the rape and murder cases by the crime lab—Biela appeared before a justice of the peace to acknowledge that he understood the charges facing him. He also claimed indigence and requested a public defender; the judge set his preliminary hearing for two weeks later, on December 10, 2008. He was taken back to the Washoe County Jail and placed in the facility's infirmary section and kept under suicide watch, which was standard for a prisoner facing charges as severe as his. According to Deputy Brooke Keast, Biela's demeanor since his arrival at the jail appeared to be one of disbelief. He also declined all interview requests from the news media.

That same morning, Wygnanski and Jenkins, along with a group of crime scene technicians, showed up at Biela's Wingfield Springs home, located on Allegrini Drive in Sparks, and began searching it for any evidence they could find that might be related to any of the crimes that Biela was suspected of committing. A *Reno Gazette-Journal* reporter watched from a distance as the group of investigators from the Washoe County Sheriff's Office dug and probed around in the backyard of the Allegrini Drive residence. The details of whatever the officers were searching the backyard for were not revealed at that time. Detectives also searched his new vehicle, and

another team of investigators had already located
the pickup he'd sold in Idaho in March 2008 and
had made preparations for it to be searched, too.

When detectives fanned out and made inquiries
throughout the neighborhood where Biela lived,
many neighbors said that they did not know the suspect and did not see him very often. Biela's next-
door neighbor told the officers that he had heard
the loud knocking of the police early that morning,
but said that he did not know what the commotion
was all about. The neighbor told a reporter for the
Reno Gazette-Journal that the only times that he had
seen Biela was when Biela either left his home to go
outside or went back indoors, coming or going from
his garage, or when he returned home from work.

"It's scary," the neighbor said. "We were not
friendly—we never talked—so we don't know anything."

"We had no idea who he was," said another neighbor. "Just looking at him, he doesn't look like he's
that type of man."

Another neighbor, who lived across the street
from the house that Biela shared with his girlfriend,
told the investigators that she recalled when the
couple had moved in, around three years earlier.
She said that she had never actually met the couple,
and had not seen them talking to others in the
neighborhood. She said that she thought it unusual
that they stayed to themselves, especially considering
the fact that they had a child.

"Normally, the kids play together and the parents
talk," the neighbor said. "He seemed like a nice,
normal guy. Isn't that what the neighbors normally
say? I guess killers don't wear a sign. . . . This is too
unbelievable. I've seen him come and go for three

years. It was a really unbelievable thing to do, and it was really unbelievable it was the guy across the street."

Yet another neighbor agreed that Biela had always kept a low profile within the community. She said that she could not recall having ever seen him or his girlfriend, and she did not know whether their child was a boy or a girl. The neighbor, who ran a day care center from her home, said that she and a friend routinely went out walking at 4:45 A.M. daily. She said that in hindsight it was scary, with him having lived so close to her.

"I carried Mace and my friend carried a baseball bat, but we were never worried about a person," the neighbor said. "We were worried about coyotes." After Biela's arrest, she and her friend must have come to feel that there had been far more dangerous predators than coyotes in the area.

A young woman who brought her son to the neighbor's day care center on a regular basis said that she often left her seventeen-year-old sister waiting in the car while she dropped off her child. Sometimes her sister would be left alone for as long as fifteen minutes or more.

"They thought [he] would be a regular guy, with a regular family, and he is," said the woman. "I never thought it would be here. We just don't think about it in this neighborhood. . . . He could have been watching me the whole time."

The woman said she would never fail to lock her car in the future, regardless of where she was.

Another Reno resident, a man who had known Biela for approximately four years, recounted a recent encounter with the accused killer.

"I just had a beer with him, sat right next to him, the other night," the man said. "He's the last person

I'd think of as doing [the things for which he was charged]. He's a really likeable guy. He's funny, great to be around."

A short time later, Joseph "Joe" Biela, James Biela's father, spoke with a reporter from the *Reno Gazette-Journal.* The heavily-tattooed, bespectacled father, with long, straggly graying hair and a Ho Chi Minh–type beard, explained that he had not spoken with James for several years. The senior Biela acknowledged that he was upset about the news of his son's arrest and the allegations facing him.

"I did not do this. He did," Joe Biela said. "And now he's going to have to suffer for it. The cops have evidence."

Joe, a former U.S. Marine and truck mechanic, said that he had moved his family to Reno from Chicago in 1990. He was long divorced from his wife, who had remarried and relocated to Spokane, Washington. Joe said that his son James had two brothers, one of whom had died, and two sisters. He explained that he had moved to Reno to find work, but he had become disabled, could no longer work, and lived on disability benefits. He said that he was rarely visited by his sons.

The senior Biela, who spent much of his time in a wheelchair inside a North Reno trailer home, said that James, whom he referred to as "Jimmy," was his youngest child. He told reporter Martha Bellisle that his children—Joey, Kristi, Jeffrey, Kimberly, and James—were all born in Chicago in the aforementioned order. Joey, he said, died while he was still an infant.

"Joey is in Heaven," he said. "He hit his head in the crib three days before he was nine months old."

Joe confirmed his son's trouble in the Marine Corps and how Jimmy was discharged for "doing drugs."

"A couple of years ago, he (James) comes here with his girlfriend and baby and says everything is okay," Joe said. "But it wasn't. . . . Why did he do this to this lady? I'd like to know why he did what he did.

"He's still my son," the father added. "He's my blood. I will always love him and back him up. But I can't help him. He did it to himself. I had no signs that he could do something like that. No signs at all."

As details of the arrest continued to circulate quickly throughout the Reno area, it was reported that local attorney David Houston, known for handling high-profile cases, had been contacted by Biela's family to determine if he was interested in representing the murder suspect. Among those Houston had defended was murder suspect Chaz Higgs, convicted of murdering his politician wife, Kathy Augustine. Houston acknowledged that he and another attorney had spoken with Biela's family about taking on the case. However, the attorney added that they had not yet decided whether they would accept or not.

"The primary concern is whether it is possible for anyone accused to get a fair trial in this case," Houston said. "So many people are ready to point the finger based on an accusation. . . . Anytime you have a high-profile case, you have a large number of people who have formed an opinion as to the guilt or innocence of an individual without having seen the evidence, having seen the evidence tested. . . ."

Houston seemed somewhat dismayed that people had already begun discussing what type of punishment should be meted out against the defendant in the event that James Biela was convicted. He said that such discussions were premature, even though detectives had linked Biela to the murder of Brianna Denison and the rapes of some of the other victims.

"How valid is the DNA sample?" he asked. "How valid is the evidence control? It is so emotionally charged that people want to believe we have arrived at an answer. Because of that, there may be a willingness to overlook what would otherwise be thought to be fair procedure."

Much to the chagrin of the populace at large, Biela did not look like a monster, like many people had thought he would look, which is typically the case in such investigations. There were no fangs, no dripping saliva, little or nothing to make him stand out in a crowd. Instead, he was reasonably good-looking, and was the father of a four-year-old child. Biela even regularly picked the little boy up from a day care center. He had an attractive girlfriend and they lived in tract housing in a Reno suburb and shopped at the malls and grocery stores, where everyone else shopped. Even though investigators had said that the killer at large might have been someone known to the victims, that turned out not to be the case. Police had found nothing to connect Biela to his victims in any way, meaning that he had selected his victims totally at random, making him an even more chilling person, given his appearance of normalcy. Residents had conjured up monstrous images of the man who victim descriptions said had kept his pubic area shaved. Biela, who they learned had a fetish for collecting women's underwear, was the picture of a normal guy to those who did not know him well.

Some of the residents of Reno had slept better after Biela's crimes ceased because many people believed, correctly, that he had left the area, thinking that he had gone in search of a new, fertile stalking ground. He had returned after only a short absence, though, and was living in their midst. He could have very well been biding his time, waiting for the right moment to strike again. Thankfully, the *unassuming monster's* world fell apart before that could happen.

Meanwhile, a Washoe County judge set December 10, 2008, for Biela's preliminary hearing. Although Biela claimed that he was indigent and asked for a public defender, attorney David Houston and another lawyer, Byron Bergeron, said that a decision had not yet been reached on whether they would defend Biela or not. It was obvious that his case would not be an easy one to defend, particularly with one large cloud looming overhead: There was no way to know whether the plumber-turned-rapist-and-murderer, with martial arts skills, could get a fair trial in Washoe County.

Chapter 14

As Jenkins and his colleagues at the Reno Police Department and the Washoe County Sheriff's Office continued building their already-strong case against James Biela, a clearer picture of the accused killer's background began to emerge. In addition to confirming some of his friends' and acquaintances' statements that he could be a "funny guy" or the "life of the party," the detectives had also established that he had a quick-tempered and bullying side, in part due to the information that had surfaced regarding his failed relationship with Angi Carlomagno. Much of the background or history they established for Biela was, of course, accomplished after his arrest and while he was on suicide watch at the Washoe County Jail's infirmary section.

Biela, they knew, had been the last of Joe and Kathy Biela's five children before their divorce—the couple divorced shortly after arriving in Reno, when James was nine. His mother later remarried and moved to Washington. Although Jenkins did not immediately determine which schools James attended as a child while still in Reno, he did learn that the murder and rape suspect had lived with his mother in the Spokane Valley area for a while and had graduated from West Valley High School there in 1999, confirming relatively strong ties their suspect had with that Pacific Northwest locale. Jenkins also learned that James Biela and Carleen Harmon, the mother of his son, had applied for a marriage license in 2007, but the license had evidently gone unused. There did not appear to be a record of an actual wedding having taken place.

With regard to Biela's martial arts training, Jenkins learned that he sometimes trained at an establishment in Reno called Charles Gracie Jiu-Jitsu Academy, owned by Gary Grate. Jiu-jitsu is a self-defense martial arts form that trains the student in choke holds, among other things, to gain control over an attacker. The academy's owner said that Biela sometimes trained alongside local police officers, but Biela had only attained the rank of blue belt, which is only one level above that of a beginner.

"He was just a guy in a big group of students," Gary Grate said. "He was under the radar. Police officers trained next to him, but nobody noticed anything about him that was peculiar."

Gary said the last time he had seen Biela was about a year earlier, at approximately the time that police began investigating the sex attacks against female students on or near the UNR campus.

As Jenkins and the other investigators continued piecing together James Biela's life, they learned that his childhood and that of his siblings was "terrifying," according to what his sister, Kristi Jackson, had said. Their terror centered around the abusive relationship they said that they had experienced due to the out-of-control behavior of their father and the violence he had allegedly inflicted on their mother on a continual basis.

"We pretty much spent our whole childhood afraid of the men in our lives," Kristi said. "I think I probably thought it was normal."

Kristi said that she and her siblings were afraid to leave their room to use the bathroom, and instead used buckets that they kept stored beneath their beds so they would not have to leave their rooms and risk going down the hallway. She said that she did not have any friends while she was growing up because she was too embarrassed to invite them to come to her house. According to Kristi, their parents were not affectionate, and a typical night at the Biela home included her dad beating her mother. On one occasion, their brother, Jeffrey, told the other kids that they needed to get out of the house and tell the police to come and do something to stop the abuse. After exiting from a bedroom window, they realized that little brother Jimmy was not with them. When they returned to the house, they found him by himself in the living room with a blank look on his face.

Kristi said that it was not until she had turned twelve or thirteen that she began to understand that the violence in their lives was unusual. She also said that James appeared to be a good father to his son, and added that he no longer had a relationship with his own father.

Another relative, Liz O'Brien, an aunt, characterized Joe and Kathy Biela's wedding as having been "more like a funeral" than a union of holy matrimony. A short time after the marriage, she said that Joe pulled Kathy's hair in a shocking display of violence. She said that Joe drank a lot of beer, and one of her memories of his drinking was that he liked to make pyramids out of his empty beer cans.

"We thought she was making a mistake," Liz said of Kathy's marriage to Joe.

On one occasion, Liz said, Joe held one of his daughters over the edge of a balcony. Witnesses believed he may have planned to drop the little girl, but family members convinced him to bring her back to safety and to let her go. After that incident, his wife left him for a while, "but she went back," Liz said.

According to the aunt's recollections, Joe allegedly beat Kathy severely one night when James was nine years old. After witnessing the beating, the children fled to Liz's house in the middle of the night; Kathy showed up later as well. Liz said she saw that some of Kathy's hair had been ripped out of her head, and she had cuts and scrapes on her legs. Because Kathy was concerned about expenses, she refused to go to a hospital for treatment of her injuries. Kathy, she said, always seemed to have an explanation for her injuries and often claimed it was not from her husband's abuse—an all-too-common response given by victims of domestic violence. She also said that Kathy did not have any teeth because "they had all been knocked out."

At another point during the inquiry into James Biela's upbringing, Kathy indicated that her husband had not spanked or beaten the children, but she claimed that he had beaten her almost on a nightly basis. He once pushed or shoved their eldest son, Jeffrey, but the violence from her husband always seemed to be directed toward her and not the children. After leaving Joe, Kathy told the investigators, she never saw him again. However, she said that the court had ordered that their children have contact with their father only by telephone—no in-person visits were to be allowed.

John Latham, a coworker of James Biela's at the construction company, told investigators that Biela was always on time for work, was a conscientious employee, and did a good job as a pipe fitter. He said there were "never any complaints" about Biela, but he indicated that Biela had appeared unhappy and frustrated during the autumn of 2007 and the early part of 2008. When John asked what was bothering him, Biela told him that he was perturbed or frustrated with his girlfriend and son. During one of their talks, John said, he witnessed Biela "put his fist through a wall." The coworker said that Biela began slacking off at work, which caused issues with his job performance. Then, around mid-January 2008, John said that Biela told him that he wanted to leave town and was "tired of the drama in his life." It was also around that time that he began talking about leaving his job.

When Brianna's body was found, Carleen Harmon was working in the human resources division of Employers, a workers' compensation firm. From her office window, Carleen could see the area near the crime scene, the field where Brianna's body was found. She called Biela at work and told him that she could see all sorts of activity in the field, with police cars, police, and crime scene tape. She told him what she was watching and that she thought Brianna Denison must have been found. He was silent, saying nothing. A short time later, when word spread that it was likely Brianna's body that had been found in the field, John Latham said that he asked Biela "how he felt about her being found." Biela responded with a couple of expletives and said that Brianna "probably had it coming."

Later that same day, James Biela approached his boss, Jeremy Coston, and requested a voluntary layoff because of "personal problems." Jeremy said that Biela's request came at a time when the construction company was behind schedule on many of its projects, which was creating significant overtime opportunities—nothing to sneeze at for a union pipe fitter. Nonetheless, Biela remained adamant that he needed the voluntary layoff.

According to Detective Ron Chalmers, who investigated Biela's work schedule, among many other aspects of the case during the times of the various crimes, Biela had worked at his job on October 22, 2007, December 16, 2007, and January 19, 2008. However, he did not work on January 20, 2008, the date that Brianna disappeared. Investigators noted that Biela left in March 2008 to travel to Spokane, Washington, where he planned to work as a pipe fitter. He and Carleen drove the truck to Spokane and she flew back to Reno from there. Biela did not return until September 2008, when Carleen flew there and came back to Reno with him.

Meanwhile, Brianna's family issued words of praise via the *Reno Gazette-Journal* to the caller of the Secret Witness telephone line, the woman without whose tip Biela's arrest might not have come so soon—if at all. The caller had said that she wanted to remain anonymous.

"It was so incredibly brave of you knowing this could possibly be the guy," Lauren Denison told a reporter for the newspaper. "We are so grateful you had the inkling that, wow, this behavior is weird and you had the courage to call Secret Witness. It's remarkable."

Lauren expressed disappointment that the call had not come from Carleen Harmon, Biela's girlfriend and mother of his child, but she also made it clear that she and the family were nonetheless grateful and did not want it to appear that they were blaming Carleen for anything.

"Love is blind and maybe she couldn't fathom that he could be that way," Lauren added. "She has got to have unthinkable emotions. She is the mother of his son, lived with him, and had a relationship with him for six years. You would hope you would know someone. It's just disappointing we couldn't reach out to everyone after we had said ten million times for women to really look hard at the men in their lives who fit the profile. But thank goodness she confided in her friend, and that friend was the vehicle that broke this case."

Lauren Denison also expressed disappointment that Biela had not been stopped in 2002 after threatening former girlfriend Angi Carlomagno with a knife. It seemed that he barely received a slap on the wrist after pleading guilty to battery and driving under the influence a year later, and then receiving a sentence to attend DUI school. Somehow it did not seem right that the people around him had failed early on to see his future possibility for violence. But what if they had seen it? What could they have done in the absence of catching him committing a crime? There were no easy answers.

There never are to situations like this, where a violent offender wasn't stopped until he had committed the ultimate crime of murder.

"He was already displaying this kind of violent behavior," Lauren said. "Someone tried to stop him when he was escalating, but it didn't happen. How do you stop something that is starting? The signs were there."

Shortly after James Biela's arrest, the investigators showed the Denison family members a photo of Biela. Naturally, the Denisons were upset.

"It sickened me that I was actually looking at the person who took my niece's life," Lauren Denison said. "We have a name and a face for the person that has completely rocked our world. This guy basically put the community on notice and . . . [held] us hostage in our own city. . . . I'm sure he drove by all the blue ribbons, posters, and banners of Bri and read the newspaper. He would have had his head in a hole if he didn't. There's no way he could have gotten away from it. He really blended in, walking amongst us and no one suspecting him. Just like the FBI profile said."

Meanwhile, Brianna's family decided that they wanted to take down the blue ribbons, which had been hung up around town, telling the community that they had only wanted the ribbons to remain in place until Brianna's killer was identified and apprehended. The ribbons had been serving as a stark reminder of the tragedy that had taken the life of the young college student, they said, and of the other rape victims, who had survived the attacks against them. It was now time, the family believed, to begin moving on and start focusing on bringing about legislation that would require everyone who was arrested for a crime to submit their DNA so that it could be loaded into a national database.

At that time, Nevada required DNA samples from those who had been convicted of a felony, not from those who had been placed under arrest for a felony but not convicted. The law requiring DNA from convicted felons had been mandated in 2007. Had it included those arrested—and if that had been done when Biela was arrested in 2002—Lauren said, "We would have had him after the first attack." At the time of the 2002 incident, she explained, on through the time of the rapes and Brianna's murder, as well as Biela's arrest, only convicted felons were required to submit their DNA without a court order. Because of the potential legal ramifications and protections under the U.S. Constitution, it seemed like their quest to get DNA samples from every person arrested for a felony would be an uphill battle.

The BBJF, which had served Brianna's family and friends as a way to take positive action toward changing the laws on DNA samples, began an all-out campaign to lobby legislators to adopt "Brianna's Law," patterned after New Mexico's "Katie's Law," the Katie Sepich Enhanced DNA Collection Act. The law, which was enacted in 2007, was named after Katie Sepich, also a student, who was raped and murdered there. A task force was formed by the foundation, the Secret Witness Program, and the Nevada Attorney General's Office to work toward getting the law passed in Nevada. Task force members made a strong case for the law by pointing out that if DNA had been required for everyone arrested in the state on felony charges, Biela could potentially have been stopped before Brianna's death. After his 2002 arrest on assault charges, if his DNA had been on file, it would have enabled him to be linked to the 2007 rape cases around a month before Brianna's murder.

The proposed law was introduced during the legislative session following Biela's arrest by the house's minority leader Heidi Gansert, R-Reno, a supporter of the foundation. However, it was not passed because of the estimated high cost of putting it into effect, a cost of likely more than $6 million dollars. Even though felons were assessed a $150 DNA testing fee, the authorities reported that only around 10 percent paid the fee.

Overtime paid to members of the Reno Police Department during the Brianna Denison investigation amounted to over $365,000, and the BBJF reported that the passage of Brianna's Law would bring about an extreme reduction of the time and money spent on such lengthy criminal investigations. It would also serve as a quick means of exonerating those suspects who were not guilty and removing them from further suspicion, stopping repeat offenders, and preventing many violent crimes when the perpetrators knew they would be speedily identified because their DNA was already on file.

Those who were opposed to the law claimed that not only would it be too expensive to put into effect, it might also be in violation of the civil rights of some of those tested, because an arrest was not a guarantee of a subsequent conviction. They also feared that the information obtained by DNA testing might be used to discriminate against some minorities or to gain access to other personal medical information about the persons who were tested. There were other concerns about funding also. In New Mexico, where Katie's Law had been passed the previous year, legislators had become concerned that their own lack of funding was resulting in slow storage of samples in databases, with criminals remaining free while backlogs grew. Nevada's attorney general admitted that funding would be the biggest challenge there.

"I am hoping we can work through the civil issues," said Attorney General Catherine Cortez Masto.

The members of the BBJF were determined to find funding sources for the law. Valerie Van Antwerp, vice president of the foundation, said, "The foundation's guiding principle is to do everything possible to ensure that no other family or individual is forced to go through what Brianna and her family had to endure."

The foundation's veep went on to say that working for the passage of the legislation was likely the most important step the foundation members could take toward achieving that goal, adding that taking DNA samples could save an untold number of lives.

Reno PD sergeant Chuck Lovitt said that DNA testing would enable detectives to save a great deal of time and effort by allowing them to home in on a suspect quickly without spending so much of their time pursuing false leads. He pointed out, however, that suspects still had to be investigated, and arrests were not made solely because of a DNA match.

Lovitt explained the theory of DNA testing for persons arrested for what he called "gateway crimes," such as burglary, that often lead to violent crimes. If those offenders were required to give DNA samples, he said, escalating crimes could be prevented.

"We have an opportunity to significantly impact

violent crime," he said, adding that the testing wouldn't work unless the system could handle the drastic increase in lab work.

"Otherwise," he said, "the system will grind to a halt because it's so overwhelmed."

The American Civil Liberties Union's Northern Nevada Chapter named potential problems with the law, saying that both it and the process by which the testing would occur were both at risk of being unconstitutional. The ACLU chapter's coordinator, Lee Rowland, said that the law would treat those arrested as though they were already convicted, then require them to pay for the testing only because they had been arrested.

"Here in America, you're innocent until proven guilty," Lee Rowland said.

A Reno assemblywoman said that legislators would have to be assured that public safety concerns would outweigh citizens' right to privacy. Sheila Leslie, a Reno Democrat, called the debate about DNA laws "a balancing act," saying that the government had no right to take a person's DNA just because a law enforcement officer had placed him under arrest.

"How would you feel if you were wrongfully arrested and your DNA was taken?" she asked.

Scientists in DNA testing labs said that the only information they could determine from a DNA sample was the person's gender, and there were no names connected with the samples, only a code number. Foundation members said that they recommended destroying samples if a person was acquitted of the crime they had been charged with. Supporters of the passage of the law believed that the testing of persons who were later acquitted was a "no harm, no foul" situation. If the innocent were protected in such a matter, the guilty would not go unpunished.

Secret Witness founder Don Richter was an outspoken supporter of Brianna's Law, and said that any legislator who failed to get behind the effort to pass the law would "personally wear the name of all future rape and murder victims. The true cost of not having this is the loss of human lives, raped women, and traumatized victims and families."

At the root of all the discussion of the potential law, both pro and con, lay one fact that could not be denied. If James Biela had been required to submit a DNA sample after his problems with his former girlfriend, which resulted in his 2002 arrest on assault charges, he would have been identified as a rapist before he ever had the opportunity to become a murderer.

Chapter 15

Before November 2008 was over, Reno police investigators again called for possible rape and/or kidnapping victims of Biela's, if any existed who had not yet been identified, to come forward with their information. Police felt that there might be additional victims who were holding back because they feared to report that they had been assaulted, like the young woman who was raped at gunpoint in the parking garage of the UNR campus on October 22, 2007, or the December 16, 2007, victim who had been rendered unconscious by a choke hold. Investigators pointed out that choke holds of that type were part of the jiu-jitsu training that Biela had been learning. If, by any chance, there were any other victims out there who had been attacked by him, the authorities wanted their information in order to supplement the case they had built against their suspect. They emphasized that Biela's attacks were all random, opportunistic assaults. It was for that reason, including the fact that Biela's most recent girlfriend, Carleen Harmon, had found small-sized women's thong panties inside his truck, that they suspected that additional victims of Biela's might be out there and had not yet come forward and reported to the authorities that they had been attacked. According to police, the panties found by Harmon in Biela's truck were a major break that was instrumental in helping detectives crack the case. Like the DNA evidence that came later, the panties were one of the common denominators linking Biela to the crimes. It was also for that reason that investigators still were urging the owner of the Pink Panther thong panties to come forward.

According to Lieutenant Robert McDonald, police in Washington and Idaho were also looking for any connections to Biela. They were carefully examining unsolved sex crimes in their states during the time frame in which Biela might have been in their locales. When Biela fled Reno in March 2008 and relocated to Moses Lake, Washington, he had likely done so when he felt that things were about to get too hot for him in Reno.

"It seems like he was waiting for things to calm down," McDonald said. "It had been six months and he had no contact with police. He still had his girlfriend and son. He came back."

According to McDonald, investigators in Reno were particularly interested in any rape or sexual assault victims in Reno or the immediate area who had been attacked in the latter part of 2007 through March 2008. It was of great importance to the case against Biela for any such victims to come forward with their information. McDonald pointed out that the October 2007 rape victim had not reported the assault against her for a time, and he reassured potential victims that it was okay if such an assault had not previously been reported. He stressed the point that had it not been for the October 2007 victim's information, police might not have obtained sufficient details to put together the composite sketch of the suspect—the sketch that bore such a striking resemblance to Biela.

"We would really love for any more victims to come forward," McDonald added. "We will do our best to keep the information confidential, but we need to know if there are more victims out there."

So far, according to McDonald, Biela had not been linked to any additional crimes in other parts of the nation through his DNA. He also reiterated how Biela had held the community hostage for nearly a year, and that residents could now "sleep easier" because of his arrest.

"But I can't stress enough that this doesn't mean you have to stop paying attention to what's around you, and protect yourself," he said. "[Biela] isn't the only bad guy out there. We'd be naïve to think he's the only predator in Reno."

According to Washoe County DDA Elliott Sattler, who was preparing to prosecute the case against Biela with his boss, DA Richard Gammick, the district attorney's office was looking to file additional charges against Biela. Authorities strongly suspected that Biela was involved in two additional sexual assaults on college students, and potentially even others, he said. That was why the investigators needed such victims to come forward.

"We anticipate filing an amended complaint in the near future," Sattler told reporters without being more specific.

What else were police doing to build their case against Biela at this point in the investigation? According to McDonald, detectives suspected that he had followed the Brianna Denison case closely, and computer forensic experts were preparing to examine computers seized from Biela's home to find out.

Following his arrest, detectives learned that Biela had traded in his Toyota Tacoma pickup to a dealership in Kellogg, Idaho, in June 2008, and investigators had seized it. Forensic experts from the Washoe County Crime Laboratory had been painstakingly processing it for clues after it had been tracked down through Department of Motor Vehicles (DMV) records. Biela had traded the Toyota pickup for a Chevrolet truck, which also had a gray interior, the same color as the fibers obtained from the December 2007 victim's clothing. Unfortunately, the dealership in Idaho had already detailed the Toyota pickup before it changed hands to a new owner, but investigators were hopeful that some forensic evidence remained despite the thorough cleaning it had been given. The truck no longer looked like it had when Biela owned it; the new owner had modified it by placing a cover on its bed and had equipped it with running boards, but DMV documents and the vehicle identification number (VIN) proved that it was the same vehicle.

Meanwhile, it appeared that defense attorney David Houston would not be defending Biela at trial. Instead, it now looked like public defender

Jeremy Bosler's office had the job, and that Richard Davies would lead the defense team. Biela had asked the court for new attorneys, claiming his relationship with his previous attorneys had been damaged. Davies was attempting to prepare for Biela's scheduled December 10, 2008, preliminary hearing in Reno Justice Court, but Bosler indicated that his office might need to request additional time.

"We are still receiving police reports and witness statements and will evaluate our ability to go forward after that process is complete," Bosler said.

On Friday, December 5, 2008, as they had indicated that they might, prosecutors filed three additional charges against Biela, including allegations that he sexually assaulted a young woman at gunpoint in October 2007 in the Brian J. Whalen Parking Complex on the UNR campus. This was an assault in which DNA had not been collected and which had resulted in part in the delay of investigators connecting the case with the others. He was also charged with battery with intent to commit sexual assault for an attack on a young woman on College Drive in November 2007. Prosecutors also alleged that he sexually assaulted Brianna Denison on or about January 20, 2008. Although DA Gammick issued a statement, he declined comment about the new charges.

"I'm not going to get into any specifics or discussions on the case at this time," Gammick said. He indicated that he might have more to say later, after the preliminary hearing that was only a few days away—still scheduled for Wednesday, December 10, 2008. Gammick did say that his office was still in the process of reviewing the specifics of the case to decide whether or not to seek the death penalty against James Biela.

Due to what they referred to as the "sensitivity of the case," the Denison family said that they would not comment on the new charges and they would likely not do any additional interviews until after the trial.

At one point, Officer Joe Robinson was brought into the case to inspect some of the evidence. Robinson had considerable training in the painstaking skill of tracing and examining cell phone records. By utilizing Robinson's well-established skills, investigators wanted to try and pinpoint as closely as possible Biela's locations at the time of Brianna's disappearance, as well as where he was during the times of the other crimes he was suspected of committing.

Robinson discovered that someone, likely Biela, had used Biela's cell phone to check his voice mail on the night Brianna disappeared. Cellular telephone transmission, simply put, goes out from the phone to a cell phone tower strategically placed in various locales; the calls placed are typically picked up by the tower nearest the phone being used. In this case, Robinson discovered that the cell phone tower related to Biela's telephone's transmission that night was located approximately 1.5 miles from the house from which Brianna was abducted.

Robinson also discovered that Biela's cell phone was also used near the home from where the December 2007 victim was abducted and sexually assaulted.

Meanwhile, Reno detective Roya Mason had conducted a forensic search of Biela's computers, which the police had seized. She had found thousands of search-term hits for the word "thong," along with hundreds of photographs featuring women wearing thongs. She later said that the forensic search findings indicated that Biela's "interest in . . . thongs and women in thongs" was thematic.

During this time, another investigator, Detective Troy Callahan, found two pairs of size-small women's thong underwear hidden inside a storage compartment during a search of a travel trailer owned by Biela. By this point in the investigation, Biela's interest in women's thongs had become a well-established fact.

Chapter 16

When court proceedings began in preparation for James Biela's arraignment, the accused killer didn't seem to take things seriously at times, smiling into cameras and often sitting with a cocky look on his face. He became more somber as things progressed, and he was totally serious by the time new evidence was presented that indicated that a pair of thongs might have been used as the murder weapon that strangled Brianna Denison. When questioned about the results of the autopsy that she had conducted on Brianna, Dr. Ellen Clark told the court that in her opinion, the cause of death was strangulation by ligature. The mark on Brianna's neck was an exact match for the strap on a pair of K.T. Hunter's panties that had gone missing the night Brianna was abducted.

Also testifying was Alberto Jimenez, who reported finding Brianna's nude body, wearing only socks, in a field near his workplace on February 15, 2008. Alberto gave a graphic description of the animal bites he saw on the body, and told the court how a discarded Christmas tree had been thrown on the remains in an attempt to conceal them from view. After discovering Brianna's body, he hurried back to work and immediately notified the authorities, he said, thinking all the while about his own children and the family of the young girl he had just found.

"If I didn't do something about what I had seen," he told the court, "it would haunt me for a long, long time."

Hearing the sickening details of how Brianna's body was found, and the condition it was in when Alberto Jimenez first noticed it, proved to be too much for the deceased's mother and brother. They were unable to stay in the courtroom and listen to some of the more disturbing details that were being brought out during the testimony.

The court also heard from Detective Adam Wygnanski, who questioned Biela following the Secret Witness tip that had finally broken the case. Wygnanski said that he began to believe that Biela could be the man that law enforcement had been searching for when, during the interview, Biela appeared "just very, very nervous" and began to sweat.

Dr. Lisa Smyth-Roam, an expert with the Washoe County Crime Lab, told the court that the DNA of seven hundred men was tested following Brianna's murder, and most of them came forward to be tested voluntarily in order to exclude themselves. There had been only one of the tests that proved to be a match for the DNA taken from the crime scenes. Neither James Biela nor any of his other paternal male relatives could be excluded from the Y chromosome DNA profile, Dr. Smyth-Roam testified.

Biela's mother and two sisters were present in the courtroom during the hearing. They sat there, stunned, as though they were in shock throughout the proceedings. It was clear to observers that they still could not believe that the man they thought they had known so well, their son and brother, could have done the things they were hearing about during the testimony. To Brianna's family members, though, the possibility was all too real.

Carol Pierce, Brianna's grandmother, called Biela a "pathetic, sick man." Her aunt Lauren was pleased when the judge bound Biela over for arraignment in Washoe County District Court to enter a plea in the charges against him: kidnapping, murder, the rape of Brianna, and the additional rapes of at least two other victims. At the time of his arraignment, he would have the choice of pleading guilty, not guilty, or not guilty by reason of insanity.

The trial would be scheduled following Biela's plea entry, but there was a likelihood of the prosecution requesting additional time to prepare for the trial. This, according to District Attorney Richard Gammick, was because there was an extremely large amount of evidence in the case. Gammick also said his office had still not decided whether or not to seek the death penalty. Until the case was ready for trial, Biela would be held in custody without bail.

Biela's defense team made several requests of the court while they waited for the legal process to continue—one of which was for the trial to be moved to another county in order to choose from an unbiased jury pool. Defense attorney Davies also wanted Biela's three trials to be held separately, claiming that each of the cases involved inconsistent weapons, unrelated victims, and differing methods of attack. He feared, he said, that jurors would convict Biela in the two rape cases, only because of the strong feelings about the Brianna Denison case. This might happen whether the evidence in the rape cases proved Biela's sufficient guilt or not. The community involvement in the case, he said, was so extensive that "the community is almost a witness at this point."

The prosecution, led by Elliott Sattler, called those claims "absurd," and said that each separate charge was a strong case in itself, saying that the evidence proved that the crimes were all related.

"The most recent case in the news is always the 'most covered' any community has ever seen," Sattler said, comparing the O.J. Simpson and the Craigslist Killer cases to James Biela's similar publicity situation.

Incredibly, Biela had been seen to have a smirk on his face occasionally during the hearing, and observers in the room said that he looked toward the back of the courtroom at one point at Brianna's mother. Bridgette Denison immediately averted her eyes, refusing to meet the stare of the man who, she believed, had brutally murdered her daughter.

Chapter 17

As expected, James Biela entered a plea of not guilty at his arraignment, and the court later set a February 22 trial date. It was not long, however, until his defense attorneys filed a motion claiming that they had none of the DNA evidence that they had planned to use in his defense. It had been destroyed by the county's crime lab, they said. When the defense had asked for access to the DNA samples for independent testing, the crime lab reportedly told them the samples had been "consumed during testing," although an earlier report from the Washoe County Crime Lab had claimed that some material was still available.

The lab furnished the defense with a copy of their directives for testing, which instructed them to use the "smallest amount possible" of the available samples.

According to the defense's motion, the amount of evidence collected from the crime scene was *70 to 100 times the amount necessary for a lab to develop a genetic profile of a suspect, so what happened to all of this unused evidence?*

The motion said: *Without the ability to conduct its*

own testing, the defense is unable to challenge the state's test results. Allowing the state's DNA tests into evidence would force the defendant into the position of proving a negative.

The chief deputy public defender Maizie Pusich said in the defense motion that the laboratory had violated its own policies when it had destroyed Biela's semen samples after they used what they had for DNA testing. Pusich claimed that *[destruction of the samples] raised the inference that arresting and prosecuting someone, anyone, in this high profile murder case may have been more important to state agents than following the procedures designed to prevent false tests.*

The state is asking Mr. Biela to disprove their own test results, while they simultaneously have destroyed the evidence in the case, which he needs to present his defense.

The motion asked that an order be issued that any DNA test evidence, when the entire sample had been used and could not be retested, be suppressed as evidence and not presented to the jury at the trial. The DNA evidence in question had been collected in the Brianna Denison murder case and in the December 2007 rape case.

The defense also said they planned to ask that the date of the trial be moved to a later time. There were two primary reasons for the request, they said: both the ruling that was to be made on their motion concerning the DNA evidence, and the fact that Biela's previous lead attorney had left the public defender's office and had since gone to work for a private law firm. Pusich said she needed more time to prepare for the case and had not yet received all of the evidence that had been requested by the defense.

Biela's defense team also asked that other key evidence in the case be suppressed, including the testimony of Carleen Harmon about his fetish for thong underwear, and also the DNA sample that had been taken from his son. The child's DNA, they alleged, had been taken from the minor with only the consent of his mother. For that reason, the defense hoped to have it suppressed as evidence.

Because of the defense's requests, a hearing was subsequently held to determine what evidence could be presented to the jury when the trial, rescheduled to start on May 10, was held. DDA Elliott Sattler told Judge Robert H. Perry that the prosecution felt that the evidence about Biela's alleged interest in thong panties and pornography should be included in the trial for the reason that it connected the evidence in the murder and sexual-assault cases. Biela's defense, however, sought to limit much of what evidence was to be presented to the jury, claiming that Biela's alleged interest in thongs and pornography was, in itself, nothing illegal. By allowing the evidence to be presented, the jurors' opinions of Biela would be affected.

Biela's onetime girlfriend Carleen Harmon told the judge that Biela spent a lot of time on pornography websites on their home computer. She said that she often searched the computer after he had used it to see what sites he had visited. She told the judge that she tried to keep him from going to the websites, to no avail, by changing the passwords on the computer.

Carleen also said that she had good reason to believe that Biela had a fetish for women's thong panties. She said that she had found two pairs of thongs in Biela's truck when she went to visit him in September 2008 when he was working in Washington. Suspecting that he might be cheating on her, she said she had searched his truck and was upset when she found the two pairs of small cotton thongs in a pastel-flowered design. She confronted Biela with the thongs, and he became very angry and defensive and threw them out the truck window, finally claiming that he had picked them up at a Laundromat, she said.

In ruling on the request regarding the thong underwear, Washoe District judge Robert Perry decided that the ex-girlfriend's testimony concerning Biela's interest in websites featuring thong underwear would, indeed, be allowed during his trial. He ruled, however, that the sites could not be referred to by the defense as pornography. In addition, Perry denied the defense's motion asking that Biela's son's DNA sample be suppressed.

The prosecution considered the rulings to be highly in their favor, even with the judge's stipulation that all their evidence would have to be officially introduced at the trial and must at that time meet all the necessary legal standards.

Chapter 18

Before the start of his trial, James Biela's mother and siblings had spoken to the media on several occasions, telling about the person they knew, the person who was not the monster that was being put on trial, accused as a rapist, kidnapper, and killer. It was almost impossible for his family to perceive Biela that way, and they tried to describe his childhood and early life in a way that would show him as they remembered.

"It's not the Jimmy we know," his mother, Kathy Lovell, said. "He's not the monster they are describing." She had come to Reno to be in court during the jury selection, and to bring her son the new black suit he would wear during the trial. However, she and the other family members could not be present in the courtroom during the trial itself because of the possibility that they might be called as witnesses during the penalty phase if Biela was to be found guilty.

Biela's other family members were upset that they could not be present during the trial because they wanted to be able to show their support for him. His sister Kristi had saved vacation days from her job since his arrest so that she could attend the trial. She worried that the public would perceive the family's absence from the courtroom in the wrong way.

"What will a jury think when they see there is no one there for him? We want people to know why we aren't there, and it's not because we don't want to be," she said. "I want people to know there are people who love Jimmy. To me, he was a good brother and a good father [to his son]. He is my best friend."

Biela's mother had been experiencing a great deal of hurt since her son's arrest, with the newspapers in the Spokane area, where she lived, carrying frequent headlines about the case. The atmosphere at the auto shop where she worked as a bookkeeper and receptionist was supportive, she said, and the men she worked with would do their best to try to reassure her when yet another story about her son would be published. "But I just end up crying," she said. "It's all guys I work with, and they try to talk to me about it, but they don't know what to say."

There had even been death threats toward her family, Kathy Lovell said, adding that she knew it would be difficult to be in Reno—what with the extreme level of public animosity toward her son. However, she said that she just tried to think of the day she would be able to hug Biela once more. She firmly believed in his innocence, she said, and thought that the police had been under pressure to find someone to blame. She added, however, that her heart went out to the Denison family. Biela, too, had told her that he felt bad for the Denisons, his mother said.

"Someone who did something like that wouldn't

feel remorse," she said. During a phone call, he had also told her, "Mom, I'm so sorry for putting you through this."

News reports had criticized Biela for having what they referred to as a smirk on his face at times during his preliminary hearings, but his mother said, "That's just Jimmy's expression, something he does when he's nervous. I can tell in his eyes how scared he is."

When Carleen Harmon had first called Kathy Lovell and told her that James had been arrested, his mom initially thought there had been some sort of terrible mistake.

"She told me Jimmy had been arrested, but I just didn't believe it," his mother said. "I thought that they got this wrong."

Biela's sister Kristi said that the time since Biela's arrest had been especially tough for the family.

"There's no one who can relate to what I'm going through. No one cares about the defendant's family. They just hate us," she said.

Kristi said that she had picked out a tie for her brother to wear with the JCPenney suit his mother was bringing to Reno for him to wear during the trial.

"What tie do you pick out that may be the tie your brother may be wearing when a jury decides whether he lives or not?" she asked.

Kristi also said she worried about her mother being alone in Reno during the trial. She expected that the streets around the courthouse would be cleared before Biela was brought there, wearing a stun belt and a bulletproof vest, but wondered what might happen to any of his family, who would have no protection from hostile crowds.

Biela's family stayed in touch with him during the

time between his arrest and the start of the trial by writing to him often. Kristi said they talked to him by phone a few times a week. Kathy Lovell said she lived from paycheck to paycheck, but the family had still managed to put money into an account for Biela so he could make phone calls and buy items from the jail store. She had added Reno numbers to her cell phone plan, she said, to save long-distance charges, and said the family kept their phones with them at all times because they never knew when Biela might get a chance to make a phone call.

At the jail, they were not able to visit Biela; they could only view him on a monitor through the jail's television visitation system. When he had first been arrested, his family could view him through a glass window.

"We all put our hands up against the window," Kristi said. "It was the closest contact we have had with him."

Kathy Lovell remembered her son, growing up, doing all the normal things in spite of his abnormal home situation with a horrifically abusive father. Jimmy had tinkered with cars, joked, helped others without being asked, his mother said, and was afraid to put worms on his fishing-pole hook. Money was very scarce; and when they were young, the children would look on the ground for change people had dropped and check every phone booth for coins people might have forgotten. When they collected enough change, the children would go to McDonald's for two hamburgers, which they divided among the four of them.

Kathy Lovell said that on one occasion, when

Jimmy was about five years old, he had insisted that the children should have a birthday party for a Japanese cartoon character that he liked. She had made corn muffins for the party, and they all had sung "Happy Birthday" to Spectreman, the cartoon superhero.

The Biela children and their mother tried to make the best of things during the years when the children were young, doing the best they could to have a happy life during the times when Joseph Biela was not on the rampage against his wife. His abuse had begun almost immediately after their marriage, and had been a constant in their lives from then on. The family was on welfare, and they had a car, but there had been little money for gas. When they moved to Reno when James Biela was nine years old, Joseph Biela drove ahead to find work and then, when he did, the rest of the family came by train.

Despite their financial situation, Joseph refused to allow his wife to work, or even to make any friends. The brutal beatings he subjected her to took place almost every night, with the children listening, terrified, afraid to come out of their bedrooms. Their father didn't hit them, but he verbally abused them. He didn't want his wife to tell the children she loved them.

"He thought it would make them sissies," she said, "especially the boys."

The family's situation finally changed in September 1990, when Kathy and the children moved in with Kathy's sister. This happened after Kathy and Joseph Biela had a particularly horrible fight. Kathy divorced Joseph, got a job, went to night school, and met Ron Lovell, the man she married in 1993. They moved back to Spokane, and Kathy was surprised at how good Ron said all the Biela children were, considering what they had gone through in their early lives.

"You would think with all that abuse and situation," he said, "you'd be dealing with kids who were really messed up."

Ron became a father figure to all the children, and took young Jimmy fishing and bowling, competing together in a father-and-son tournament.

The family said that James Biela had been an average student in high school. He didn't date, they said; he was shy but had a great sense of humor. He worked at a pizza parlor, at Target, and at the auto shop with his mother while he was in high school. He enjoyed Spanish class, jazz and heavy metal music, and playing video games.

"He really was a normal kid," Ron Lovell said. "He didn't kill the family pets or do anything that would indicate he is a person who could do something like this."

After graduation, James Biela joined the Marine Corps and did well, until his discharge for drug use. Then he returned to Reno, where he eventually had problems with the police due to his dust-up with former girlfriend Angi Carlomagno, her neighbor, and her boyfriend. Then he met Carleen Harmon; and when they had a son, Ron Lovell said, Biela's life changed.

"He really grew up and loved being a father," Ron said. "He wanted to provide for his family and went to school to be a plumber's apprentice."

While Reno waited for Biela's trial to begin, all his

family could do was wait for the time when, if he was to be convicted, they would get the opportunity during the penalty phase to tell about the Jimmy they knew and loved. They would have only one chance to convince the jury that he was still their gentle, beloved little brother, who deserved mercy, not the monster that could very well be sentenced to death for kidnapping, raping, and murdering Brianna Denison without a second thought.

Chapter 19

The public's interest in the Biela trial had remained extremely high since his arrest. When the trial finally began, the courtroom was packed with reporters and cameramen from newspapers and television stations around the region. Preparations were made for the press to make their reports from inside the courtroom by posting updates online, and from outside the courthouse with live on-camera reports at the close of proceedings each day. Delays had pushed the start date of the trial to May 10; on that date, jury selection finally began, and the community's intense interest in the trial had only increased as time passed. By the official starting date, the Biela trial was the featured story on every newscast, in every newspaper, and on countless Internet sites.

Biela's attorneys had asked the judge to screen all potential jurors with a seven-page list of questions to be certain that they had no preconceived opinions about Biela's guilt or innocence. The defense also requested that the jurors be questioned individually in the judge's chambers so that they could speak freely about their own personal feelings on the death penalty.

Judge Robert Perry denied the defense's requests, saying that the use of a jury questionnaire might, in fact, result in Biela's ability to get a fair trial being jeopardized.

"The notice to jurors sent before trial, telling them that they would be involved in this highly publicized case, would encourage discussion with others, and possible independent research about the case," Perry ruled. "The risk that these potential jurors would be 'infected' with the opinions of family and friends is high."

Perry also said that he agreed with Biela's lawyers that almost all those people residing in the Reno area were very aware of Brianna's murder and rape.

"The court believes that it is pure fantasy to imagine that it is probable that any juror in any location in the state of Nevada will not have heard of this case, particularly by the time the case comes to trial in any venue," he said. "The reality of the modern jury selection requires the focus to be on finding jurors who will set aside 'preconceived notions' and the opinions of others, and render verdicts based on the evidence presented at trial."

Judge Perry therefore denied the defense's request for individual questioning of each potential juror. The court would rely on the jurors it chose to deliver a fair, unbiased verdict.

Deputy District Attorney Elliott Sattler told the media that the judge's order "speaks for itself." The DDA said that he believed the court would be able to seat a fair and impartial jury in Reno, adding that it was important to conduct any trial in the jurisdiction where the crime occurred. The people in any community in which a crime occurred, he said, should have the ability to have that trial in their community.

When jury selection was completed and the official jurors and alternates who would hear the cases against James Biela were seated, the panel was made up of five women and seven men. They were described by one reporter as a typical group of middle-class, middle-aged people, ready to hear the testimony of the large number of witnesses who were scheduled to present evidence. As the trial began, Brianna Denison's family sat on the prosecution's side of the courtroom, and Biela's family sat on the other side, behind him and his defense attorneys.

Spectators in the room during the trial proceedings claimed that they could always hear a steady, clicking buzz from all the laptop keyboards being used by the large number of reporters covering the trial. The members of the press were constantly updating the reports they were sending back to their news agencies or adding to their Internet reports as the prosecution began its presentation. The courtroom was packed to its maximum capacity with spectators, but thanks to the many reporters posting to the Internet, thousands more people were able to follow the trial, live and in its entirety. The interest in the case was not confined to Reno; every day that court was in session, people from all over the nation and around the world logged on to the wide range of Internet coverage to keep up with each development as the trial progressed.

In his opening statement, Deputy District Attorney Chris Hicks told the jurors that when the DNA and other forensic evidence in the case was presented, there would be no doubt in their minds that James Biela was guilty as charged. Hicks claimed that Biela had initially begun his crimes as a serial rapist, but he had soon "graduated" to murderer.

Jay Slocum, one of Biela's public defenders, said that the jurors should look at the evidence in what he called the "cold light of reason," because he claimed that the DNA evidence against Biela was not conclusive. He said that even though law enforcement and the prosecution was alleging that Biela was the sole assailant in all of the three cases brought against him, each of the cases had enough differences to cast doubt on his responsibility for all three. Each case, Slocum said, had "very distinct facts" and could very well have been the work of three different perpetrators.

When the time came to begin testimony about the two rape cases, DDA Hicks called the alleged victim from the October 2007 incident to the witness stand. The assault had taken place in a University of Nevada, Reno, parking garage. The woman in that case, Amanda Collins, testified that she was taking a class that met on Monday evenings between seven and ten o'clock. On these nights, she would park in the university's Whalen Parking Complex, which was located near the education building.

Amanda was on campus to take a midterm in that class. After the exam, she walked back to her car in the parking garage. As she got near to her car, Amanda was attacked from behind by an unknown male. He grabbed her, putting one hand on her back and the other hand up and over her breast.

She was pulled to the ground and pushed down between vehicles in the parking garage. The man straddled her and put a gun to her head.

Amanda could only see part of his face; he was wearing a hoodie, and the hood was over most of his face. She was raped at gunpoint, she said; the man raised her skirt, opened her legs, and inserted his penis into her. Then her attacker ejaculated on her skirt; then, she said, he moaned and said it felt good. Incredibly, he then complimented her on her skirt, telling her that it made her "look good." After the rape, she said that the man got up and pulled up his pants, and told her to stay put until he was gone. Then he left, taking her thong panties with him.

Amanda drove straight to her sorority house, where she took a shower. Then she drove to her home in Spanish Springs, where she threw away the clothes she had been wearing. She was understandably traumatized by the attack and chose not to report it to the authorities at that time, saying that she didn't "want her body to become a crime scene." She initially didn't tell anyone what had happened. She later told a roommate, Deborah Johnson, who contacted the police after news of Brianna's disappearance had been published. Amanda agreed at that time to meet with police detectives, and she assisted the police sketch artist in drawing a picture of the suspect who had raped her. But when Biela was arrested for Brianna Denison's murder, she recognized him and came forward and identified him to the authorities as the man who was her rapist. There was no DNA evidence available in that assault because, in addition to failing to report the rape immediately, Amanda had thrown away the clothes she had been wearing at that time.

Her testimony was challenged by the defense, because prior to Biela's arrest, she had told one of her friends that she couldn't describe her attacker.

The woman presented as being Biela's second rape victim had been interviewed extensively by Detective Jenkins about her kidnapping and subsequent rape, which took place on December 2007, two months following the assault on the first woman. At the time of her assault, Virgie Chin, the second victim, was a Chinese exchange student at UNR, studying marketing. She lived by herself in an upstairs apartment on North Virginia Street, which was across the street from the UNR campus.

In the wee hours of December 16, 2007, Virgie gave two of her friends a ride from her apartment, where they had been visiting, to their residences nearby. She got back to her apartment around three in the morning. She parked in her assigned parking spot, but at the door to her apartment, she realized that she had left her keys in the car. She went back to the car, found the keys, and got out of the car again. Before she could lock the doors, she was grabbed from behind by an unknown male. His left arm was wrapped tightly around her body, holding her arms down, while his right hand was covering her mouth and nose. It was almost impossible for her to breathe, and she couldn't scream. She started to hit and kick at her car, and he picked her up off the ground and started walking backward, carrying her. He tripped and fell to the ground, landing hard on top of her. Virgie's face hit the ground, and she lost her glasses. The man kept holding her tight with his hand over her mouth, and she lost consciousness and woke up, sitting in the man's truck. She didn't have her glasses, and her jacket hood was covering her eyes. The man told her, "Don't do anything stupid," and told her not to look at him.

Virgie had been hurt from the fall and didn't think she could get away from him, so she tried to remember everything she saw in the truck. As the man began to drive, he asked Virgie what her name was. When she asked him for a tissue, he gave her one. She remembered that he had a deep American voice and didn't have any particular type of accent.

The man drove for only a few minutes to an open area nearby, which had parking spaces. There he asked her to use her mouth and her hand to help him achieve an erection; then he made her perform oral sex on him. Then he kissed her vagina and put a finger deep inside her. He asked her if her breasts were real; then he touched her body and finally masturbated himself to a conclusion. Afterward, he got back into the driver's seat and told Virgie to put her clothes back on, but he took her underwear. He drove her back to her apartment and told her not to tell anyone, or he warned, "I'll be back."

At the apartment, a neighbor helped Virgie find her keys, and she called the police, who took her to the hospital for a sexual-assault examination and some minor medical treatment. At the hospital, a registered nurse, Denise Engel, conducted the exam and confirmed that Virgie had been sexually assaulted. A Sexual Assault Response Team (SART) kit was prepared from the exam, containing samples and swabs in sealed envelopes from the examination. The completed kit was delivered to Suzanne Harmon, a criminalist with the Washoe County Sheriff's Forensic Science Division, to be processed.

Dr. Lisa Smyth-Roam, a senior criminalist and DNA analyst in the Washoe County Crime Lab, handled the DNA testing that was done following Biela's arrest, which revealed that a DNA profile from the kit matched a reference sample of James Biela's DNA. Based on those results, Dr. Smyth-Roam concluded that neither Biela nor any of his male paternal relatives could be excluded from the results matching the ones developed from the swabs taken in Virgie Chin's SART kit.

Virgie testified that while she was being held in the vehicle, she saw a child's shoe in the floor of his truck. She also said her attacker had a shaved pubic area, which coincided with information Carleen Harmon had given describing Biela's shaved and trimmed genital area. Virgie had been able to give other valuable identifying information to the authorities. She described her attacker as white, with brown hair, a medium build, a little bit of a belly, and arms that were darker than his chest and stomach areas from being in the sun.

When she was asked if her attacker's physical build matched Biela's, he was made to stand up in court so she could get a good look at him. She confirmed that he fit the description of the man she so well remembered.

Unlike Amanda Collins, Virgie Chin had reported the assault. According to testimony, the DNA obtained from her rape kit matched Biela's DNA. His defense attorneys had attacked the DNA-testing method used to make the match, earlier having claimed, to no avail, that it was inaccurate and should not be allowed. Now, however, it served as a positive link that undeniably tied Biela to that assault.

Chapter 20

A video that had been made at Mel's Diner was presented during the trial as evidence. It had been made when Brianna Denison and her friends went there to eat on the night she was abducted, a few hours before she settled down on K.T. Hunter's couch and began texting her boyfriend, Cameron Wilson Done. The video was shown in court, and those in the courtroom leaned forward, watching and listening intently to get a look at that one last image of Brianna, alive and well. Deputy District Attorney Elliott Sattler asked K.T. Hunter, who was on the witness stand, to confirm for the record that the petite, lovely girl shown yawning on the video was Brianna.

"To the best of your knowledge, was that the last time Ms. Denison was photographed alive?" Sattler asked.

"Yes," K.T. answered.

It was a very emotional time for many of the spectators, and it grew much more so as other witnesses took the stand. Several of Brianna's friends, the people she had spent time with at the rap concert and at the diner, were called to testify. They all said that nothing unusual had happened that evening, and that none of them had seen James Biela at any of the parties and events they had attended that night.

Jessica Deal said that she had returned to the house before Brianna and K.T. because she had to work the next day, and had already gone to sleep and did not hear the other two girls when they came in later. She and K.T. began making breakfast when they got up the next morning, and initially they were not alarmed when they saw that Brianna was not on the couch, thinking she had gone upstairs to the other bedroom. Then, Jessica said, they noticed Brianna's phone was on the counter.

"It was vibrating," Jessica said. "Probably a text message."

The girls noticed the spot on the pillow, but thought it could have been made by K.T.'s dog. Jessica then drove K.T. to pick up her car, and went to work.

The other students testified that they'd had an enjoyable time that night, spending time with Brianna, and Ian McMenemy said that he and another friend had given Brianna and K.T. a ride home and watched until they saw the two girls go into the house. Biela's attorney Maizie Pusich asked him if Brianna had been upset with someone that night and sending text messages. Ian told her that Brianna had been on the phone with her boyfriend.

Some of the people in the courtroom cried while they listened to the testimony of Bridgette Denison

Brianna Denison.

Mel's Diner in Reno, where Brianna was seen and captured on security video only hours before her abduction. *(Author photo)*

The house from which Brianna was abducted, near the University of Nevada, Reno campus, where a series of rapes occurred in the months before Brianna's abduction. *(Author photo)*

MISSING PERSON

Brianna Zunino DENISON
19 years old
5'00", 90 lbs., Long Dark Brown Hair, Blue Eyes

R.P.D. CASE # 08-2284: Date / Time: January 20, 2008 at 0400 hours.
Last Known Location: 1395 Mackay Court, Reno, Nevada.

Brianna was last seen at the listed location at approximately 4:00 am on January 20, 2008.
Her disappearance is suspicious at this time.
She was possibly wearing light blue or pink sweat pants and a white tank top.

Anyone with information is urged to contact the Reno Police Department.

Searchers examine a vacant lot in South Reno where a female body believed to be that of Brianna Denison was found on Friday, February 15, 2008. *(Photos courtesy Tim Dunn/*Reno Gazette-Journal*)*

Investigators search the area in South Reno where a female body was found. *(Photo courtesy Tim Dunn/Reno Gazette-Journal)*

Prior to Brianna's abduction, another woman was attacked in this parking garage. *(Author photo)*

The University of Nevada, Reno campus, site of a series of rapes later attributed to murder suspect James Biela. *(Author photos)*

People gathered at a memorial erected where Brianna Denison's body was found. *(Photo courtesy Marilyn Newton/Reno Gazette-Journal)*

Part of the memorial erected where Brianna Denison's body was found. *(Photo courtesy Marilyn Newton/Reno Gazette-Journal)*

James Biela's arrest mug shot, 2008.
(Photo courtesy AP Photo/Reno Police Department)

Artist's composite of suspect, issued by Reno Police Department.

(Photo courtesy AP Photo/Reno Police Department)

The coroner's office. *(Author photo)*

Washoe County Courthouse, Reno, Nevada, where James Biela's trial was held. *(Author photo)*

Murder defendant James Biela, right, sitting next to one of his attorneys, Jay Slocum, deputy public defender, glances toward the gallery on Wednesday, May 12, 2010 during the first day of his trial for the murder of Brianna Denison. *(Photo courtesy Marilyn Newton/Reno Gazette-Journal)*

Judge Robert Perry listens carefully to the testimony of the first witness in the James Biela murder trial. *(Photo courtesy Marilyn Newton/Reno Gazette-Journal)*

Lisa Smyth-Roam, a forensic expert with the Washoe County Sheriff's Office, reacts to a question posed by Washoe County assistant district attorney, Chris Hicks. *(Photo courtesy Marilyn Newton/Reno Gazette-Journal)*

During the second day of Biela's trial, Reno police Detective David Jenkins describes how a hood covered the face of one of the victims allegedly raped by James Biela. *(Photo courtesy Marilyn Newton/Reno Gazette-Journal)*

Prosecutor Elliott Sattler shows the jury a photo of a pillow used by Brianna Denison that has a large blood stain. *(Photo courtesy Marilyn Newton/Reno Gazette-Journal)*

Reno police Detective Troy Callahan shows a pair of women's thong underwear found in a travel trailer owned by James Biela. *(Photo courtesy David B. Parker/Reno Gazette-Journal)*

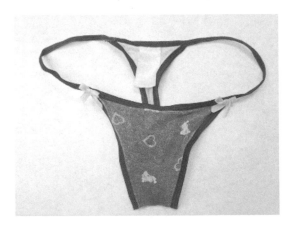

Pink Panther thong panties were discovered at the scene where Brianna's body was found. Police later determined they had not belonged to Brianna. *(Photo courtesy of Reno Police Department)*

James Biela, convicted of the murder of Brianna Denison a day earlier, enters the courtroom for the penalty phase. *(Photo courtesy Marilyn Newton/Reno Gazette-Journal)*

James Biela, convicted on all charges, glances toward the courtroom gallery during the start of the penalty phase on Friday, May 28, 2010. *(Photo courtesy Marilyn Newton/Reno Gazette-Journal)*

Washoe County Sheriff's Sergeant Tom Green talks with defense attorneys James Leslie and Maizie Pusich during the noon break at the start of Biela's penalty hearing. *(Photo courtesy Marilyn Newton/ Reno Gazette-Journal)*

Elliott Sattler, deputy district attorney, makes a statement during a press conference on Wednesday, June 2, 2010 after Biela was sentenced to death. *(Photo courtesy Marilyn Newton/Reno Gazette-Journal)*

telling about the last night that she had seen her daughter alive.

When Bridgette took the stand to testify about what happened when she first learned of her daughter's disappearance, she told the jury how things had been at their home on the final night of Brianna's life. Brianna had made plans, Bridgette said, to go out with K.T. Hunter that night and would be spending the night with her friend after their evening out. Brianna had gotten together a bag, filled with some clothes and other items, her mother said, and had left for K.T.'s house to get ready to go out to a rap concert.

"January 19, at eight forty-five P.M., was that the last time you saw your daughter?" Deputy District Attorney Elliott Sattler asked Bridgette.

"Yes," she said.

"What would Brianna wear when she went to bed?" Sattler asked.

Bridgette told him that Brianna hated being cold, so she usually would wear sweatpants, a sweatshirt, socks, and would sleep under "a couple of down comforters."

The next morning, Bridgette testified, K.T. called her, worried and upset, telling how Brianna was not asleep on the couch. When K.T. had gone to bed, that was where Brianna had been, staying up and texting her boyfriend. K.T. had searched the house and Brianna wasn't anywhere to be found. A moment later, Bridgette said, K.T. had called back, crying and hysterical.

"She said she had looked further at everything in her apartment. She said there was blood on the pillow that Brianna was sleeping on," Bridgette testified.

Bridgette immediately headed for the apartment. "I told her to call 911, and I went to her house."

When Bridgette got to the apartment, one of the first things she found was that all of the things Brianna had left home with, on the evening before, were still there: her shoes, her cell phone, all of her clothes, and personal items.

"I saw the blood on her pillow," Bridgette said. She followed the police around, inside and outside the apartment, helping them in any way that she could while they searched for any trace of Brianna. She gave them a DNA sample for exclusionary purposes, she said.

Bridgette told Detective David Jenkins, who arrived to investigate the disappearance, that Brianna was a very petite girl and was sensitive to the cold. She told him that she couldn't believe that her daughter would go outside at that time of the winter dressed in only a T-shirt and sweatpants. After she and Jenkins went through Brianna's clothing, they decided that the only items missing were the pieces of clothing she wore to bed: a thin, sleeveless camisole top, with *Bindi* printed on the back, and a pair of worn pink sweatpants.

There was nothing else missing: Brianna's purse had been left behind, containing her wallet, credit cards, driver's license, lotion, sunglasses, and lip balm. The bag of clothing and cosmetics was still there. She had disappeared without taking her phone, shoes, or coat.

Detective David Jenkins testified that when he had first arrived at K.T. Hunter's apartment that morning, his first order of business had been to try and determine whether Brianna had left voluntarily from the residence or if she perhaps had been kidnapped. After meeting with Bridgette Denison, he decided that the fact that Brianna's cell phone had been left behind was a very strong indication that she had not left of her own free will.

"Mrs. Denison described her daughter as not being the type of person who was prone to unusual behavior," Jenkins testified. "Mrs. Denison said she couldn't fathom her daughter could go anywhere without her cell phone."

"So she has no shoes, no coat, no telephone. No way to get around. Just gone," said DDA Sattler.

"That's correct," Jenkins told him.

When K.T. Hunter took the stand, she told the jurors how she and Brianna had met some of their friends to go to the rap concert that evening of Brianna's disappearance; then they had returned to the Sands Regency Casino and Hotel. Following that, they went to Mel's Diner, where Brianna had French fries and a milk shake before they went back to the apartment for the night.

K.T. described how Brianna had gotten ready for bed by changing into a T-shirt and sweatpants; then she had taken the pillow, a teddy bear, and a couple of pink blankets, which K.T. brought for her to use to sleep on the couch. Brianna was texting her boyfriend, Cameron Wilson Done, when K.T. took her dog and went to her own room to go to bed. She told the jury that Brianna had told her earlier that night that she and Cameron, who was spending the winter break at his family's home in Eugene,

Oregon, had been arguing because he had not wanted her to go out to the concert.

"She said to me earlier that night, 'I don't know if me and my boyfriend are together anymore,'" K.T. said.

The next morning, K.T. woke up to find that Brianna was not on the couch. Her first thought was that Brianna might have gone upstairs to sleep in the bedroom of another roommate, who was not at home that weekend. K.T. went to check to see if Brianna was in that room, but the door was locked. When K.T. knocked, there was no answer. She grew more worried and went back downstairs.

"I saw that there was a red stain on the pillow," she said, but she thought at first that it was something her dog had chewed on "and made a mess of." On closer inspection, she realized that the stain looked like blood, she said.

At this point, Elliott Sattler handed K.T. an evidence bag and a pair of rubber gloves, asking her to put the gloves on and see if she recognized the contents of the bag. When K.T. pulled the cut-up pieces of a pair of pink thong underwear out of the bag, she said that they belonged to her. She said that until that time, there in the courtroom, she hadn't realized that they were missing.

K.T. didn't know that the pair of thongs she was holding in her hand were the same thongs that Sattler had said previously, at another hearing, were most likely the murder weapon that had been used to strangle her friend Brianna.

When Cameron Wilson Done took the witness stand and began to testify about the last time he spoke with his girlfriend, Brianna Denison, his grief made it difficult for him to tell the jury about their relationship. He was in tears, running his hands over his face, while he told how the two had argued back and forth in text messages. The last text probably came only minutes before Brianna was kidnapped from her friend's home.

Brianna had gone to the rap concert with her friends that night against his wishes and he was upset at her for going out without him, he said. She had gone to Reno over the winter break, and Cameron had gone to his family's home in Eugene. He had been irritated at her for making plans to go out for the evening with her friends. They had argued about it before she left home to go to K.T. Hunter's apartment. Brianna tried to call him at 3:00 A.M., he said, but he didn't take the call. When she got back to K.T.'s at 4:10 A.M., they resumed their argument via texting, with Brianna saying she had done nothing wrong by going out. Cameron, however, remained angry with her.

"I said I was fucking pissed off and I would talk to her later," Cameron told the court.

She texted him, again, at 4:13 A.M., wanting to know what she had done wrong. At 4:17 A.M., he swore at her and texted, I'm over you right now.

Two minutes later, Brianna texted back and asked if she could call him.

"I said no, don't call me," he said, and at 4:23 A.M., she texted him for the last time and told him once again that she didn't do anything wrong. She said that he was "messed up."

Cameron cried while he told the jury that he had expected that Brianna would keep trying to get in touch with him so they could make things up, which was their usual pattern during arguments. He said that he had never heard from her again after that final text message.

Brianna was Cameron's first girlfriend, he said, and they had met while they were both going to Santa Barbara City College. They remained in their relationship after he transferred to the University of Oregon. They had planned to live together whenever they were both finished with school, he told the court.

"It was a privilege to be able to date her," he said, choking back tears. "She truly was the sweetest, kindest person I've ever met."

Cameron said that he had expected Brianna would call him in the morning after their texted argument, but she never texted any further that night or tried to call him again. Rather, when morning came, instead of hearing again from Brianna as Cameron Wilson Done had expected, the shocking phone call he got told him that she had vanished without a trace in the dead of night.

Chapter 21

One of the first of many law enforcement witnesses who had been scheduled to testify during the trial, Detective David Jenkins told the court about the more than five thousand tips that his office received after Brianna's disappearance. He testified about the number of documents that had been created during the investigation, which exceeded 39,000. He also told of the extensive police search that took place starting immediately after Brianna was reported missing.

The search process included an exhaustive check of the license plate numbers of countless numbers of vehicles that matched the description that had been given by one of the rape victims. There were also the very many thorough and repeated checks of a tremendous number of fields, wooded areas, vacant houses, and much more, even down to checking the manholes in the area. Hundreds of members of the public joined in the search and combed likely locations throughout the area; then, once Brianna's body was found, an equally large number of people offered DNA samples in order to eliminate themselves from any suspicion. Several people had contacted the police to claim they believed an ex-spouse was the murderer/rapist, Jenkins told the court, and the news of the receipt of those particular tips served as a great deal of incentive for many men who submitted their DNA samples to the authorities in order to be excluded. State and federal law enforcement agencies from several parts of the country had helped a great deal with the case and were involved in the search efforts, he said.

When John Latham, a foreman at J.W. McClenahan Co., Biela's workplace, testified about his own personal knowledge of James Biela, he told the court what a good employee he thought that Biela had been and how he was one of the best pipe fitters on the job. The foreman clearly had no suspicion of Biela, not even when he noticed a child's shoe in Biela's truck, even though police had released that information to the public as part of the description that one of the rape victims had provided about what she had been able to see inside her attacker's vehicle.

John Latham also didn't suspect anything out of the ordinary when Biela asked him to lay him off from his secure, well-paid job on the same day that Brianna's body had been found. John said he didn't find it strange when he and Biela had discussed the case and John asked Biela how he felt about the body being found. According to the witness, Biela had said that "the bitch probably had it coming"; then he smiled. John said it never occurred to him to report the remark to police; he said that he thought

Biela's remark was one that a lot of men with Biela's sense of humor might have made, despite its extreme inappropriate nature. Like so many others around Biela, John Latham had no idea whatsoever that his employee might have been involved in murder, rape, and kidnapping.

When Alberto Jimenez spotted Brianna's body in a vacant field of thick, tall, dry grass adjoining his workplacc, EE Technologies, his manager, Scott Ferris, testified that he had immediately returned to the location with Alberto to see what the man had found. Alberto led his boss through the high grass to where he had noticed Brianna's body in a ditch, covered with a discarded Christmas tree. Scott Ferris said that when he walked up to within five feet of the body, he could see that the remains were those of a young white female, naked except for socks, lying flat on her back, faceup. He said that there was very little flesh left on the face, apparently the work of animals. The teeth were showing, he said, and it caught his attention that they were a very bright white. The rest of the body showed very little damage and "looked like a body," he said, but "the face from the neck up looked different. You could see the teeth distinctly."

Scott had brought along his cell phone in the event that he might need to report whatever Alberto had found. He immediately called the police to tell them a body had been located. He was questioned again by the authorities later on in the investigation, when it was discovered that Biela had actually worked for EE Technologies at one time. Scott checked the records and said that Biela's employment with the company had lasted only two and a half months, and he did not know Biela during that time.

One of the officers who initially responded to Scott Ferris's phone call described for the court what the authorities had found when they arrived at the scene.

Officer Victor Ruvalcaba observed quite a bit of decomposition on the head and face and much deterioration of the skin tissues. The body appeared to have been there for a period of time, he told the jury. He photographed Brianna's body, describing the orange socks with yellow flowers, which were the only items of clothing she wore. He collected the two pairs of thong underwear that were found lying underneath her body. A large photo of Brianna's legs, from the calf down and wearing the orange socks, was shown to the jury. Biela took several brief glances at the photo of his alleged victim's dead body while it was being shown in court.

Ruvalcaba testified in a great deal of detail about the thong underwear. After donning gloves, he pulled the pair out of an evidence bag. He showed the jury where the DNA experts had cut the thong into pieces for analysis. Brianna's mother, Bridgette Denison, was unable to remain in the courtroom when Ruvalcaba told the jury how Brianna's socks had been removed and her body had been bagged for transport to the coroner's office. Bridgette rose and walked out of the courtroom, stopping briefly at the door and leaning her head against the wall for a moment in an attempt to compose herself before leaving. Several concerned and equally upset friends and family followed her.

Forensic pathologist Ellen Clark testified that

she could not say for a certainty exactly how long Brianna had been dead, but she said that in the course of her examination she had found stomach contents that would have been consistent with what Brianna had eaten at Mel's Diner prior to her disappearance. Clark also testified that autopsy results confirmed that Brianna had been raped and strangled—and a pair of thongs likely used as the weapon of strangulation. It might have taken as long as four minutes for Brianna to die, Clark told the court.

Detective Jenkins testified about the search for Brianna's killer and how it took a sudden turn in November 2008, when the investigators received a Secret Witness tip about a man who fit their profile almost exactly: James Biela. Biela was said to be obsessed with thong underwear; his truck matched the description given by Virgie Chin; his driver's license picture showed a man who looked very much like the sketch made from Amanda Collins's description.

"You put all that together, and this person shoots up to the top of the list," Sattler said to Jenkins, who agreed with him.

Jenkins also said that the location of Brianna's body, the field next to EE Technologies, was also a telling factor in the investigation. Biela had worked there, he said, and Carleen Harmon worked at a business that was "a stone's throw" from the intersection next to the field.

After the Secret Witness tip was received, Jenkins said that he and some of the other detectives met with Carleen Harmon and asked her if they could take a DNA sample from her little boy, Biela's son. She agreed and allowed the sample to be taken.

The prosecution's witness, with arguably the most wrenching, emotional evidence against Biela, was Carleen Harmon. She spent several long and very difficult hours on the witness stand. After her testimony, spectators in the courtroom told the press that it was "impossible" not to feel sympathy for her. The judge had ordered the media not to show Carleen's face and to disguise her voice, but that afforded her almost no concealment of her identity.

Carleen was nervous, embarrassed, and humiliated by the questions she had to answer in front of so many people about the extremely graphic detail of her sex life with Biela. At one point, she even apologized to her father from the witness stand for having to describe some of the sexual acts she didn't want to have to discuss in his presence. It was undoubtedly an extremely painful experience for her, but Carleen showed a great deal of courage on the witness stand. She did what she felt that she had to do. She gave full and straightforward testimony against the man she had once loved, with whom she'd had a child.

The prosecution asked Carleen to start at the beginning with the details of her relationship with Biela. She said she first met him at Brew Brothers at the Eldorado Hotel Casino. She initially thought he was shy and quiet, but she said that she realized that he was "really funny," once they began having a conversation.

Their relationship quickly progressed. Biela moved

into her house a short time later; Carleen paid most of the bills. She testified that when she sold her house and bought a new one in Sparks, Biela's name was put on the deed, even though he didn't contribute anything toward the purchase. She also told the jury that she had bought Biela a Toyota truck so he could get to his job at Lake Tahoe in the winter.

When she told him she was going to have a baby, she said he seemed to be really happy about the news. She told the court that he was a good dad to their little boy. They continued to get along "fairly good," she said, and their sex life was normal. He didn't show any particular interest in women's underwear, or in the thong underwear that she personally wore. Carleen said, "He never asked me specifically to wear them." But things began to change around October 2007, she said, when he began to be "gone a lot. We were fighting almost every day." He sometimes slept in the guest room when they were arguing, she told the court.

Biela had become very short-tempered, Carleen said, and was angry very often, sometimes leaving the house and being gone for several days at a time. When she asked where he had stayed while he was gone, he claimed he had been sleeping in the truck, she said. He also became very physically aggressive, throwing things and punching holes in the walls with his fists. Carleen claimed that even during these violent incidents, he never hit her.

When she followed Brianna Denison's case online, Carleen said, the only remark Biela had ever made to her about the case was to claim that "if she wasn't hot, nobody would care. That's why it's getting so much attention." He said, "Her parents have money, and there are other people getting raped and nobody ever talks about those cases."

Carleen said that she had followed the case closely from the day that Brianna had disappeared. "I read everything that came out about it," she said. "It was scary."

Biela's employer had earlier testified that Biela had come to him and had requested to be laid off from his pipe fitter's job on the day that Brianna's body had been found. Carleen told the court that Biela never told her he had been laid off by his own request.

The following month, he moved to Washington State to work, and Carleen helped him clean out his truck prior to the move. She found a pair of her son's shoes in the truck, which she threw away. She also helped Biela buy a travel trailer to live in while he worked in Washington. She and their son and her daughter went to spend two weeks with Biela while he lived there, and everyone enjoyed the visit and got along well, she said. Biela told her that he had to have a bigger truck to pull the trailer, so he traded in his Toyota before he moved back to Reno in September 2008. She was not in favor of trading in the truck, but she said that he had already made a down payment on another truck without telling her.

When Carleen went to Washington to help Biela move, she said she immediately got suspicious that he had been cheating on her while he was working away from home.

"The minute I got there, I started searching the truck," she said. Under the front-seat armrest, she found two pairs of thong underwear. They were size small and pastel colored, used but clean.

"I was superpissed," she told Elliott Sattler when he asked what her state of mind was at that point. She called Biela at work, she said, and asked him if he wanted to explain the panties she had just found in his truck.

Biela was silent. "I was upset," Carleen said, adding that since she had found the panties, she now was certain that he was cheating on her. She met him at his job site and he was angry with her, she said. She yelled at him as he sped off, driving haphazardly.

"Tell me where you got them," she said that she had shouted, telling the court she was "going crazy the whole time." She testified that Biela had only pointed his finger to his forehead in a shooting simulation; then he grabbed the thongs and tossed them out the window of the speeding truck. Finally, Carleen said, the explanation that he came up with was that he had stolen the panties at a Laundromat.

After they returned home and resumed their now-strained relationship, Carleen saw descriptions on the news of the suspect's truck in the Brianna Denison murder, along with police sketches of the suspect in the case. It never occurred to her that Biela could be a suspect, she said; she claimed that she didn't notice any resemblance between the sketches and her boyfriend.

Carleen also testified that she had frequently searched their home computers after Biela had been online. She said that she found that he had spent quite a lot of time at various porn sites. She often changed the passwords on the computers, she said, in an attempt to keep him from going to those websites—a tactic that apparently had not worked.

Biela had previously made it a point to show a lack of interest in the Brianna Denison case;

however, he became very nervous when he was called in and questioned about the murder by Reno police detectives. As soon as he returned home from the interrogation, he called for Carleen to come to him. She said that she found him upstairs in the bedroom, pacing back and forth. He told her what had happened and said that she was going to have to give him an alibi.

She didn't question his demand for the alibi, even though she couldn't—and didn't—give him one. She tried to reassure him that he had nothing to be concerned about and everything would be all right. She still believed he was innocent and told him that being called in to talk to the police about the case was nothing to worry about; lots of people were getting questioned, she said. He started drinking heavily during the next few days, but Carleen still tried to support him. Even after she gave her consent for their son's DNA to be tested, she still didn't believe the man she lived with—her son's father—could have possibly been involved in Brianna Denison's death. It came as a complete, shocking surprise to her when she learned that Biela had been arrested.

On that day, her child's day care center had called and told Carleen that she would need to come and pick her son up. When she told the center's employees that Biela was already on his way to get their son, she was told that she would have to come for the boy because the police were at the center. The center's staff would not give her any further information over the phone. Carleen's first thought, she said, was that there had been a car accident. To her complete shock, she soon found out otherwise.

Biela called her into the police station after he

was arrested. She tried once again to calm him down and assure him that he would not be charged. She met him in an interrogation room.

"As you walked into that room [to talk to Biela], did you think he had done something then?" asked Deputy District Attorney Sattler.

"No," Carleen answered.

"You were going out of your way [to support him] because you still believed in him?"

"Yes."

Sattler asked her if her opinion had changed since that time, and the defense immediately objected to his question. But before Judge Robert Perry could rule on their objection, however, Carleen quickly answered. She told Sattler that yes, her opinion had, indeed, changed.

Chapter 22

Carleen Harmon had gone to meet with Biela at the police station in an interview room following his arrest. One of the items of evidence shown to the jury during the trial was the video that had been made of the meeting. Biela's face was shown, but Carleen's face had been blurred on that copy of the video by the judge's order. The effort at concealment made little difference in protecting Carleen's identity, however. The video was released to the press after it was shown in court and entered into evidence at the trial. The meeting in the interrogation room had been highly emotional. The tape showed Carleen walking into the room where Biela waited. She was holding her head in her hands, crying. She became nearly hysterical when she saw him, saying again and again, "Did you do this? Oh, my God, did you? Did you?"

She walked over to Biela and they hugged, but she continued to ask him if he was guilty, crying the entire time. There were stretches of the conversation that were unintelligible; but at one point, Biela asked her why she had lied.

"About what?" she asked, and Biela answered that she'd lied to him about their son's DNA. Carleen asked him if the boy's DNA had matched that of the killer, and Biela said he didn't know. Then he asked her not to let the boy forget him.

He told Carleen he didn't want to live anymore. He had wanted to buy a gun the previous week, he said, but he couldn't. When she asked him why he wanted one, Biela told her he was going to shoot himself.

"I'm not a piece of shit," he told her. "I don't know what to do."

Carleen pleaded with him, crying, to tell her the truth. "Tell me, please."

Biela began apologizing to her for ruining "Thanksgiving and your birthday," evidently trying to sidetrack the conversation. Carleen, however, still wanted some straight answers.

"Your DNA matches," she told him.

Biela then claimed, "They threatened to kill me tonight. They're listening right now."

"I don't care," Carleen told him, "let them listen."

"I don't want to be alive anymore," Biela said, beginning to sob.

Carleen still begged for the truth. "Please! I need to know. Please!"

Biela was full of self-pity. "You're going to leave," he told her. "You're going to leave me."

Carleen again begged for an answer. "Please," she said again.

"I can't right now," Biela answered, telling her, "They're going to kill me, anyways."

"Tell me," she told him, "tell me. I can help you."

"You can't help me," Biela said. "At this point, it

doesn't matter. I'm sorry I fucked it up. It doesn't matter."

"It does matter to me," Carleen sobbed.

Then Biela asked a telling question: "If I told you, 'I did it,' would you still love me and be with me?"

Carleen's answer to that question was inaudible.

After more unintelligible conversation and mutual crying, Biela asked Carleen again not to let their son forget him, and he said once more that he was sorry.

"I'm sorry for everything," he said. "I'm sorry for being a fuckup."

Later, following their meeting, Biela was taken to the Washoe County Jail by Detective David Jenkins, who had heard Biela saying to Carleen that he didn't want to live anymore. Jenkins told him that he shouldn't hurt himself, but Biela told Jenkins and the other officers present that he was evil and he hoped his son "wouldn't be fucked up like him."

As witness after witness took the stand and testified, the evidence against James Biela continued to mount up in all three cases.

When the prosecution called the police expert on tracking cell phone records, the officer testified about calls made from Biela's phone on the dates of the December 16, 2007, rape of Virgie Chin and the January 20, 2008, abduction and murder of Brianna Denison.

Officer Joe Robinson had reviewed Biela's cell phone activity and found that Biela had called his friend, Carl Jaeger, two times on December 16, 2007, around two hours before the rape. Jaeger had previously testified that he had received a call from

Biela that night, but he had not answered his phone. The cell phone tower that was used for the calls to Jaeger was in Northwest Reno, Robinson told the jury.

Another call that Robinson testified about had been made from Biela's phone to his voice mail on January 20, 2008, the morning when Brianna was taken, Robinson said. The call had been made using a tower located northwest of Virginia and North McCarran, about a mile and a half from the apartment where Brianna was spending the night.

Verizon network operations technician Mike Metcalf testified that if someone had been calling voice mail from the vicinity around the Brianna Denison abduction site, it was highly likely that the cell phone they were using would have connected with the tower northwest of Virginia and North McCarran.

DNA expert Brittany Baguley offered her findings on the tests she had run on the human hair that had been found in Biela's truck and the DNA results of those tests. FBI trace evidence examiner Stephen Shaw testified about finding fibers from Biela's truck carpet on Brianna's socks.

Detective Zachary Thew told the court that when he searched Biela's truck, he found two boxes of nine-millimeter ammunition and a receipt from Scheels sporting-goods store for a nine-millimeter Glock pistol. The receipt indicated that before Biela could take possession of the gun, he had to pass a background check.

Detective Troy Callahan testified that he had searched Biela's travel trailer, which had been stored at EZ Storage near Lemmon Valley. Inside the trailer, hidden inside a storage compartment, Callahan told the jury that he had found two pairs of thongs: one was brown, with pink polka dots, and the other was a multicolored fruit design. Both thongs were size small. Biela had purchased the 1972 Road Ranger trailer for $600 on June 18, 2008, and the woman who sold him the trailer told the investigators that the thongs weren't hers. She had never seen them before.

When Detective Roya Mason, of the Reno Police Department, took the witness stand, she testified about the forensic searches she had done on the three computers belonging to Biela. Thousands of hits had been found for "thong," she said, along with hundreds of photos of women wearing thongs. There had been 1,408 hits on one computer and 1,164 on another, Mason said, with one typical site called "Buy used dirty thongs." Many of the website pages that were involved had been viewed between May and November 2008; some of the pages had even been viewed on the morning of Biela's arrest.

Deputy District Attorney Chris Hicks asked, "Based on your review, did you find any appetites or themes?"

"I thought an interest in the thongs and women in thongs was a theme," Mason answered.

Detective David Jenkins testified at length about several aspects of both the assault cases, as well as Brianna Denison's murder. He told the jury that several things linked all three of the cases. The DNA evidence from the December assault case was a match for the DNA that had been taken from the doorknob at the house where Brianna disappeared,

Jenkins said. After Brianna's body was found, the sperm taken from her body was found to be a positive link to both the doorknob sample and the DNA from the December assault.

Jenkins also told the court that if a circle had been drawn around the location of all three of the crimes, it would have been a little smaller than four hundred yards in diameter.

"There was something about that neighborhood," Jenkins said. "The offender either worked or lived in the neighborhood or had some connection with that neighborhood. If he struck again, he would likely strike in that same neighborhood."

Jenkins said that following the crimes, additional police patrols had been added in that area because of the likelihood that it was the assailant's chosen "hunting grounds."

Through the prosecutors, jurors had been allowed to ask Jenkins questions about the December 2007 sexual-assault case. In one of those questions, Jenkins was asked if the investigators had considered any vehicles other than Biela's Toyota Tacoma truck. Jenkins responded that a wide range of similar vehicles had been looked at, but it had been determined that a 2008 Toyota Tacoma had been the best fit for the very detailed description given by one of the assault case victims.

Another question for Jenkins was why the attacker in the case had apologized to his victim, and Jenkins said that many sex offenders often did the same.

"Even in the midst of unspeakable violence, offenders will often apologize, or say, 'This isn't really what I want to do.'"

When a juror asked Jenkins about Biela's stated attempt to buy a gun, as he had said in his meeting with Carleen Harmon, that particular question resulted in the defense calling for a mistrial when court resumed the following morning, before the jury was seated.

The juror had wanted to know Jenkins's opinion as to why Biela would have wanted to buy a gun if he already owned one, which he had allegedly used in the assault/rape case in October 2007. Biela's victim in that assault had testified earlier in the week that he had raped her at gunpoint in a parking garage.

The juror's question prompted James Leslie, the deputy public defender, to claim that Biela should be granted a mistrial. The question, he said, suggested that the juror who had asked that question had already determined Biela's guilt in that sexual-assault case.

Deputy District Attorney Elliott Sattler, however, was not of the same opinion. He told the judge that the question only showed that the juror was paying attention to all the details of the three cases. The juror had heard testimony about Biela using a gun in the sexual-assault case; then she had heard other testimony saying that he had tried to buy a gun prior to his arrest.

Sattler told the judge, "The question itself doesn't suggest that, at this moment, she believes Mr. Biela is guilty."

The judge called the juror into the courtroom alone to ask her about her question and to find out whether or not she had already formed an opinion about Biela's guilt or innocence.

"Is there anything about this note [containing the question for Detective Jenkins] that we should be concerned about indicating you have made your mind up about the attack?" Judge Perry asked the juror.

"No, sir," she promptly answered, "not at all."

Perry thanked the juror and sent her back into the jury room, ruling that the trial would continue and a mistrial would not be granted.

Maizie Pusich, the other public defender for Biela, later told the press that it was too soon to decide whether the judge's decision would be a point for appeal if Biela was convicted. If it got to that point, Pusich said, the defense team would be looking at every possibility for appeal.

When Eric Marconato, an instructor in martial arts and a Sparks police officer with whom Biela had studied, heard about Biela's arrest, he contacted the investigators. He harbored serious suspicions that the jiu-jitsu move that was used on one of the sexual-assault victims sounded to him like something that he had taught Biela during their classes.

As a witness, he told the court that the move he had shown Biela, grabbing a person from behind and holding him around the neck and shoulders in a certain position, could render the victim unconscious in seconds. The "rear naked hold," as it was called, was very similar to what one of the victims had described in her testimony during the trial when she told the court that she was grabbed from behind and quickly taken down to the ground by her attacker.

Biela had a blue belt, the instructor said, and had been training in martial arts for around three years. When he found out that Biela had been arrested, he said, he had become concerned that some of the moves and maneuvers he had taught during the training might have been used by Biela in the assaults.

Anthony Napierski, a friend of Biela's who had taken the jiu-jitsu classes with him, also testified about Biela's martial arts experience and training. Anthony testified that Biela was skilled with the hold in question, the one that had been used in the assaults. When asked what the effects of that move by a man of Biela's size would be against a small woman, Anthony said that the woman would be defenseless; she wouldn't be able to do anything. "She wouldn't be able to get away," he said.

When the prosecution finished calling all its witnesses, the state rested its case. The defense then began with its first witness, DNA and paternity expert Roger Vincent Miller. Miller started by criticizing the Washoe County Crime Laboratory for their decision to use all of the swabs they collected in the case to establish DNA profiles. This, Miller said, made it impossible for anyone else to check the crime lab's results.

"A better way of doing this would have been to split [the samples] in half," said Miller, of Chromosomal Labs, based in Phoenix, Arizona. Miller said that the lab could have started with half; then if that was not enough, it could have added the rest.

"The question is, was there a justification for [using up all the samples], and I'm not sure there was," Miller said. He said that national standards required using only a portion of the samples so that the other side could retest.

Miller told the court that he had seen what might have been additional DNA in one of the samples found on Brianna's body, but he could not retest to determine what he had seen.

"We did find one peak that did not correspond with either the victim or the defendant in this case," he said. It raised the question, Miller said, that if they had been able to do an additional test, they might have found someone else's DNA on the swab.

To the surprise of the court, Miller was not only the first defense witness to testify—he was also the last. Following his testimony, to the amazement of the spectators in the courtroom, the defense rested its case.

There had been a total of fifty-nine witnesses for the prosecution, and their testimony had taken nine days to complete. The defense had called only one witness, DNA expert Roger Vincent Miller, before resting. Now James Biela's fate would lie with the prosecutors and the defense attorneys who would present their all-important closing arguments to the jury, beginning the following morning.

Chapter 23

The defense and prosecution were prepared and ready to begin their closing presentations on the following day, hoping to successfully make their final points to the jury. First, however, when court was called into session, Judge Robert Perry asked Biela if he was sure that he did not want to testify in his own defense. Biela had turned down the opportunity to speak on his own behalf earlier. The defendant had told Judge Perry that he would like to, but he said that he had chosen to decline the opportunity to address the jury on the advice of his attorneys. Biela once again told the judge that he was still certain that he did not want to testify at that time. "I would like to," he said, "but I will follow their advice not to do it."

There was a large crowd on hand to listen to the closing arguments, with over a hundred spectators packed into two courtrooms. Since that number of people could not have been accommodated in the main courtroom alone, a live video feed had been run to a second courtroom down the hallway.

Behind the defense table, in the first row of seats, Biela's mother, stepfather, and brother were seated directly behind Biela. His mother fought back tears during the prosecution's presentation, as she had also done during the other occasions she had been allowed to be present in court.

Behind the prosecution table, Bridgette Denison and her son and other family members and friends sat with several of the police officers, investigators, and detectives who had worked the case and who all had a keen interest in its outcome.

When the jury came into the courtroom, Judge Perry read them their instructions before Deputy District Attorney Elliott Sattler began his closing arguments. Sattler started with a shocking statement that immediately got the attention of everyone present.

"The bitch probably had it coming," Sattler said, quoting Biela's remark when he was told that Brianna's body had been found.

"Think about a more chilling insight into the mind of the defendant," Sattler said to the jury. They could probably assume, he said, that Biela had that same attitude toward all three of his victims.

Starting with the first victim, he told the jury that she had been raped at gunpoint by Biela in October 2007. "He shoved her underwear aside and brutally raped her," Sattler said, adding that when the assailant got up, the victim saw his face.

"The face that haunts her dreams," he said, pointing to Biela. "The face right over there."

Sattler told the jury that DNA testing had proved that none of the other men in Biela's paternal line— no one but Biela himself—could have been responsible for the assaults on Virgie Chin and Brianna Denison.

Virgie, who was assaulted in December 2007, didn't see her attacker's face, Sattler said, but she had been able to give the authorities many more details that pointed to Biela. While she was being held in her attacker's truck, she saw a child's shoe on the floorboard. Both the statement of Carleen Harmon and that of a coworker of his included the fact that they, too, had seen a child's shoe in the truck.

The victim also said that her rapist had shaved his pubic hair, and Carleen had testified that Biela kept his genital area shaved or trimmed. And the victim had also asked for Biela to stand up in court so she could see his height and weight, and she then told the court that he was a match for the physical build of the man who had raped her.

Sattler then began a long and detailed account of what the prosecution believed had occurred on the night that Brianna Denison had been kidnapped and murdered. The final image of Brianna, he said, was in the video that had been taken at Mel's Diner on the last night of her life. She was seen yawning, tired and ready to go home. She and K.T. Hunter went into K.T.'s unlocked house, and Brianna started getting ready for bed. She was texting back and forth with her boyfriend, Sattler said, who was unhappy that she had gone out that night with her friends.

"We know at that point the last time anyone, besides the defendant, sees Brianna Denison alive is when

K.T. Hunter gives her that brown pillow, those two blankets, and a teddy bear so she can sleep on that couch," Sattler said. Sometime after that, he said, "she's snatched off that couch."

Sattler said that Biela had seen her through the windows from outside, lying in full view on the couch in the unlocked house.

"Seeing her lying there, [Biela] decides this is an opportunity he can't pass up," Sattler told the jury, adding that Biela previously had raped a woman in October and another one in December.

"He decides he's going to rape again," Sattler said. "He opens the unlocked door, takes that pillow, and he shoves it over her face, and he pushes and he pushes and he pushes." Sattler told the jury that Biela had pushed so hard that an investigator testified that she could see teeth marks on the pillow.

"He pushes so hard that it causes her to throw up blood," Sattler said, adding that the hard part was what Biela then did to Brianna.

"It is reasonable to assume that Ms. Denison was taken into the defendant's truck and he sexually assaulted her," Sattler said. Instead of breaking Brianna's neck, Biela used his obsession with women's thong underwear to kill her.

"Biela wrapped [K.T. Hunter's] underwear that he had just stolen around that woman's neck and strangled her to death because she saw his face," Sattler said, reminding the jury, "Dr. Clark testified that it may have taken four minutes to die."

Sattler said that Biela then took Brianna's body, carried it to the field near the place he had once worked, and threw a discarded Christmas tree over it.

Sattler reminded the jury of Carleen Harmon's testimony that following that night, Biela became increasingly restless and "antsy." When she called him on February 15 and told him she believed that Brianna's body had been found in a field near her office—a field that she could see from the windows in the building where she worked—"his reaction was stone-cold silence," Sattler said.

Biela asked that day to be laid off from his job. He soon moved to Washington State, Sattler told the jury, and things "cooled down" then.

"What does he do? He disposes of the truck," Sattler said. Carleen Harmon was unhappy with Biela's decision to sell the truck; she had just paid it off and did not think it made sense to sell it.

Biela sold the truck so that he could distance himself from the evidence in the case, Sattler said, but investigators had been able to retrieve some of the evidence, anyhow. They examined the fibers recovered from the carpet of the truck and found fibers that were linked to the socks that Brianna was wearing when she was killed, Sattler said.

When Biela moved back to Reno and met with a police detective who told him that he was a suspect in the Brianna Denison murder, his first question to the detective was "Who reported me?" Sattler told the jury.

After his meeting with the detective, Sattler said, Biela had called for Carleen Harmon, upset and crying, and told her what had happened. Carleen had told him that he shouldn't worry, because police had talked to so many other people who were considered to be potential suspects during that time. Since she still believed in his innocence at that point, she allowed the authorities to take a DNA swab from their son. But instead of clearing Biela, as Carleen had believed would happen, police had made a positive match.

Biela was subsequently arrested for the murder. He told police that their evidence against him was "horseshit," Sattler said.

It was Biela's DNA that was found on Brianna's body, Sattler said. "That's him."

Sattler had already mentioned Biela's obsession with thong underwear, and he reminded the jury that Biela had looked at used thong websites on the very same day that he was arrested.

In the defense's closing argument, public defender Jay Slocum used his presentation to explain to the jury the principle of reasonable doubt. He claimed that the crime lab should have saved half of the DNA samples so that the defense could have had them independently tested. If the crime lab needed to consume an entire swab for DNA testing, they should have videotaped the process, he said.

"It's not a crime to have women's underwear in a travel trailer," he told the jury in an attempt to lessen the impact of Biela's thong fetish and the fact that he had allegedly used a pair of thongs to strangle Brianna Denison.

Slocum claimed that Biela didn't try to avoid the police when they contacted him about the case. The defense attorney said that Biela initially thought that they wanted to speak to him because his father might have gotten in trouble.

There was little that Slocum could do in his closing remarks other than attempt to insert even a fragment of doubt in the jury's mind about something—anything—that had been presented as evidence against Biela.

"That defense attorney could only do so much [with what he had to work with]," one courtroom observer would say later.

During rebuttal DDA Sattler said that Biela had tried to buy a gun because he was planning to kill himself. Sattler also said that the analyst at the crime lab knew that he was only going to have one shot at testing the samples, so he did the right thing and used them all.

If the jurors believed the October 2007 rape victim when she pointed out Biela in the courtroom and identified him as the man who had assaulted her, Sattler said, that was all they needed to convict him of those crimes.

In closing his rebuttal, Sattler said, "We've heard testimony that the defendant fancied himself as a kind of comedian. He was a funny guy. 'The bitch probably had it coming' might be a very poor attempt at humor from anyone other than the person who strangled the life out of Brianna Denison. It might, in fact, apply to all three of the victims in this case, 'They probably had it coming.'"

Finally, after several hours, with all the closing arguments finished, the three cases against James Biela were turned over to the jury. It was now solely up to them to decide his fate. They would have to reach a decision on five different counts:

Count 1: *sexual assault, from the October 2007 rape in the University of Nevada parking garage*

Count 2: *kidnapping, the incident involving the December 2007 victim, who was taken from outside her apartment building*

Count 3: *the sexual assault, which occurred in Biela's truck after he had abducted the December 2007 victim*

Count 4: *the murder of Brianna Denison (It would be up to the jury to decide whether it would be first degree, second degree, or manslaughter.)*

Count 5: *sexual assault against Brianna Denison*

If Biela was found guilty, the trial would immediately move into its penalty phase and the prosecution would begin to present the evidence that would support their call for the death penalty. There would be more testimony from the defense during this phase than there had been during the trial itself. The attorneys would tell the jury the whole, terrible story of Biela's traumatic childhood. The defense team would hope to convince the jurors that there were mitigating circumstances caused by the abuse he had suffered as a child that would justify a sentence of life in prison instead of death. That testimony would be the only card the defense would have left to play in its attempt to save Biela from the death penalty.

Only six hours after beginning their deliberations, the jury returned with their verdict: guilty on all counts.

"'We the jury in the above entitled matter find the defendant, James Michael Biela, guilty of sexual assault,'" the court clerk began to read aloud from

Biela's verdict sheet. All of the other counts against him were named, one by one, and the clerk read the guilty verdict for each of them. Biela and his attorneys stood, motionless, receiving the verdicts without reaction. It was likely that the jury's decisions didn't come as any surprise to them.

Biela would now be eligible for the death penalty, and the sentencing phase of his trial would begin immediately.

While those in the courtroom took a short break as they readied themselves for the trial process to continue, a few people remaining in the room noticed a remarkable meeting taking place between Brianna's grandmother Barbara Zunino and Kathy Lovell, the mother of James Biela. Only moments after the guilty verdict was announced, Mrs. Zunino stood and walked across the courtroom toward Mrs. Lovell, reaching out to her. Mrs. Lovell took her hands and the two women stood for a moment, speaking softly to each other with tears in their eyes.

When asked what she had said to Biela's mother, Barbara Zunino would only say, "She's a mother. I'm a mother." She would not comment further except to say that she would share their remarks, "maybe, someday." It was an emotional, private moment between the two women—each of them grieving for a loved one—and those who witnessed it were touched by the kindness and empathy that Barbara Zunino displayed.

Chapter 24

Unlike in some other states, it is a requirement in Nevada that the jury, not the judge, is responsible for deciding all sentences in murder cases. Both the defense and the prosecution were ready to begin their presentations, and the jurors were ready to do their duty to the best of their ability. The seriousness of the decision they would have to make weighed heavily on each of them, and they all clearly realized the importance with which they were tasked.

The prosecution, calling Biela a "serial rapist" and a threat to society, was preparing to ask the jury for the death penalty. Biela's attorneys, however, would attempt to convince the jury that Biela's traumatic childhood had been largely responsible for his actions. There was no question that he and his siblings had endured terrible things during their early lives, and the defense would take the fullest advantage of that fact.

Public Defender James Leslie began his presentation by telling the court about his client's early years, saying, "He witnessed things no child should have to witness. No child should have to be down the hall with his brother listening to what is happening to his mother night after night."

Leslie described James's childhood household as "frankly, bizarre" and said that it kept all the children continually frightened and dreading the coming of night, listening from their rooms while their father, Joseph Biela, beat their mother with chilling regularity. Leslie recalled the earlier testimony about James Biela and his siblings being so afraid to come out of their bedrooms at night that they kept buckets in the rooms to use as toilets.

Dr. Melissa Piasecki, a medical doctor specializing in psychiatry and forensic psychiatry, began her testimony for the defense by calling Joseph Biela's daily behavior "unusual and abusive." She described the atmosphere in the family's apartment in Chicago as one where psychological and verbal abuse were continual and harsh. Dr. Piasecki told the jury that Biela's mother was tied to the bedpost and viciously whipped and beaten almost every night while her husband loudly ranted about his sexual fantasies. This took place in the room next to the one where James Biela slept with his brother, Jeff, who told the court that he could still hear the beatings in his mind, with his father mercilessly whipping his mother with a belt while she begged him to stop. He said that he could still hear, he said, the whistling sound the belt made as his father brought it down, over and over.

Kathy Biela's abuse included having her hair and earrings pulled out, numerous broken ribs and teeth, and being tied so tightly on so many occasions that she eventually had to have wrist surgery because of her injuries. Sometimes Kathy went to try and hide in the children's rooms, crawling under their beds in unsuccessful efforts to keep her husband from finding her. The terrified children would watch while their father came into their rooms, found their mother hiding, and dragged her out from under the bed and back to his bedroom to start his vicious attacks against her once more. The beating and the abuse would continue and they would hear the screaming begin again.

Citing an example of Joseph Biela's "bizarre" behavior, Dr. Piasecki said that one of the things he did that fell squarely into that category was an unbelievable incident that took place on one occasion when he put a pet cat into the freezer and then proceeded to relieve himself in the cat's litter box.

After the court recessed for the day, with the psychiatrist scheduled to return to the stand the following morning, a large number of people and an equally large number of media representatives gathered outside the courthouse and talked about the outcome of the trial and what they thought the sentencing might bring. Reporters took the opportunity to interview many of the spectators who had been in the courtroom during the trial, asking their opinions on what had taken place, what they thought of the verdict, and what they thought the outcome of the penalty phase of the trial might be.

Most of the people said that they thought that the defense "didn't have much of a chance."

"He should get the death penalty," one young lady told reporters.

"I'm kind of mixed on the death penalty," another

bystander said. "Honestly, if they're going to pursue the death penalty, then, yeah, eye for an eye."

Adam Wygnanski, the retired detective who was the first to finger Biela as the likely suspect in the rape cases and Brianna's murder, due to the Secret Witness tip he investigated, was one of those interviewed outside the courthouse. He had been in the courtroom, along with a large number of other law enforcement personnel who had worked the case, when the guilty verdict had been read. He said the verdict came as a relief for all of them.

"The victims, the people who worked so hard on the case, we all spent a lot of time," he said, recalling what he called "ten months of agony" for law enforcement, as well as for the victims and their families.

Detective David Jenkins told the reporters that he was very satisfied that the jury had done what he called "the right thing."

District Attorney Richard Gammick and his team had successfully brought the case to trial, and Gammick told the press that he was "tickled to death" that James Biela had been convicted. "No matter what happens, he's going away for a long, long, long time."

Upon learning that his family members had testified in court about the vicious beatings he handed out to his wife on a daily basis, and that his household had been deemed "frankly, bizarre," Joe Biela grew very indignant and hostile when he was contacted by the media for a statement.

The whole thing was "a bunch of lies," he said, justifying his statement by adding that "everything was fine. I beat my wife, but not my kids." When asked if the beatings were severe, he told his interviewer, "That you will have to ask her." Apparently, he believed that it was perfectly fine to hand out horrible abuse and vicious beatings to his wife, as long as he didn't beat his children.

The elder Biela's behavior toward the press, along with his opinion about his son's situation, always seemed to change drastically from one interview to the next, likely due to his mental-health situation. He told one reporter, who spoke with him while the trial was in the penalty phase, that he hoped his son's life would be spared. He said, "Let him spend the rest of his life in jail. If they let him out, he might do that again."

But on another occasion, on video with another interviewer, Joe Biela looked and acted differently. He appeared very disoriented and angry toward his son, and he appeared to be quite emaciated and ill, even more so than in his previous interviews. Looking at a photo of his son in a family album, he snarled, "There's that little ass wipe that killed that girl."

When the reporter pointed out another photo in the album, a snapshot of James Biela with a little boy, the reporter asked, "Is that his kid?"

Joseph Biela snorted and flung his arms out dismissively.

"Hell if I know," he said.

When court resumed the next morning for the continuation of the defense's penalty phase testimony, Dr. Melissa Piasecki returned to the stand to complete her testimony about James Biela's dreadful childhood. When time came for cross-examination, Deputy District Attorney Elliott Sattler pointed out that he agreed that the experiences Dr. Piasecki had described on the witness stand must have been terrible for the Biela children. He said that none of the other children, however, had grown up to be a convicted murder and rapist.

Sattler said that despite the fact that James Biela had been court-martialed out of the U.S. Marines for being AWOL and using marijuana, he was still a good student, a hard worker, and a good provider for Carleen Harmon and their son. Things changed in the fall of 2007, Sattler said, when Biela embarked on the series of sexual assaults that led to Brianna Denison's murder.

Sattler asked Dr. Piasecki how she could explain Biela's suddenly starting to rape women, stealing their underwear, breaking into their homes, and "violating women in the most despicable ways possible and choking women to death. How do you explain that?"

"I can't explain that," the psychiatric doctor answered.

"How is it that, sixteen years removed from this horrible father, he snaps and starts raping and killing people?" Sattler asked.

Dr. Piasecki told him that there was not yet a good understanding of the way that early experiences can affect people later in their lives. There was usually more of an "association" between such things, instead of a "cause and effect."

Also testifying for the defense was a former director of the Nevada Department of Corrections

(NDOC), who described for the jury the conditions of prison life for prisoners who were sentenced to terms of life in prison without the possibility of parole. Richard Nelson, a deputy Washoe County sheriff who worked in detention, and Tom Green, a sergeant in the Washoe County Sheriff's Office, both took the witness stand and testified on Biela's behavior while in custody. They said that he had been a model prisoner during that time. Several members of Biela's family testified, including his brother, sisters, mother, aunt, and uncle. His friends, David Bouch, Shawn Hardiman and Zach Flores, and former girlfriend Carleen Harmon also spoke to the jury.

James Biela finally changed his mind about speaking on his own behalf and decided that he would address the jury himself at this point. He stood at the defense table to speak. He had been told by his attorneys that he could address the jury at sentencing without having to be sworn in or facing cross-examination by the prosecution. The process, called an allocution, had some very clear limitations, however, in what he could say. He could express remorse, or he could plead for leniency, but he could not deny the crimes he had been convicted of or discuss the evidence in the case. If he did so, his attorneys told him, the prosecution would then get a chance to cross-examine him, and that would definitely not be in his favor.

Biela looked at the jury, but instead of speaking to them or to his victims and their families, he seemed to be addressing his young son and his own family. He said, "I just wanted to say I'm sorry that this incident has destroyed several families," and he began to shake and choke back sobs as he said that no matter what the jury decided, he would never be able to see his son grow up and be a father to him.

Biela said he was sorry if he'd failed his son and that he just wanted the boy to know that he loved him.

"This might not be the time or place, but I love you," he said about his son.

The news media reported that all in all, Biela said he was sorry four times, with tears rolling all the while. Never once, however, did he say he was sorry for what he had done to his victims, nor did he apologize in any sense to their families for his crimes. Obviously, this didn't escape the attention of the media, whose video reports of his statement were posted on the Internet, nor the attention of those who were listening in the courtroom. He seemed to be sorrier for himself than for anyone he had committed such violent, vicious crimes against, they reported, and most of those who heard his statement felt only disgust.

One of the most dramatic times of the trial came later that day, when Brianna Denison's family and friends took the witness stand to address the jury to make their victim impact testimony and plead for justice for the young girl whose loss they felt so keenly. One by one, they spoke, and Brianna's mother directed her remarks straight to James Biela.

"I am here before you today," Bridgette Denison said, "suffering more than any mother should. The horrific acts you perpetrated on my daughter have impacted me, my son, my family, and people who have been there for me . . . words cannot describe.

It sickens me to think that my poor baby girl spent her last moments of life alone with you. I will never live to see her complete her life's journey. I feel like the life has been sucked out of me."

Then Brianna's grandfather Bob Zunino addressed the jury.

"I know Mr. Biela wants mercy, but I don't think he deserves mercy," he told them. "I hope that no one in this room ever has to go through the experiences, the horror, the pain, and the sorrow my family is going through and has gone through for the last two and a half years. I am also hoping that the decision you make today or tomorrow will bring justice and peace to my little Brianna."

In closing remarks, public defender James Leslie spoke of the mitigating factors the defense had presented in the hope of convincing the jury to spare Biela's life.

"Nothing we say is meant to lessen the tragic loss of life or take away the pain so many people have suffered on a very human level," Leslie told the jurors, "but there are reasons not to vote for the death penalty in this case." Leslie said that Biela's childhood, filled with mistreatment and neglect, witnessing and hearing violence down the hall night after night, was reason to vote for life in prison without parole.

"That is an appropriate and sufficient punishment," Leslie said.

Deputy District Attorney Chris Hicks countered the defense's contention that Biela deserved mercy because of his childhood trauma or any other mitigating factor.

"All the emotions, all the travesties of this case, all of the impacts on friends and families, it's all because of him and nobody else," Hicks said to the jury. "We will be asking you to give him the death penalty."

Defense attorney Maizie Pusich told the jury that sentencing Biela to life in prison without the possibility of parole would be sufficient punishment for him and would serve to protect the public by keeping him permanently unable to harm anyone else. She told them that killing Biela was not the way to prevent such tragedies from happening in the future.

"Death does not bring peace or renewal to anyone," she said.

After Pusich finished presenting her final remarks to the jury, the defense followed up with a short rebuttal. DDA Sattler said that he agreed with the defense that the death penalty should be reserved for the "worst of the worst." He said that Biela fit that category, however, because he had strangled Brianna with a pair of thong underwear.

"He could have used his bare hands. He could have snapped her neck and killed her if he wanted to. He chose not to do that. He killed her in a sick and sadistic way that was directly tied in to what he had done earlier," Sattler said.

Then the case was given over to the jury. Their task was straightforward and simple; the prosecution had asked the jury to choose the death penalty, and the defense pleaded for their client to be sentenced to life in prison without the possibility of parole. There was enough time remaining for the jury to spend a couple of hours of deliberation that

evening; then Judge Robert Perry sent them home
for the night, with instructions to return the following morning and resume their deliberations again at
8:30 A.M.

The jury had taken around six and a half hours to
find James Biela guilty, and the amount of time they
were taking on the sentencing phase was running
past that when they took a lunch break and ordered
sandwiches and salads from the Pub'N'Sub, a restaurant near the courthouse. Their lunch order arrived
at approximately the eight-hour mark in their deliberations, but it took only a short time after the jury
finished their lunch break and resumed their work
for their final verdict to be reached. Court was
quickly called back into session; everyone took their
places in the courtroom; the verdict was announced.
Despite the arguments from his defense team, the
jury had decided that James Biela would receive the
death penalty.

On their verdict form, the members of the jury
said that they realized Biela had endured a hurtful
and traumatizing childhood. However, they still
agreed with the prosecution's argument that he
should be put to death by lethal injection for Brianna
Denison's rape and murder.

The clerk polled the jury individually. As they answered, one by one, Biela and his attorneys stood,
stoically and motionless, as they listened. It seemed
as though it took a very long time for each juror to
be asked if the death penalty was his or her decision.
During that time, Biela never moved. His attorneys
occasionally looked over at the jurors or looked
down at the floor, but the man who was in the
process of receiving a death sentence showed no
reaction of any kind. He stood like a statue with his

hands folded in front of him, staring straight ahead and occasionally shaking his head slightly, showing none of the emotion that he had displayed earlier when he made his tearful statement to the jury. Like the guilty verdict, it seemed as though it came as no surprise to him or to his defense team.

Following the polling of the jury, Judge Perry made his own statement to the courtroom: "My heart goes out to all the innocent people who have been touched by this tragedy."

The judge then set a date of July 30 for sentencing on the sexual-assault and kidnapping charges. State law demanded that the jury would determine the sentences in death penalty cases, but Judge Perry would be responsible for deciding the sentences in the other cases himself. Until those other sentences were imposed, Biela would remain in the custody of Washoe County authorities, in the special housing unit at the Washoe County Detention Center.

Biela was handcuffed and led out of the courtroom by a deputy, and others in the room saw that he turned to his family on the way out, telling them not to cry, apologizing to his mother, and saying, "I'm sorry. I fucked up. I love you."

They called back, "I love you, Jimmy" as he left the room.

Once James Biela left the courtroom, Brianna Denison's family began to realize that the long nightmare of the trial was finally over and Brianna would, indeed, receive the justice that the entire community was so determined she would have. Some of Brianna's family members had cried with relief when the sentence was announced. Outside the courtroom, a celebratory air began to take shape. Bridgette Denison hugged the prosecution team and gave several of the courtroom observers the BRING BRI JUSTICE buttons, which had been worn by so many people, family, friends, and total strangers during the quest for the apprehension and punishment of Brianna's killer. All over the courthouse, Brianna's beautiful, smiling face began to appear on the lapels of people who were elated that Brianna's killer had finally received the sentence they had been hoping for.

There were many others the Denison/Zunino family members hugged; a great number of law enforcement personnel who had worked so long and hard on the case had been in court that day, and the hallway outside the courtroom was full, with everyone being congratulated and thanked. Retired detective Adam Wygnanski had invested much hard work on the case from the time that he had first sat down across from James Biela, looked him in the eyes, and realized that he was the man the authorities had been searching for.

"Justice was served," Wygnanski told the media. "The jury had a tough job, and they did it."

Washoe County DA Richard Gammick told reporters that he was extremely happy with the jury's decision, saying it was "well-deserved. Cases like this strengthen my faith and belief in the jury system." Gammick announced a press conference with Brianna's family that would be held that afternoon. The family had repeatedly told the media that once the verdict was reached and the sentencing was done, they would have statements that they would be making, but they had chosen to wait until the conclusion of the trial and sentencing to speak to the press.

Chapter 25

At the news conference that afternoon, Bridgette Denison said, "Together we lost a beautiful, vibrant, and promising life, and my family and friends have suffered unimaginable tragedy, but we can and will turn this loss into something positive and good. When James Michael Biela messed with my little girl," she said, "he messed with the wrong families, the wrong group of women, and the wrong city and state."

Bridgette said that her family, through the BBJF, would continue to work to toughen laws against offenders in an effort to prevent others from experiencing the same heartbreak her family had suffered.

Brianna's grandmother Carol Pierce said of the verdict, "I didn't expect that." It hadn't set in yet, she said, and added that she would have accepted either a sentence of life without parole or a death sentence.

"As long as you get him off the streets so he doesn't hurt anybody else," she said.

"It's what we wanted," said Lauren Denison, and Brianna's maternal grandmother, Barbara Zunino, who earlier had shown kindness and compassion to Biela's mother after the guilty verdict, said, "It turned out right."

A statement from Virgie Chin, the woman who was raped by Biela in December 2007, was read by her mother. *A simple thank-you is not enough to convey how I feel,* the young woman had written. She had special thanks for one particular victims' advocate who had helped her: *for taking such good care of me.* Virgie had decided to become a victims' advocate herself because of the support she had received from that person, her mother told the people at the press conference.

Don Richter, the founder of the Secret Witness hotline, also spoke about the tip the authorities had received through his organization, the information that had resulted in James Biela finally being positively identified as the man that law enforcement had been so desperately searching for.

"The message we're trying to get out is that police fight crimes with guns and tear gas, but all you need is a telephone," he said. He praised all those who had called in tips to the hotline during the long investigation into Brianna's disappearance and death. He encouraged the community to continue their participation in solving crimes.

Deputy District Attorney Elliott Sattler, the lead prosecutor in the case, commended the jury for their hard work and had praise for the Denison family and the families of the other victims. He saluted the strength they had exhibited throughout the trial.

"It touches you emotionally when you deal with good people, and the three victims in this case were outstanding women," he said. "It's gratifying to know that I was a part of producing justice."

District Attorney Richard Gammick expressed the pride he felt in the law enforcement personnel and the people of the community for working together in such a dedicated and determined manner and bringing about the solution of the two sexual assaults and Brianna's rape and murder. The case had brought everyone together to get positive results, he said, adding that Brianna's disappearance had "started one of the most massive manhunts I've ever seen for a missing person in this community. Nothing we do here can bring Brianna Denison back, but I think I can stand here now and say we did bring Bri justice. A sexual predator was removed from our midst permanently," he told the press.

Shortly after the press conference, Biela's family told the media that his attorneys planned to try and set up a meeting so that they could see him briefly. They also issued a statement: *Our hearts go out to all the families involved in this tragedy. This tragedy has robbed several families of their children and grandchildren, and a son of his father.*

After the verdict had been announced, Biela's mother and stepfather had declined to comment, saying, "Maybe tomorrow." Later, Kathy Lovell told reporters some of what her son had said to his family.

"He said, 'Don't cry.' He said he loved us," Biela's mother said.

After James Biela was sentenced to death, he was placed under suicide watch observation at the Washoe County Jail, Sheriff's Deputy Armando Avina told the media. The special watch was to ensure that Biela didn't hurt himself, and he was checked by camera every fifteen minutes. He would remain at the county jail until after the sentencing on the rape and kidnapping charges; then he would be sent to the Northern Nevada Correctional Center for a twenty-one-day intake process, then on to Ely State Prison, where more than eighty other death row inmates were all housed.

Chief deputy public defender John Petty had already been tapped to handle Biela's first series of appeals, and Petty told the media that all capital murder cases in Nevada automatically went to the state supreme court for review. Petty said that he planned to submit a notice of appeal immediately after Judge Perry sentenced Biela and entered his written judgment.

"That's because the defense wants the supreme court to review all five of the charges," he said, "not just the murder. We want to ensure that we are able to raise issues in the other counts."

Petty said that he had not yet reviewed the trial transcripts, but one issue that concerned him was whether or not there had been sufficient evidence to convict Biela on the sexual-assault charges.

Petty said that after the case record was sent to the supreme court, his office would have sixty days to file its opening brief, with the option of a sixty-day extension. Prosecutors had forty-five days following that time to file their response; public defenders would then have forty-five days to respond. Petty said that the briefing process should be complete by the end of that year, and could possibly be ready for consideration by the supreme court by January of the following year. The justices would then decide whether or not they would allow oral arguments. If the defenders were to lose in the supreme court, Petty said, the case would be sent to a different group of lawyers that would then start an appeals process in Washoe County District Court.

Between the end of James Biela's murder trial and his sentencing hearing on the additional rape charges he had been convicted of, a long, unpleasant exchange occurred that had taken place back and forth between Judge Robert Perry and District Attorney Richard Gammick concerning a remark Gammick was said to have made about Biela's guilty verdict.

Judge Perry was sharply critical of Gammick after hearing that the district attorney had been quoted in the *Reno Gazette-Journal* as saying that *"some people say that decision day is better than sex."*

Judge Perry promptly issued a court order to reprimand the district attorney for his comment, saying that the remark, comparing a guilty verdict to sex, *undermines public confidence and respect in the criminal justice system,* and was highly inappropriate. Gammick then filed a motion asking that the judge withdraw his court order, but Perry issued a second court order refusing to recant his criticism. He would not order sanctions against Gammick, he said, but neither would he take back his original reprimand. Perry continued to say that such inappropriate and unprofessional statements made by those in the legal profession not only could cause appeals, but also were detrimental to the public's respect for the legal system.

Learning of the court order, Gammick said that

he disagreed with the judge, saying, "We'll leave it lie and see what develops." He added that he and the judge "have a history."

For Gammick to say the two men had "a history" was quite an understatement, and it quickly became evident that neither was willing to "leave it lie." It seems that in the 2008 elections, DDA Elliott Sattler had run against Judge Perry. Gammick and Perry engaged in an e-mail feud during the campaign, with Gammick claiming that Perry had made false statements about Sattler. Gammick also went so far as to accuse Perry of using cocaine.

Perry responded to the e-mails with an attack of his own, accusing Gammick of trying to muddy the waters in order to disguise what he called Sattler's inexperience and his lack of qualifications for the judgeship. Perry won the election, and a six-year term on the bench.

Between the time that Biela was found guilty and before his sentencing, the Gammick-Perry feud was renewed with vigor when Gammick made the remark to the newspaper about decision day being "better than sex." During the height of the dispute, Gammick wrote a letter to the editor of the *Reno Gazette-Journal,* claiming that he was only repeating a quote from a former district attorney, Mills Lane, who allegedly had once said that a guilty verdict was better than sex. Gammick claimed that he had repeated Lane's remark during a private conversation with reporter Siobhan McAndrew, who had written the story.

An experienced and highly professional reporter, McAndrew stood by her story. She countered Gammick's claims by stating that the conversation had not been a private one; she had been obviously acting as a reporter at the time, since she was asking questions and writing Gammick's answers in the notebook she was carrying. The entire conversation had taken place in the Washoe County Courthouse's media room following the announcement of Biela's guilty verdict, she said.

A few weeks later, on June 25, Judge Perry prepared and released a court order dealing with the disclosure of personal jury information. Following the release of the court order, Perry told the media that he felt it necessary to remind all the attorneys in the case that they were required to follow Nevada's Rules of Professional Conduct. He said that the "better than sex" comment had been highly inappropriate and that such a remark could even lead to an appeal of the verdict.

Gammick was not pleased to have been singled out by the judge once again for criticism and censure. He filed a motion four days later asking Perry to revise his order and leave out mention of his comment. Judge Perry might have "misapprehended" the situation, Gammick said, and complained that he didn't see how his remark could be grounds for an appeal. It was made outside the hearing of the jury or the judge, and was supposedly off the record, Gammick said. He claimed that Nevada's Rules of Professional Conduct forbade statements that might affect a legal proceeding, or *have a substantial likelihood of heightening public condemnation of the accused*. Gammick clearly believed that his comment had been innocuous and would not have affected the case. He said that the jury had been ordered not to read or view any news items, so what he said to McAndrew—

in what he claimed had been a private conversation—could not have had any bearing on the jury's decision in the penalty phase of the trial. And in closing his motion with one last word on the subject, Gammick said that his remarks were not specifically about Biela, so there was no question of slanting public opinion against him.

In response to this, an obviously angered Judge Perry issued a second court order: *The victims in this case were forcibly subjected to sexual assault. To imply that some people, arguably including [Gammick], would receive satisfaction comparable to sex from a guilty verdict in such a case was thoughtless and could be viewed as disrespectful by at least some rape victims and their families.*

Perry went on to state that it was his belief that Gammick had undermined the seriousness of the cases against Biela by his remark: *This litigation was not a game. Neither was there anything remotely funny about what happened to the victims nor in the thoughtful imposition of the death penalty by the jury.*

It was a great credit to both Judge Perry and to District Attorney Gammick that they did not allow their animosity toward one another to have any bearing on the Biela trial. Both men managed to put their personal differences aside in the courtroom during the period of the trial and conducted themselves with the highest professional standards, working together to ensure a fair, unbiased trial and bringing justice for the victims and their families.

While the Gammick-Perry feud was taking place, with statements, motions, and court orders volleying back and forth, a much more cordial and productive meeting was taking place between Nevada Democrat senator Harry Reid and Bridgette Denison. Reid wanted to talk with Brianna's mother about the Katie Sepich Enhanced DNA Collection Act of 2010, which increased Byrne grants for states that undertake DNA sample collection programs for people who are placed under arrest for committing violent crimes.

The Edward J. Byrne Memorial Justice Assistance Grant (JAG) Program originates from the U.S. Department of Justice, Office of Justice Programs, Bureau of Justice Assistance. The JAG Program is authorized by the Omnibus Crime Control and Safe Streets Act of 1968, as amended, and was designed to provide seed money to support a broad range of activities to prevent and control crime based on local needs and conditions.

One of these many activities supported by the Byrne grants was the funding of DNA collection of those arrested for violent crimes in eligible states. Bridgette had been lobbying the state legislature for the passage of a similar bill to require DNA collection from those arrested for violent crimes in Nevada, which would make Nevada eligible for the increased Byrne funding.

Reid said that he felt that what had happened to Brianna was "an absolute tragedy. I believe we must do more to capture DNA samples from criminals, and I respect her mother's efforts to honor her daughter's memory by advocating for law enforcement funding that will save lives by identifying violent offenders earlier through

DNA cataloging. I encourage the state legislature to pass a bill in their next session that will enable Nevada law enforcement to collect samples from violent offenders, so we don't have to lose another bright, young Nevadan like Brianna."

Chapter 26

Once again in Judge Robert Perry's courtroom for sentencing on July 30, 2010, James Biela looked quite a bit different than he'd presented himself during his trial. He came to receive his additional sentencing wearing prison clothes and shackles instead of a suit and tie. The difference did not go unnoticed by the people in the courtroom. Lauren Denison took note of his changed appearance. She said that Biela had gone out and raped and pillaged the community and had run amok, and consequently, he was now "dressed for the success he created for himself." She and other Denison/Zunino family members were attending the sentencing to show their support for the two rape victims and their families.

Jury members, who gave Biela the death penalty for Brianna's rape and murder, also were present for the sentencing in the rape cases, even though they were not required to be. They told reporters that being a part of a trial that was so important to the community had been an experience that would always stay with them. They felt that being there in court, present for the additional sentences, was a necessary part of their seeing it through to the end.

The hearing lasted thirty minutes, with only one woman taking the witness stand. Amanda Collins, Biela's victim of October 2007, who had been raped at gunpoint in a parking garage on the UNR campus, testified that she and her husband were now several months pregnant with a baby girl. She told the court that their joy was diminished, however, by the life-altering experience of her rape. During her testimony, Biela sat with his head down, staring at the floor, refusing to look up and meet her eyes as she read from the statement she had prepared.

"Mr. Biela, I wish you would look at me," she told him. Then she read: "'Though you didn't murder me, you killed the trusting and vivacious woman I was, moments before you turned my world upside down. Despite the fact that you committed the most unforgivable act, I forgive you for everything you put me through. I pray you find peace with God, because he's the only one who can save you.'"

While she had gone on to graduate from UNR, got married, and had become pregnant with her first child, she said that her Christian faith had been the only thing that had helped her to deal with the unshakeable memories of the "actions of evil" that she had been subjected to.

Following the victim's testimony, Judge Perry acknowledged James Biela's horrific childhood, growing up as a witness to the abuse his father subjected his mother to on practically a nightly basis, and living in poverty. However, the judge told Biela, "It's an obligation to play with the cards we're dealt with."

Sattler told the judge that the prosecution believed it was important to sentence Biela to the maximum sentence on each charge in order to honor each one of his victims. He told the judge, "You probably have to know that he's one of the most dangerous people you could ever have before you."

Judge Perry was then ready to pronounce his decision. He announced that he was sentencing Biela to four additional life terms for the three sexual-assault charges and the kidnapping charge. The minimum time served would be ten years each for the rape charges and five years on the kidnapping charge, and it was possible that the judge also would decide that another year could be added to one of the rape sentences because Biela had used a firearm in its commission.

Deputy District Attorney Sattler explained to the media that in the unlikely event that an appeal should overturn Biela's death penalty, the four life sentences would insure that it would be a minimum of thirty-six years before he would be eligible for parole. Sattler also explained that Virgie Chin, the December 2007 rape victim and a native of Thailand, had chosen not to testify because she wanted to move on and leave the assault behind her. She had returned home to Thailand, Sattler said, and Detective Jenkins had traveled there at one point to interview her about her case.

"Not only were these people terrorized, but the community was terrorized," Judge Perry said about his sentencing decisions, adding that he felt the additional sentencing had been necessary to honor the two other rape victims, despite the fact that Biela already had received the death penalty for Brianna Denison's rape and murder.

Perry said that he planned to sign the formal death warrant and set Biela's execution date by August 16, and his doing so would then trigger the process that would begin Biela's first automatic appeal to the Nevada Supreme Court. In the meantime, he said, the prisoner would be returned to the Washoe County Detention Center to wait there until the time came for the NDOC to take custody of him.

Biela declined to make a statement during the hearing, much as he had during the trial. He sat quietly, wearing his orange prison jumpsuit and a bulletproof vest. He listened to the proceedings but said nothing. His family, who sat behind him in the courtroom, did not have any comments following the hearing and did not answer any of the media's questions.

Following the hearing, attorneys representing both the defense and the prosecution met with the media to give statements. DDA Elliott Sattler said that his office had asked for the maximum sentence possible for the protection of the community, in order to insure that Biela would be kept off the streets permanently. That way, despite whatever might happen with any of the individual cases, he would still remain behind bars for the rest of his life.

"One never knows what will happen to the death penalty," Sattler said, "but I have no reason to believe he'll ever be released from the Nevada state prison system." He went on to say that he applauded Judge Perry's decisions.

"If anyone deserves the maximum possible punishment," Sattler said, "it's James Michael Biela."

Chris Hicks, the state's co-counsel, agreed, saying that Judge Perry had listened to all the testimony.

"He's well aware of the kind of guy that Biela is," Hicks said. "I commend him for the sentence."

Lauren Denison, who had come to court for the

sentencing to show support for the other victims, said the family was pleased that the judge had ordered a separate sentence for each crime.

"Judge Perry made it count for them. He validated the attacks on them," she said.

Defense attorney Maizie Pusich said her client was "holding up pretty well," saying that Biela was a model inmate before, and still was.

"He's easy to talk to," she said, telling reporters that Biela was always polite and professional.

"It actually makes me feel pretty bad," she said.

The day following the end of the trial, the Bring Bri Justice Foundation made a statement so that people would know that they planned to be around for years to come. Only the focus of the foundation had changed, they said, with mandatory DNA testing coming to the forefront of their attention and efforts.

Foundation and family members were "finding our way, what we were going to be about, how we were going to carry Brianna's name and not let her die in vain," Lauren Denison said. Part of the foundation's goal would remain as working with local law enforcement and being the "go to" location for people to find out what they could do to help locate a missing person.

Members of the foundation put together safety kits they planned to pass out to the public at fairs and other similar events, consisting of door alarms, whistles, pepper spray, and other such items.

"We're really going to kick in now, now that we don't have to be quiet any more," Bridgette Denison said of the foundation that had been created to honor her daughter's memory.

The Denison-Zunino family members and their friends were not the only victims' advocates who were hard at work to do everything possible to make life safer for individuals who might someday become prey for rapist-murderers, like James Biela. Another one of his rape victims was also doing everything that she could to increase the odds of safety for other young women like her, even at the cost of constantly having to relive Biela's attack on her in October 2007.

After Biela's trial and conviction for raping her at gunpoint, Amanda Collins became an outspoken advocate of the movement to allow college and university faculty and students with concealed carry permits to bring their guns onto college campuses. She became one of the first actual victims of an on-campus rape to speak out publicly in support of the growing effort to change the laws regarding gun-free zones on campuses.

When she testified before Nevada's Government Affairs Committee, Amanda told the committee members how she felt about the laws that had kept her from carrying her legal handgun on the night that James Biela raped her in a UNR parking garage.

Amanda had held a concealed carry permit for years before she was attacked, but because of the laws at most public colleges and universities (with the exception at that time of Utah and Colorado) that forbade firearms on campus, she had to leave her gun at home when she was going onto the UNR campus for classes or activities. When she was grabbed from behind by James Biela in the parking garage, less than three hundred yards from a campus police office, while returning to her car after a night class, she had no way of defending herself because she didn't have her gun.

"He put a firearm to my temple, clocked off the safety, and told me not to say anything," she said of Biela's attack, "then he raped me.

"On October 22, 2007," she told the committee, "my right to say 'no' was taken from me by both James Biela and the Nevada Legislature. If the purpose of the current law is to ensure safety to those on university property, then it is not serving that objective."

The fact that the school was a gun-free zone didn't mean anything to Biela, Amanda said, and she continued to speculate that it might have even made him bolder, since he would not have to worry that his potential victim might be armed. Having been an earlier victim of Biela's, she said that she believed that if she had been able to defend herself that night with her firearm, Brianna Denison might still be alive and Virgie Chin might not have been raped.

After she was attacked, Amanda was finally given permission by the university's president to carry her gun on campus. She later testified to legislators in favor of Senate Bill 231, a proposed state bill introduced by Senator John Jay Lee, D-North Las Vegas, that would allow concealed weapons to be carried at Nevada's public universities and would do away with the requirement that the university president would have to approve permit holders—an approval that was usually denied.

Lee said that the bill was not about campus security; it was about personal security: "This scenario is perfect for a would-be assailant, knowing they have minutes to commit a crime and their victims would be defenseless."

Amanda had received her approval for concealed carrying on campus—too late, though, to save herself or Biela's further victims. According to the Nevada System of Higher Education, in the eleven years preceding the hearing, only six permit holders had requested permission to carry their weapons on the campus of the University of Nevada, Las Vegas. All six were denied. And the only time permission was given at UNR was to Amanda Collins, after she was raped and under the condition that it would remain a secret.

There were many people on hand to testify in favor of the bill; gun rights activists, a member of the team that had prosecuted Biela, as well as others who were in support of the bill. The NRA offered a written statement in favor of the bill, but some of the most powerful testimony came from a nurse who was also a UNR graduate, Stefanie Utz. She told of treating gunshot wounds, all inflicted on assault victims.

"It wasn't the good guys," she said. "It was the bad guys who injured those individuals." Utz went on to tell the meeting that she, herself, had been assaulted while she was a student at UNR. She testified that a weapon would have, at least, given her a chance to defend herself.

Scott Durward, a firearms trainer for Blackbird Tactical Training in Reno, told the committee that he felt it was unfair to single out students and faculty and leave them more vulnerable than the rest of the population. And Assemblyman Scott Hammond, R-Las Vegas, said students in the night classes he taught at UNLV admitted that on occasion, they felt unsafe leaving his class. He himself would feel safer, Hammond said, if some of the students in his classes were trained permit carriers.

There was strong opposition to the bill from several powerful organizations, as well as from Reno law enforcement and state legislators. UNR police chief Adam Garcia said that he felt campuses were less dangerous than the communities around them, and he and other police organizations opposed the bill, saying it would make campuses less safe if guns were allowed. Garcia pointed out the sporting events and other activities held routinely at colleges and universities that involved alcohol, and he felt that guns and drinking, if combined, could pose a definite security threat.

"These events could become killing fields," Garcia said.

The Nevada Sheriffs' and Chiefs' Association, represented by Frank Adams, felt that the bill would pose "grave concerns." He asked the committee what would happen in regard to where and how guns would be kept in dormitories and how security would be maintained with guns present at sports events.

A group that called itself the Nevada Faculty Alliance was also opposed to the presence of guns on campus, saying that it was important to maintain security and reduce the risk of gun-related accidents and other incidents by retaining the gun-free–zone status of campuses. Even guns that were legally carried on campus, they believed, would translate into more violence in schools.

A state senator also agreed with the group, saying that he felt that guns in the hands of students could prove to be highly dangerous. Senator Michael Schneider, D-Las Vegas, said that students were not trained professionals.

"By the time that any student could get a gun, when they were attacked by someone else with a gun, if they went for their gun, it could be a bad outcome," Schneider stated.

Others questioned what outcome might be seen as worse: being attacked with no means of defense, or having at least the chance of fending off the attacker with a concealed handgun.

John Lott, a gun advocate, pointed out that seventy schools, at that time, allowed faculty and students with permits to carry weapons; and in those schools, not one single permit holder on those campuses had been involved in a gun accident or crime. The gun opponents' predictions of disaster, he said, had simply not occurred. At that time, more than a dozen other states were considering lifting their prohibition of carrying guns on campus—with Texas, Idaho, and Florida actively debating the issue. Clearly, other states besides Nevada had issues they were debating, and time would tell how many of those states would support the passage of Katie's Law or the allowing of legally carried concealed weapons on campus, and how many would not.

Schneider was intent on blocking the bill when it made its way to the Nevada Senate, but Amanda Collins remained just as determined to continue speaking out at every opportunity to promote the issue. Whenever and wherever she was needed to go, she testified about her deep conviction that all people deserved a chance to defend themselves.

"The criminals who are intent on committing a crime don't care about what the rules and regulations are," Amanda said, adding that the only ones who did respect the rules were the law-abiding citizens, who should be permitted to carry protective firearms.

"I don't understand why good, responsible people are trusted to be able to have their firearms across the street, and as soon as they cross an arbitrary line, they somehow lose all reason and ability to be able to be competent with that responsibility," she said. "It makes no sense to me at all.

"Why does it take somebody being assaulted in order to be able to defend themselves?" Amanda asked, referring to getting permission finally from the university president to carry her weapon on campus.

"Is it because I was assaulted at gunpoint in a gun-free zone? The unanswered question of my life is, and will remain to be, 'What would have changed if I was carrying my weapon that night?' It is a question that continually keeps me awake at night as I replay the worst ten minutes of my life, over and over again, with several different possibilities."

It is a certainty that two of those possibilities Amanda lay awake at night, considering, were how things could have been so very different—for Virgie and Brianna—if she'd had her handgun with her that night in the parking garage.

Chapter 27

On September 16, 2010, the BBJF held a "Spread Safety" event in downtown Reno featuring live local music, gourmet food, drink specials, and, most important, self-defense demonstrations and safety talks from Reno police officers and UNR representatives. The event, the foundation said, was a part of its mission of keeping the community safer through constant education. It was held at the Spread Peace Café. Like all the other events that had thus far been held by the foundation, it drew a large and enthusiastic crowd and was viewed as being very successful in promoting safety awareness.

On October 14, during a "Tapas and Teddy Bears" luncheon fund-raiser at the Eldorado Hotel Casino, which benefited the foundation, Nevada's Republican governor Jim Gibbons proclaimed the day, October 14, as "Brianna Denison Day." The proclamation said that its purpose was to create awareness against violent crime and recognize crime victims and their families.

Keynote speaker at the event was Democrat Nevada attorney general Catherine Cortez Masto, a staunch supporter of the Bring Bri Justice Foundation. She said that Nevadans must not forget the impact that violent crime makes on the surviving family members of victims. The Denison family, she said, had been instrumental in creating the public's increased awareness of DNA collection and the laws surrounding it.

If a law requiring DNA collection of all those individuals who were placed under arrest for violent crimes had been in effect before Brianna's kidnapping and murder, Masto said, her murder would have been solved sooner because Biela would have been linked by DNA evidence to the December 2007 sexual assault, which he was eventually convicted of—the attack that took place in October 2007 had not been reported at the time and his DNA evidence had been cleaned away by the victim.

Biela had been arrested initially for felony assault in the incident that had occurred with his ex-girlfriend years earlier. The charges were subsequently reduced to a lesser offense, which did not require DNA collection on conviction. If that reduction hadn't happened, and his DNA had been attained, there is a strong chance that he would have been arrested and incarcerated after his rape of Virgie Chin.

Attorney General Masto supported the foundation in its efforts to pass legislation requiring DNA submission to see if those arrested for all felonies were linked to any other unsolved crimes. In this manner, criminals like James Biela would not slip through the cracks and go on to commit further offenses.

The foundation experienced a very busy and productive fall season, with fund-raisers, events, and excellent publicity. In late October, *Dateline NBC* aired a follow-up episode on the Brianna Denison case. A previous episode had covered the investigation of Brianna's disappearance prior to Biela's arrest, when the authorities were still searching for the killer. The follow-up, according to *Dateline* correspondent Josh Mankiewicz, took viewers from James Biela's identification as the likely killer, his arrest, and through the trial to the final verdict.

While efforts were under way to allow guns on campus and DNA testing in felony arrests, Biela's attorneys were already busy preparing their presentation to attempt to get either a new penalty hearing before a newly impaneled jury, or to have his death sentence set aside in favor of a sentence of life without possibility of parole. Judge Perry had entered his written judgment on August 18, 2010, along with an Order Staying Execution of the Judgment of Death Pending Direct Appeal. Both were filed that morning, and a Notice of Appeal was filed that afternoon by Biela's appeal attorneys.

Those actions began the long and often very tedious process of Biela's first appeal; after this initial appeal was concluded, there would be others. The appeals process in death penalty cases could continue for years, and would result in costs to the state of hundreds of thousands of dollars, paid by the taxpayers of Nevada.

In fact, the first round of appeals before the Nevada Supreme Court alone could stretch out for as long as six years. Then, as the case made its way into the federal appeals system, where it could last for a far longer time, it would allow Biela to challenge his conviction for decades to come. This long, drawn-out procedure, many people contended, was unfair to the victims' families, law enforcement, and the judicial system, while others claimed that the process was essential to guaranteeing the death row inmates' constitutional rights. However, it also forced them to live out their lives under "inhumane conditions" on death row. The current average amount of time spent on death row by inmates in Nevada is over seventeen years, with one inmate's time already well over thirty years.

ACLU staff attorney Lee Rowland said that the isolation of the Ely State Prison and its conditions on death row had made Nevada the leading state for voluntary executions. Rowland said that it amounted to state-sponsored suicide. Over the past thirty-five years, eleven out of twelve prisoners who have been put to death in Nevada have been voluntary executions. These were the executions of inmates who had given up on their appeals process and had chosen to die rather than continue living as death row prisoners. Rowland said her organization was disturbed by that number; she said that it had begun to look more like a human rights issue.

A timeline of Biela's first appeal ran as follows:

08/30/2010   *Notice of Biela's appeal filed, and*
             docketed in the Nevada Supreme Court
09/14/2010   *Record on Appeal filed, volumes 1*
             through 8 and volumes 11 and 12

09/15/2010   Record on Appeal filed, volumes 9 and 10

11/24/2010   Motion filed for extension of time to file opening brief

11/29/2010   Order issued granting extension of time, opening brief due January 24, 2011

01/21/2011   Another motion filed for extension of time to file opening brief

01/28/2011   Motion granted for extension of time to file opening brief, due February 24, 2011

02/24/2011   Final motion filed for extension of time to file opening brief, due March 28, 2011

03/28/2011   Opening brief is filed

05/25/2011   Stipulation for extension of time (answering brief) is filed

05/26/2011   Order filed disapproving stipulation/answering brief, brief due June 27, 2011

06/27/2011   Motion filed for extension of time

07/05/2011   Motion granted, answering brief due July 27, 2011

07/20/2011   Respondent's answering brief filed

09/02/2011   Reply brief is filed

09/02/2011   Case Status Update: Briefing completed/to screening

04/02/2012   Notice issued scheduling oral argument for Monday, May 7, 2012, at 10:00 A.M. in Carson City, Nevada (Argument limited to one hour)

05/07/2012   Oral argument held, and case submitted for decision

08/01/2012   Order of affirmance issued; judgment of conviction is upheld

08/17/2012   *Motion filed for extension of time to file petition for rehearing*

08/20/2012   *Motion granted, petition for rehearing due, August 24, 2012*

08/23/2012   *Appellant's petition for rehearing is filed*

09/19/2012   *Order denying rehearing is filed*

10/15/2012   *Case Status Update: Remitter is issued, and the case in the Nevada Supreme Court is closed*

Despite the avalanche of legal paperwork, it must be noted that this was only Biela's first round of appeals. The process would then move on to the Washoe County District Court. If unsuccessful there, he and his defense team could take many other routes of appeal that might well last for the rest of James Biela's natural life, which he would be spending in prison.

As several people had pointed out during and after the trial, a sentence of death did not necessarily mean that the condemned prisoner would ever be executed. Far more convicted murderers would die of natural causes on death row while waiting on appeals than would ever be subjected to execution by lethal injection. The last such execution had been held in 2006, when inmate Daryl Mack had been put to death for the murder of his wife, Charla Mack. In fact, as the ACLU had pointed out, most who had been executed in Nevada in recent years had been put to death by their own request as opposed to spending their lives in prison.

* * *

In the text of Biela's many motions, arguments, and appeals, the various points raised by his defense involved complaints about several sections of the trial: the penalty phase, the jury instructions, and the combination of the three cases into one trial. One of the first items to be addressed in the lengthy and detailed opening brief, which was filed on March 28, 2011, was the defense's belief that the charges in the case should have been severed. The five charges in the case involved three separate victims, and the defense asked that the charges be separated into three individual trials. The request was based on the argument that the events involving each of the individual victims were separate from one another and were not part of a common scheme or plan, and were also not cross-admissible at trial.

The failure to sever these charges into separate trials resulted in a substantial and injurious impact on the jury's verdict because of confusion of evidence between the cases and the piggybacking of a weaker case onto a stronger one, claimed the defense.

The brief went on to claim that the evidence in Biela's conviction on count 1—the sexual assault of Amanda Collins—had been insufficient to support the conviction that had been returned by the jury. The conviction rested entirely on the testimony of the victim, with no other collaborating evidence presented. The argument continued to say that given the circumstances surrounding the Brianna Denison investigation, Amanda had found herself "swept up" and felt that she was a part of something "bigger than herself." For that reason, the defense claimed, her identification of Biela as her assailant, following the very public arrest for Brianna's murder, would have to be seen as being suspect and unreliable. The fact that Amanda found closure in identifying Biela as the man who had raped her: *[It] should not equate to a finding that her identification was correct.*

The brief also criticized Judge Perry's decision to allow jurors to ask questions throughout the trial.

Not every criminal trial is appropriate for juror-inspired questioning, even when the defense acquiesces to the process, the defense stated. The defense team said that without a change of venue or severance into three separate cases, the case was not an appropriate case in which to enlarge the jury's traditional, neutral role of fact finder. As a result, the brief said, there was an abuse of discretion that had affected Biela's right to a fair and impartial jury.

When one of the jurors asked Detective David Jenkins for his opinion on why Biela would try to buy a gun if he already had one that he had used in Amanda's assault, his defense counsel had moved for a mistrial on the basis that the form of the question made it appear that the juror had already decided his guilt on that charge. To determine whether this was true, Judge Perry questioned the juror, asking, "Anything about this note that we should be concerned about as indicating that you have made your mind up about one of the ultimate issues in the case, specifically whether or not the defendant is guilty of the attack on Amanda Collins?" The brief stated, *[This was a] poorly worded, woefully inadequate and closed question that did not get to the heart of the matter. Thus, Judge Perry's denial of the motion for mistrial, based on the juror's response, was an error.*

* * *

In the Biela case, prior to the start of the trial, Judge Perry had specifically ordered that neither the prosecution nor the state's witnesses would be allowed to refer to the photographs and the Internet website information that were part of the evidence against Biela as being pornographic or adult in nature. He also ordered that a *Playboy* magazine that had been found underneath some thong panties was not to be shown in any of the photographs or mentioned in testimony. Despite this order, the brief stated, the prosecution referred to the *Playboy* magazine in its opening statement, then characterized some of the photographs as "adult" and elicited testimony from more than one witness that specifically described the material as pornography and as adult or sexual in nature. This violation of the judge's order, according to the brief, was plain error affecting Biela's substantial rights.

Another point brought into question concerned Nevada's instruction of reasonable doubt, which requires a jury to define reasonable doubt as that kind of doubt that would "govern or control" a person in the "more weighty affairs of life." That instruction, the brief said, constituted structural error:

As a measure or standard, Nevada's reasonable doubt instruction fails to define reasonable doubt with an emphasis on the prosecution's burden, is not worded in simple, clear language, and does not convey the requirement that the jury must be subjectively certain of the defendant's guilt in order to convict.

Accordingly, the instruction constitutes structural error and Mr. Biela is entitled to a new trial where the evidence can be assessed and evaluated under a constitutionally proper standard of reasonable doubt.

Finally the trial section of the brief stated that the

accumulation of error in the case denied Biela a fair trial.

In the penalty section, the brief stated that in Nevada, in order to obtain a death sentence, the state must prove beyond a reasonable doubt that at least one aggravating circumstance exists and that the aggravating circumstance or circumstances outweigh any mitigation evidence:

In this case, the jury was instructed explicitly in at least two instructions, if not in four instructions, that it must find that the mitigation evidence presented in this case had to outweigh beyond a reasonable doubt the aggravating circumstances in order to preclude consideration of the death penalty.

That inadvertently reversed instructional error, the brief said, mandated that the death sentence should be set aside and that Biela should be given a new penalty hearing before a newly impaneled jury, or that the death sentence should be set aside and a sentence of life without the possibility of parole should be imposed, instead.

Finally the brief argued that even without the instructional error in the case, the court's independent review of the death penalty based on the crime and on Biela himself should convince the court that the death sentence in the case was excessive and was the product of passion, prejudice, and other factors. That conclusion should lead, at a minimum, to an order by the court setting aside the death penalty and ordering that a life sentence without the possibility of parole should instead be imposed.

After this section of the brief, a very long and detailed argument section followed. It made the argument that the case should have been severed into three separate cases. The following points were presented in support of this claim:

1. The assaults took place at separate locations at or near the University of Nevada, Reno, and were within four football field lengths of each other, but the locations themselves were not similar. One took place in a parking garage at UNR, the next happened in the parking lot of an apartment close to UNR, and the third happened inside an apartment near UNR. The fact that each assault involved a college student was unremarkable, since all of the incidents occurred at or near UNR.

2. The attacks supposedly took place under different situations. In one case, the alleged victim testified that a gun had been used, that she had not been actually removed from the parking garage, where she had been attacked, and that she had been vaginally assaulted. On the other hand, another alleged victim said that she had been kidnapped from a parking lot and driven to another parking lot several miles away, that she had been forced to have mutual oral sex with her assailant, and that she was digitally penetrated. In addition, she said she had been brought back following the assault to the location from where she was kidnapped, and no weapon was ever used or seen during the assault. In Brianna Denison's case, she was in her friend's home when she went to bed and was not there the next morning;

she was taken away from her original
location and was never brought back.
There was evidence in her case that a ligature was used to subdue her. The claim
that the victims were all of a similar
height and weight was insignificant, the
brief stated, because they were all people
who were of average height and weight,
and Virgie was ethnically different from
either Amanda or Brianna.

3. The original locations in each of the
three charges, despite being fairly close to
each other and in the same area of the
city, on or near the UNR campus, were
each unique. In the October 2007 assault,
the crime took place in a public parking
garage. In the December 2007 rape, the
assault began on an open street-side
public parking lot. In the charges involving Brianna, the crime began inside an
apartment.

4. The brief detailed the movements involved in each of the three charges, which
it claimed involved different actions of
the assailant. In the charge involving
Amanda, she was not taken away from the
original site of the crime. Virgie was
moved from the beginning location to a
place that was several miles away, then returned to the place from which she was
originally kidnapped. Brianna was moved
from her friend's house and was never returned there.

5. The actions of the assailant in each of these
cases, said the brief, were substantially

different. In the first case, the victim was
grabbed from behind, a gun was used to
force her to submit, and the crime involved penile penetration. In the second
case, the victim was grabbed from behind,
but the attacker covered her mouth and
nose with his right hand and placed his
left hand around her body, holding down
both of her arms. No weapon was used in
that case, and the victim was subjected to
forced mutual oral sex and digital penetration. In the cases involving Brianna,
the attacker was believed to have pushed
a pillow over her face; the weapon used to
subdue her was a ligature; forensics believed there to have been some degree of
penetration, but DNA had only been
found on the outside of her body.

The brief contended that none of the cases was an
integral part of any of the others, and its belief was
that the fact that each of the victims was sexually assaulted in some fashion had not been enough to
render them part of a common scheme or plan. Neither, it claimed, was the fact that they had occurred
in a variety of locations in close proximity and near
the university, nor the fact that each case had involved young women. Even combining all the
common elements together was said to have been
not enough to make the allegations part of a
common scheme or plan, when considering the
large number of differences that had occurred in
each case. Therefore, the brief said, the district
court's conclusion that the individual cases were
part of a common scheme or plan was an abuse of

discretion, as was its denial of Biela's motion to sever the cases.

Another point argued in the brief stated that Biela's lawyers were concerned that there might be confusion between the cases, specifically mentioning that the DNA evidence could be confused by the jury from one case to the other. The fact that the judge himself had confused the DNA evidence in the cases at one point was noted, with the brief saying that when even the district court could not keep the facts straight—after having read and reviewed the evidence in written form and hearing it presented again in argument—it was evident that it could not be logically expected to expect the jury to perform more accurately than the judge when presented with the evidence during the trial.

Biela's convictions should therefore be reversed, the brief said, and three separate trials should take place: one for the assault against Amanda Collins, one for Virgie Chin's assault, and one for the charges involving Brianna Denison.

The next listed item was a challenge to Amanda Collins's identification in court of Biela as her assailant. The challenge was based on the fact that her identification had allegedly been made after she had looked at photographs of him in public media news accounts on the Internet following his arrest for Brianna's murder. The arrest was attributed in part to a police sketch that Amanda had helped create, which had been released to the media and the public. That was claimed to have caused her identification of Biela to be suspect and, therefore, not sufficient to sustain his conviction for her assault.

Amanda had testified that she had kept her eyes closed for most of the time that her assailant was on top of her. She felt that she could "completely dissociate" if she kept her eyes closed. He also had a hood pulled over most of his face, she had testified, and she could not see all of it. After the assault, she showered and threw away her clothes; so nothing of evidentiary value was saved, and the only evidence against Biela was Amanda's identification of him.

The brief claimed Amanda's identification was also questionable because she did not report the assault until four months after it had occurred, after reports of Brianna's possible abduction had blanketed the local news. Amanda had agreed to come forward at that time and cooperate with the police because she stated, "There was something bigger than myself at hand. It was more than just me at that point."

Amanda had not told her parents of the assault until after Brianna's body was discovered, saying, "In the event that something like this would happen, or they caught him, [my parents] would be aware."

The brief contended that in Amanda's mind, she had already tied her assault to Brianna's case. Then, when her parents called her and told her a suspect had been arrested in Brianna's murder, Amanda went on her computer and looked at a local news channel, saw Biela's photos, and concluded that he was her assailant.

Detective David Jenkins had stated that Amanda was very upset and confided to him during his questioning that she had been alerted by other people that an arrest had been made recently. She and her husband had been directed to the Internet, where they had looked at some media coverage of recent events in Reno. She told him, Jenkins said, that based upon her reviewing those media accounts—and specifically photographs of an individual—she was certain that was the individual who had attacked her.

She had also directed the detective to *a specific photograph for James Biela that she had viewed on the Internet as part of a media release.*

Further information was listed in the brief about the extensive coverage of the Brianna Denison case and the attention it garnered for months in the northern Nevada area. Amanda had come forward, helped the police develop the sketch of her assailant (which one officer said bore a remarkable resemblance to Biela), and experienced what the brief described as "motivated cognition," which is the tendency of people to form perceptions and to process factual information in a manner congenial to their values and desires. It was not beyond reason, the brief said, that given Amanda's personal investment in the Brianna Denison case, she would have identified anyone arrested in that case as her assailant. There was no other evidence that connected Biela to her sexual assault. As a matter of law, the brief stated, Amanda's identification of Biela should be discounted as suspect. With no other evidence supporting the allegations contained in her case, the brief contended that his conviction should be reversed.

Chapter 28

The next point addressed in the opening brief of Biela's appeal said that by the court allowing unrestrained juror questioning without administering adequate safeguards, the jury's role as a neutral finder of facts had been compromised, and Biela's right to trial by an impartial jury was prejudiced.

Juror questioning should have never been permitted in the first instance, according to the brief, because the risk of prejudice in this sensitive trial outweighed the practice's utility. Although some lower courts were accustomed to allowing it, juror-inspired questioning was not a mandatory part of trial practice in Nevada. It was, instead, a case-by-case practice that could be allowed at the discretion of the trial court.

Brianna's case, along with that of the two other victims, captivated the attention of an entire community for months. The blue ribbons, the foundation, the media coverage—all those things combined to make it an inappropriate case in which to allow the jury to become advocate and inquisitor, stated the brief:

Even though defense counsel acquiesced in allowing jurors to pose questions to witnesses, allowing the practice at all was an abuse of discretion in the first instance and plain error.

At no time, Biela's appeal attorneys claimed, was there a hearing to determine the propriety of allowing jurors to have the power of interrogation. There was only a cursory mention that the jurors would be allowed to ask questions. Judge Perry did state that he would rule on jury questions "just like if a lawyer asked it. If it's permissible, I will allow it. If it's not, under the law, then I can't."

However, Biela's attorneys pointed out in the brief that the judge's statement came after thirty-three juror questions already had been asked, out of the total of ninety-nine questions that had been posed during the trial. This oversight, they said, was significant. The number of questions asked by the jury was excessive, they added.

Their claim was that the sheer volume of questions asked at trial was extreme, reflecting a practice that was unrestrained and inherently dangerous, with even the prosecutor implicitly acknowledging the abnormal number of questions that were being asked by the jury. The prosecution even went so far as to request an instruction to prohibit jurors from asking questions during closing arguments. The brief stated that the expectation that the jury would do so at all during that time made little sense, unless there was a perception by the prosecution that the number of questions asked by the jury during trial was extreme.

The brief claimed that the jury did not simply welcome the enlargement of its traditional role. No, it readily abandoned it. There was no other explanation, it stated, for the jury's extreme amount of questioning of witnesses, and the judge's admonishment, coming after thirty-three questions already had been asked. It did nothing to stem the tide of further questions, since sixty-six more questions were asked after the admonishment. The excessive questioning continued, it said, and nothing had been done to try to correct the resulting harm to Biela's case.

The one specific juror question that had prompted the defense to ask for a mistrial was examined in detail by the appellate attorneys.

During the direct examination of Detective David Jenkins, he had testified that Biela had recently attempted to buy a gun and had said that he was planning to kill himself. That prompted a juror to ask if the detective had any thoughts on why Biela would try to buy a gun, if he already had one, which he had allegedly used in Amanda Collins's assault.

This question had resulted in Biela's defense asking for a mistrial, saying it presupposed guilt in Amanda's case, and saying that the juror asking the question had evidently already come to a conclusion as to Biela's guilt in that count. Judge Perry subsequently asked the juror about the question sent to Detective Jenkins, about whether or not he had thoughts on why Biela would try to buy a gun if he already had one, which was used with Amanda. Judge Perry said his question was not meant to suggest that he had a belief one way or the other about this. He just simply had to ask, he said, if there was anything about this note that he should be concerned about as indicating that the juror asking the question had made up his or her mind about one of the ultimate issues in the case: whether or not the defendant was guilty of the attack on Amanda Collins.

The juror answered, "No, sir, not at all."

There were no follow-up questions asked by either the judge or the defense counsel, and the juror was excused to go back into the jury room and rejoin the other jurors, with the court moving on to other matters. The following day, Judge Perry put on the record that the motion for mistrial had been denied.

The brief stated that, respectfully, neither the judge's question nor the juror's answer had satisfied the concerns raised by the question, which it said had presupposed that Biela had a gun because Amanda's assailant had a gun—therefore, he was the assailant. For a juror to have reached that conclusion in the middle of the trial was grounds for a mistrial and had violated Biela's right to an impartial jury. And because the judge took no further steps to determine the nature and quality of the juror misconduct, Biela should therefore be entitled to a new trial.

The brief then addressed another major point of its concern, claiming that the state's repeated violation of the district court's order prohibiting characterization of the other bad act evidence as "adult," "sexual," or "pornography" was plain error that had affected Biela's rights.

Judge Perry had entered an order prior to the

start of the trial saying that he was concerned about the prejudicial effect that referring to some of the evidence as "pornography" might have. He explicitly directed the parties that no witness, counsel, or other person speaking on the record was to use the word "porn" or similar characterization to reference the evidence that might be mentioned in that manner. Neither could the Internet materials be described in any such way without the use of actual examples.

During the trial, the defense asked if that earlier ruling was being maintained, and the judge said it was. The prosecution said he had told all of his witnesses that they were not supposed to use that language, and the judge had spent some time making things perfectly clear. He specifically said that the detectives could not testify that they had found thong underwear lying on top of "an adult magazine," specifically the *Playboy* magazine. He also said again that pictures presented as evidence during the trial could not be described as "adult," "pornographic," "dirty," or "sexual." He warned on several occasions to "be very, very careful" in how the pictures were described.

The appeal attorneys stated in the opening brief that despite the clear and explicit directions that had been given, the judge's order had been violated on several occasions. In the opening statement, they said, the prosecutor had said that two pairs of thong underwear had been found lying on top of a *Playboy* magazine, and they said that the search of Biela's computers had revealed *"hundreds of adult images, many of which depicted young women in poses displaying their thong underwear."*

During the testimony of Detective Roya Mason,

she stated that she had found 1,146 instances of the word "thong" on Biela's computers, going on to specify that the instances included the phrases "dirty thongs," "buy used dirty thongs," "dirty thongs and asses," and "fetish thongs." She was asked if she was able to view images that had been found because of those keyword hits, as well, and answered that she was, saying that they were images of adult women wearing thong underwear.

"Were the images like you might see in a Victoria's Secret catalog?" the prosecutor asked.

"Perhaps," the detective answered, "but not Victoria's Secret."

"Did they appear to be shopping-type websites?" asked the prosecutor.

"No," Mason answered.

The detective continued to describe a list of links found in the computer search, including fourteen separate instances of the phrase "thong fetish," with descriptions such as "Coming on mom's thongs," "Sexy candid girls in thongs and see-through," "Mother's dirty thongs," "Dirty comments about my slutty mom, thongs and butts, thongs, Bree Olson, sexy thongs//sexy string."

The defense had objected during the trial to one additional violation of the judge's order: Detective Wygnanski had testified about the Secret Witness tip that he had received. In the tip, the caller had said Biela was looking at "pornographic websites." When the defense objected, the prosecutor said that he believed that it had been an inadvertent slip on the detective's part. He then conceded that he might have failed to tell the detective not to use the word "pornography."

The brief stated that those errors were plain on

the record. It said that the judge had been very specific in his order, and it was very clear that the order had been violated numerous times. The descriptions of the websites clearly conveyed the exact inferences that had concerned the judge, and it claimed that the prosecution had gone out of its way to get testimony from Detective Mason that showed the websites were not the uncontroversial shopping-type websites.

The comments by the prosecutor and the testimony by Detectives Mason and Wygnanski were in direct violation of the district court's order, the brief stated. It claimed that the error was plain on the record and violated Biela's substantial rights. Therefore, it said, the error called for a reversal of Biela's convictions and remand for new trial.

The next point stated in the brief was still in reference to the violation of Judge Perry's order forbidding the use of terms like "pornography" during testimony at the trial. It claimed Detective Wygnanski had violated the order and reversal was required. While testifying, Wygnanski had said the Secret Witness tip that he received had said that Biela was "looking at pornographic sites."

When an objection was made outside the jury's presence, the judge said, "I'm satisfied at this point it's appropriate to go forward," and did not declare a mistrial.

The prosecution acknowledged that Wygnanski's testimony was a clear violation of the court order, and admitted that he had not been instructed beforehand not to refer to pornography, saying that it was a "joint mistake on both our parts." Therefore, the brief stated, even though the state did not deliberately encourage Wygnanski's statement, neither did it adequately instruct him ahead of time about the order, a duty that the brief said lay squarely with the state.

Wygnanski, co–lead detective on the case, was familiar with every detail of the investigation, and the Secret Witness tip that he had received from a friend of Carleen Harmon's had been its critical break. He stated that he recalled the tip "like it was yesterday," including the remark about pornography. For that reason, the brief stated, the state should have anticipated he would include it in his testimony. Reference to it was highly prejudicial and should have triggered a mistrial. The reference, it said, had a substantial and injurious effect on the jury's verdict, and Biela's conviction should be reversed.

The next point addressed in the brief was a highly technical criticism of Nevada's reasonable doubt instruction, which required the jury to see "reasonable doubt" as the kind of doubt that would "govern or control a person in the more weighty affairs of life." The instruction, the brief contended, did not emphasize the prosecution's burden, was not worded in simple and clear language, and failed to convey to the jury the proper subjective level of certainty it must have in order to convict.

In Biela's case, in both the guilt and penalty phases, the trial court instructed the jury that reasonable doubt is one based on reason, and not "mere possible doubt"; and that to be reasonable, doubt must be actual, not mere possibility or speculation.

To be a meaningful safeguard of the presumption of innocence, the brief stated, a reasonable doubt instruction must have a tangible meaning capable of being understood and applied correctly by a jury. Nevada's reasonable doubt instruction, which contained the "more weighty affairs of life" measure, failed that test.

Moreover, the brief claimed that it failed to define reasonable doubt in a fashion that emphasized the prosecutor's burden. The standard "more weighty affairs of life," said the brief, was anything but clear and simple, and the instruction as a whole did not convey the requirement that the jury should be subjectively certain of the defendant's guilt in order to convict. Nevada's reasonable doubt instruction, claimed the brief, was "structural error."

The brief next addressed the fact that Biela's appeal attorneys believed that a segment of the jury instruction issued by the judge invited the jury to convict on first-degree murder so as to get to a death penalty hearing.

During the first day of jury selection, Judge Perry provided written instructions to the jury and then read aloud the following section, Jury Instruction 29, to the jury once again before their first deliberations:

Perry told the jurors during jury selection that the case might be divided into two phases. During the first phase, about which he told them they were about to deliberate, they would be asked to decide the defendant's guilt or innocence in the five charges against him.

If the jury then found Biela guilty of count 4, murder, and only if the jury made such a finding, then it would be called on to decide whether or not to impose the death penalty. In order to facilitate a fair and orderly process, Perry told the jurors that the trial of the case would occur in two distinct phases. The first phase would be limited to the question of whether the state had proven the accused's guilt in any of the charges, including count 4, murder, beyond a reasonable doubt, which was defined by the judge. He told the jury that a reasonable doubt was one based on reason. It was not mere possible doubt, he told them, but was such a doubt as would govern or control a person in "the more weighty affairs of life."

If the minds of the jurors were such that they could say they felt the charge was true after comparing and considering all the evidence, the judge said, then there was not a reasonable doubt. Doubt, to be reasonable, must be actual, he said, not mere possibility or speculation.

The judge then told the prospective jurors that at the end of that phase, the jury would deliberate and render a verdict limited to whether or not Biela was guilty of any, or all, of the offenses with which he was charged. There would then be a second phase—if, and only if—the jury found Biela guilty of murder in the first degree. During the second phase, evidence of aggravating and mitigating circumstances would be submitted upon which the jury would separately decide whether or not it found this to be an appropriate case in which to impose the death penalty.

Judge Perry continued his comments from that point by telling the jurors that a sentence of death is not automatic, and the jury could impose a sentence of a definite term of fifty years, life with the possibility of parole, or life without the possibility of parole, instead.

Biela's appeal attorneys stated that they believed that the judge had invited the jury to convict on first-degree murder in order to get a death penalty hearing. This instructional error, they said, required a remand for a new trial.

Finally, to close the brief's comments on the trial phase, it claimed that the accumulated error in the trial denied Biela his right to a fair trial:

It is respectfully submitted that the cumulative error noted above denied Mr. Biela his right to a fair and impartial jury and a fair and impartial trial.

Chapter 29

The next section of the opening brief then moved on to the penalty phase of the trial, and the first argument presented in the brief concerning the penalty phase held that the penalty instructions had misleadingly informed the jury that it had to find "beyond a reasonable doubt" that the mitigating evidence outweighed the aggravating circumstances in making its death penalty determination.

In Nevada, the brief said, the death penalty was an available punishment only if the state could prove beyond a reasonable doubt that at least one aggravating circumstance existed, and that the aggravating circumstance or circumstances outweighed the mitigating evidence offered by the defendant. The jury instructions in Biela's case, however, seemed to have been inadvertently reversed. The jury was told that they had to find that the *mitigating* circumstances offered by the defense outweighed beyond a reasonable doubt the prosecution's *aggravating* circumstances in order to preclude consideration of the death penalty.

As an example, the Biela jury was instructed that first-degree murder was punishable by death, but *only if one or more aggravating circumstances are found beyond a reasonable doubt and any mitigating circumstance or circumstances which are found do not outweigh the aggravating circumstances.*

The jury was also told that if they found unanimously and beyond a reasonable doubt that at least one aggravating circumstance exists and *each of you determines beyond a reasonable doubt that any mitigating circumstances do not outweigh the aggravating,* then the defendant is eligible for a death sentence.

Those instructions and others along the same line, which were repeated at several points during the trial, told the jury that it had to find, beyond a reasonable doubt, that the mitigating circumstances did not outweigh the aggravating. Those instances of instructional error on a very pivotal factual determination, the brief stated, undermined the reliability of the jury's verdict. Consequently, then, Biela was entitled to a new penalty hearing before a properly instructed and newly impaneled jury. Alternatively, the brief said, the court could set aside the sentence of death and impose the sentence of imprisonment for life without the possibility of parole.

In the final point that was made in the opening brief, it stated that a law, NRS 177.055(2), required that the court conduct an independent review to determine whether the death penalty was imposed under the influence of passion, prejudice, or any other arbitrary factor; and whether the death penalty was excessive, considering both the crime and the defendant. This would prove to be the most lengthy of the arguments presented in the brief. The law named above required the court to review the record to consider:

1. The errors which had been listed in the appeal
2. Whether the evidence presented had supported the jury's finding of aggravating circumstances
3. If the jury had imposed the death sentence under the influence of passion, prejudice, or any other such factor
4. If the death sentence could be deemed excessive, taking into account both the crime and the defendant

When the state filed its Notice of Intent to Seek Death Penalty, it had identified the four counts against Biela, if proved, as its aggravating circumstances. The jury found that the state had proved the murder charge and each of the other counts beyond a reasonable doubt. In this appeal, Biela's attorneys challenged the sufficiency of the evidence offered to prove count 1, sexual assault against Amanda Collins. They submitted that even in the face of all the aggravating circumstances, death was still not the appropriate penalty.

The brief first elaborated on why the sentence of death was excessive considering both the crime and the defendant.

The facts that were presented to the jury concerning the Brianna Denison case allowed them to find that Brianna had been sexually assaulted and murdered. The evidence was not clear if the assault had taken place in the MacKay Court residence or in another location. It did not appear from the evidence that there was a great deal of time that had passed between Brianna's abduction and when her body had been left in the field.

One interpretation of these facts could conclude that this was a case where the sexual assault had gone terribly wrong and Brianna's accidental death occurred during the commission of a felony. This interpretation would remove the fourth aggravating circumstance from consideration by the jury. The brief went on to contend that the homicide involved only one victim, did not involve torture, depravity (clearly, this was the opinion of the appeal counsel, not the vast majority of the general public), poising, or lying in wait, and did not take place over an extended period of time.

The things that took Brianna's murder out of the ordinary were three things: Brianna herself, who became known by the media and the public as "Reno's Daughter"; the span of time between when she was first reported missing and when her body was found several weeks later in a field, even though the body had clearly been placed there on the same day she was taken; and the span of time between the discovery of her body and Biela's arrest, aided by the assault of the other two victims and the information they had been able to supply to the investigation.

Because of the tremendous amount of media coverage, the flood of Secret Witness tips received over time, the public blue ribbon campaigns, and the BBJF's work, Brianna Denison's murder became a "media case," resulting in it also becoming a death penalty case, according to the brief.

The jury found twenty-two out of the twenty-four

specific mitigating circumstances that the defense identified in regard to James Biela, along with one other mitigating factor—that being the fact that he had allegedly shown kindness to Virgie Chin by giving her a tissue when she asked him for one. It was proved that he had no significant criminal history before the joined charges in this case, and Dr. Piasecki's testimony had established that he was not a high risk for any dangerous behavior in the future. And finally, the brief contended, the evidence had shown that Biela had been a good employee, a good father to his little boy, and a good provider for the child and his mother.

According to the brief, the death sentence was imposed under the influence of passion, prejudice, and other arbitrary factors. It was made very clear that the Brianna Denison case received an extraordinary amount of publicity from the time of her disappearance through the discovery of her body and then on to Biela's subsequent arrest. This was made clear in the testimony of Detective Jenkins and many other witnesses, along with the other evidence that had been presented at the trial. It was reported by the *Reno Gazette-Journal* that the Bring Bri Justice Foundation had been set up by the middle of 2008, and the Reno-Sparks area was covered with blue ribbons, along with the surrounding communities in northern Nevada.

An avalanche of Secret Witness tips had come in, and the media received details about the suspect they were looking for. Descriptions of the vehicle possibly driven by the suspect, and details about the baby shoe spotted on the floorboard, along with the police sketch created with the help of Amanda Collins, were all reported in the media. The brief also mentioned what it called the publication of "suggestive details," such as the suspect's shaved pubic area, and told of the information released about the thong panties found at the crime scene, calling it significant. According to the brief, it was fair to say that the media's publication of this story dominated the local electronic and print news cycles for months, especially when Brianna's body was found.

The community had been in fear that a sexual predator was at large before Biela was arrested, and it made headline news when he was apprehended. When jury selection was taking place, many jurors were let go because they admitted to having already made up their minds about Biela's guilt and how he should be punished. The brief stated that, as it had said earlier, nothing about the actual murder took it out of the range of an ordinary first-degree case. What had caused it to be perceived as a death penalty case, claimed the brief, was Brianna and the interest of the public in her case, the time span between her death and the discovery of her body, and Biela's arrest.

According to the massive publicity surrounding this case, the brief said, Biela was singled out for the death penalty. Put another way, to uphold the death penalty in this case allowed the death penalty to be *cruel and unusual in the same way that being struck by lightning is cruel and unusual* and allowed the *unique penalty that is the death penalty* to be wantonly applied. The brief stated that by asking the crucial question: *"Are the crime and the defendant before us on appeal of the class or kind that warrants the imposition of death?"* The court would have to answer its question in the negative and set aside the death penalty in the case.

The death penalty in this case is excessive and is the product of forces beyond the crime itself and Mr. Biela, stated the brief. *This court should set aside the sentence of death and impose the sentence of imprisonment for life without possibility of parole.*

The conclusion of the brief stated that, based on the information presented and the record as a whole, James Biela's convictions should be set aside and the cases remanded for a new trial. And even if the court affirmed his convictions, it must still set aside the sentence of death and either remand for a new penalty hearing or order that a sentence of life without the possibility of parole be imposed in the place of the death sentence.

The brief was submitted on March 28, 2011.

On July 20, 2011, when filing their Respondents' Answering Brief, prosecutors contended that no court errors were made during Biela's trial, and his convictions and death sentence should be affirmed by the state supreme court. In their statement of the case, they said that the opening brief's version of the history of the case was accurate, but not complete. One of the main points—the opening brief's stated objection to the combination of the three cases into one trial—was not valid, the prosecution said.

Appellate DDA Terry McCarthy, who wrote the response, made his statement of the facts, beginning with the apparent acceleration of Biela's crimes. He noted that they all took place over a three-month period, all of the victims were of college age, and the crimes all occurred within a four-hundred-yard radius, resulting in a "sufficient connectedness" between the crimes to try them before the same jury at one time. The investigations and the evidence all overlapped between the three cases, the response said, and that overlap was what allowed all three cases to be cleared. For example, the sketch Amanda Collins had helped detectives to prepare when she came forward had become an integral part of all three investigations.

The close proximity to Virgie Chin's assault in relation to the place where Amanda was attacked, "scant yards" away, was another connecting factor. And Virgie had recalled enough details from her assault that she was able to provide other clues and information that proved connectedness between the cases. She had also been able to recall many details that would, after Biela's arrest, link DNA evidence between her case and Brianna's.

When the initial motion to sever was made prior to the trial, the motion was decided based on predictions as to what evidence would be presented, with the district court predicting that substantial amounts of the evidence would be cross-admissible in the three cases.

The state contended that there was no error made by the court in allowing the cases to be combined for trial. One of the factors weighed by the district court, the state said, was the inefficiency and cost of separate trials. The expense of multiple separate trials was a legitimate consideration, the state said, and, ultimately, the question of whether charges could be tried together was also whether there was a logical connection between them. In another case, the state supreme court had previously ruled that cases were connected whenever evidence of one crime was admissible in a trial concerning another crime.

One way in which crimes can be connected, the state said, is by temporal and geographic proximity. Biela's crime spree covered a three-month period; and each of the attacks, always on college-aged young women, took place within only a four-hundred-yard radius.

The response said, *That is a connection. A very close connection. It is difficult to envision a trial on any one of these crimes that would not have had at least some reference to the others.*

The overlap in the identity of the witnesses was extreme, the prosecution claimed. The detectives in each case were the same; the crime against Amanda came to light because of the crime against Brianna; the crime against Brianna was solved by simultaneously investigating all three of the cases.

There is zero reason to believe that the decision [to connect the cases] was whimsical, or random, or based on a toss of the coin. Instead, there is every reason to believe that Judge Perry carefully evaluated each appropriate factor, the response said. *Under those circumstances, the court should find no abuse of discretion.*

The response also said that Biela's attorneys had failed to demonstrate prejudice with his claim that the jury must have used the stronger cases to convict on the weaker case, and saying that the jury must have "gone rogue" because the evidence in the Amanda Collins case was insufficient to convict. The other claim of prejudice was a contention that the DNA evidence was confusing. Since there was no evidence that any juror had been confused by any bit of evidence, or that such confusion would not have also occurred, had there been separate trials, the fact that the judge was confused by the DNA evidence for a moment prior to the start of the trial should not be seen as a valid claim of prejudice.

The next claim made in the response was that Biela's attorneys felt there was not enough evidence for conviction on the Amanda Collins case because her identification of him as her rapist was "suspect." Nothing was said in Biela's opening brief that the identification had been wrong, but because it was referred to as "suspect," and therefore there was reason for cross-examination, the jury should not have heard the evidence at all, claimed the brief.

That is not the correct standard in any court, the response said. *Since Amanda pointed out Biela in court and swore that she recognized him as the man that raped her, the evidence is sufficient.*

The next series of issues addressed in the response dealt with the arguments in the opening brief that had to do with juror questions, with the brief saying that they must be considered as plain error. Biela's attorneys first argued that even though the defense wanted jurors to have the opportunity to be active participants (by asking questions during the trial), the judge should have overruled the decision. The attorneys next said that Biela's conviction must be reversed because the judge did not caution the jurors not to put too much weight on their own questions.

The attorneys stated that the court should rule that the weight to ascribe to evidence depends on the nature of the evidence, not on the identity of the person asking the question that leads to the evidence. The court should get out of the deliberations business and simply tell jurors to consider all the evidence, collectively evaluate the evidence, and seek a unanimous decision. The rest, the attorneys said, is up to the jury.

The opening brief's next argument had been that the sheer volume of juror questions was excessive. The state contended, in contrast, that fixing an absolute number of allowable questions prior to the trial would be an abuse of discretion.

It would be irrational for a trial judge to just pull a number out of the air and limit the questions to that number, without even knowing the subject matter, the state said.

The response then said that the district court did not err in denying the defense's motion for a mistrial because of the question posed by a juror concerning Biela's attempt to purchase a gun. During the trial, Amanda Collins had testified that she had been raped at gunpoint. Then, later, Detective Jenkins testified that Biela had attempted to buy a gun and was suicidal. One of the jurors had asked about the apparent conflicting facts that Biela had a gun at the time of the rape and then had been attempting to buy one later. The defense did not object at that time; but the following day, it moved for a mistrial, saying that the juror had obviously predetermined Biela's guilt on count 1, Amanda Collins's rape. The next day, the judge asked the juror if that had been the case, and she said it was not. Then, the day after that, the motion for a mistrial was denied. In the opening brief, the appeal attorneys said that a mistrial should have been mandatory; and the state, in its response, disagreed.

The premise of a mistrial, said the state, was faulty. The opening brief claimed that the question revealed that the juror had already made up her mind that Biela was guilty, and the juror denied that this was the case. The second flaw in the brief, said the state, was the fact that the judge had inquired into the possibility of predetermined guilt, and the juror denied it. The defense did not ask any further questions at that time, but now seemed to think that the judge should have determined the juror was lying. Since this was required by no rule of law, the state said the court should find that the district court did not err in concluding that no further action was necessary. The court should find no error in the district court's failure to declare a mistrial.

Chapter 30

On the matter of the characterization of websites, photos, and other materials as "pornography," and other similar terms, prior to the trial, the judge had ruled that the jury could see examples of the websites, but the above terms could not be used in describing them. In his opening statement, the prosecutor had used the term "adult" in a description. Biela's appeal attorneys argued in their opening brief that the conviction should be set aside because they claimed the prosecutor had violated the ruling.

The state contended that the alleged error involved the authority of the judge, not the evidence code. The leap to the conclusion that Biela had any remedy coming did not seem to be warranted, the state said, adding that there was nothing in the evidence code that allowed the district court to regulate the terminology used in opening statements by the prosecutor. The state claimed that the gag order itself was an error. Instead, *the proper course is to recognize that when counsel predicts in opening statements that the websites will be "adult" sites, he assumes the risk that the jury will disagree. Such a tactical decision, however, is not an appropriate concern of the district court,* the state contended, *and the district court should not have attempted to regulate the rhetoric of the prosecutor. When viewed under the guise of plain error, there is no presumption of prejudice.* The state said that the party asserting plain error has the burden of explaining that there is no other explanation for the verdict than that single word in the opening statement.

Another point of contention in the opening brief was that a witness had testified that the websites showed "adult women wearing thong underwear." The state responded that was not a violation of the order, because it did not prohibit mentioning that the models on the sites were adults, as opposed to children.

The opening brief also argued that Biela was entitled to have his conviction reversed because a witness also mentioned the nature of the evidence. A detective testified that the person who called in the Secret Witness tip said Biela had been looking at "pornographic" sites. The state responded that no relief was warranted because the district court did not have the authority to regulate the testimony of witnesses who were relating the words of others, for that would give the court the authority to command the witness to commit perjury. If the court had ordered the witness to use another word, that would have been a gross misuse of discretion.

The state said that if the court had the authority to "regulate the rhetorical excess" of lawyers, that did not extend to witnesses, and if the judge had told the witness how to testify, that would have been error. The testimony described the statement of an informant, the state said, and was admitted to show the progress of the investigation, not for the truth of the matter asserted.

The district court judge had noted that the detective had merely told the jury what the informant had said to him; therefore, the detective did not violate the order with his testimony. Therefore, the court should find that if the defense had sought any relief, it would not have been error if the judge had denied that request, the state said.

The appeal attorneys had next taken issue with the standard definition of a reasonable doubt. The state countered by pointing out that the reasonable doubt instruction had been repeatedly approved, and Nevada's standard definition was not contrary to constitutional standards. Accordingly, the state said, the court should affirm the judgment of the district court.

The opening brief had next addressed the issue of what it referred to as cumulative error. The simple response, said the state, was that there was no error. The state pointed out that an analysis of cumulative error should only include errors leading to the same remedy. It is inappropriate, for example, to combine a claim of insufficient evidence with a claim of admission of improper evidence, because the remedies for each are different.

The next item of contention was the instructions given to the jury in the penalty phase.

The state contended that there was error, but not the error asserted by Biela. The instructions to the jury made it clear that, even if the defendant is eligible for the death penalty, any one juror can prevent the death penalty by simply deciding not to impose it.

Each juror was informed that they individually have the discretion to prevent the death sentence for any reason or for no reason at all, the state said.

Finally the state pointed out that the defense had specifically denied having any objections to the instructions.

As the net effect of the instructions would work to the benefit of the defense, this court should find no "plain error" and certainly no specific prejudice to the defendant, the response said. *Thus, the judgment should be affirmed.*

The last argument in the response concerned the opening brief's claim that Biela's verdict was the product of passion or prejudice. The record, the response said, did not support that contention. The basic contention seems to be that *if* this murder was a felony murder, a kidnapping and rape that went wrong and resulted in an accidental death, the state said, then the death penalty would be excessive. The state contended that first, kidnapping and rape are not generally seen as mitigating circumstances; and, second, that the verdicts reveal that Biela intentionally murdered Brianna Denison by strangling her with some sort of garotte, possibly with her own underwear. Therefore, the premise underlying the argument was legally flawed and factually incorrect.

The state continued to say that the jury was not considering the hypothetical case of a kidnapping and rape followed by an accidental death, but the actual case of a kidnapping and rape coupled with a premeditated murder. The jury was not required to ignore its own factual finding that this case consisted of a premeditated murder and a separate kidnapping and rape.

Another premise of the opening brief was their contention that the jury had been influenced by pretrial publicity. The response answered that the jury selection process was part of the record, and all parties had been satisfied at the end of the process that the jurors would not be influenced by the publicity.

Again, the state said, *the premise is flawed.*

Finally the opening brief had contended, *This is but an ordinary run-of-the-mill first-degree murderer.*

In responding to that contention, the state drew again on some of the earlier statements from other court documents, with its response that the jury, representatives of the conscience of the community, seem to have disagreed. Perhaps it was because of the evidence that Biela was a serial rapist who then graduated into murder, said the state, adding that it seemed most likely that the community avoided a serial killer only because the authorities were able to catch the killer before his next graduation ceremony.

The conclusion of the state's response to Biela's opening brief said that there were errors in this trial, as there are in every trial, but they uniformly favored the defendant as the trial court bent over backward, even going so far as to regulate the rhetoric of counsel. The state said that there was no error affecting any of Mr. Biela's rights, and so the judgment of the district court should be affirmed.

This was submitted on July 20, 2011.

Chapter 31

On September 2, 2011, Biela's appellate attorneys filed his Argument in Reply, an answering brief to the state's response, saying that it was addressing only some of the answering arguments made by the state, and that it should not be taken as a concession of the legal merits of those arguments it did not address:

Rather, Mr. Biela submits that those issues have already been fully joined in the briefs on file and need not be revisited here.

Starting with the trial, the first issue addressed was abuse of discretion, with the district court failing to sever the three cases into separate trials. In the opening brief, it was claimed that in order for the cases to be tried together, they must be connected together, or be part of a common scheme or plan.

The Argument in Reply said that the state appeared to have abandoned the argument that these separate acts were part of a common scheme or plan and focused solely on whether the acts were "connected together." Therefore, it said, Mr. Biela requested that this court deem the abandonment of the argument as a concession by the state that the common scheme or plan basis for refusal to sever charges was error.

The reply said that the fact of the matter was that the cases should not have been joined; the opening brief had spelled out the similarities and differences between the three cases and had shown that they were not connected together. It claimed that under the abuse of discretion standard, the district court had abused its discretion as shown in the opening brief.

Also addressed in the reply was the fact that the judge had, prior to the trial, confused the DNA evidence between two of the cases, and had admitted that he had been confused about it. The reply said it could not be assumed that an experienced jury, hearing the evidence one time, would somehow do a better job than the judge of keeping the facts straight. The reply said that while the state suggests that the only way to make this claim of prejudice was to show that a *juror* was confused and not the judge, the reply claimed that the state then again runs up against the fact that jurors are not permitted to impeach their verdict and therefore a defendant could never show proof that a juror was confused by the evidence.

The reply went on to say that while the state might prefer such an impossible standard, the Constitution did not. The district court erred in refusing to sever the charges because the cases were not "connected together." This error, the reply claimed, wreaked substantial and injurious effect upon Mr. Biela, both by the confusing nature of the DNA evidence and the combination of the weaker case with the two stronger ones.

The reply contended that Biela's convictions should be reversed and the matter remanded for three separate trials: one for the charges involving Amanda Collins, one for the charges involving Virgie Chin, and one for the charges involving Brianna Denison.

The reply also claimed that Amanda's credibility had been destroyed because there was no physical evidence in her case, and her identification of Biela as her assailant was suspect. It stated that Amanda had destroyed all the direct evidence of a sexual assault after it had occurred, did not report the rape when it occurred, and that she had stated, when she did report it, that she did not get a good look at her attacker's face. When she did report the rape, the reply said, the police had sought a connection between her assault and Brianna's investigation. She later helped police create a likeness of her rapist, which was used in Brianna's case.

According to the reply, this participation caused Amanda to become invested in the Brianna Denison arrest. Due to having convinced herself completely that the man she saw arrested and taken into custody for Brianna's murder was the same man who had raped her, Amanda's subsequent identification of Biela as her assailant was a foregone conclusion.

The reply stated that Biela asked this court, as a matter of law, to find that Amanda Collins's identification of Mr. Biela as her assailant could not be pried from her investment in the Brianna Denison case, thereby rendering her in-court identification "incredible" and not reliable. As such, the reply said, the remaining evidence was far too thin to support the conviction on count 1 and the court, therefore, must grant the relief requested by Biela. The court must reverse the jury's verdict, the reply said.

The reply then tackled the issue of jury questions, saying that the district court's decision to allow the questions was subject to plain-error review. The state had missed the mark in its contentions regarding juror questions, or else failed to respond meaningfully to the issues on appeal, the reply said, adding that jury questioning was presumptively disfavored and therefore never appropriate as a matter of course.

This was followed by several pages listing a large number of references to prior state supreme court decisions regarding jury questioning in various situations and degrees.

The next point in the reply addressed what it called the state's failure to refute error associated with the district court's untimely undue-weight admonition.

According to the reply, while the state agreed that this jury was admonished regarding undue weight only once, and only after the jurors had asked a third of their questions, the reply said that it appeared to assume without explanation that this admonition was nonetheless sufficient because it took place well before the time came for the jury to deliberate. At this point, the reply also repeated its criticism of the amount of jury questions that were permitted during the trial, saying that the state's argument in regard to that excessiveness was "non-responsive."

Then the reply addressed the issue of references to "pornography," saying that the prohibited reference to pornography required a mistrial, and therefore required reversal. This referred to the hearsay contents of the Secret Witness Program informant's tip, which the state had claimed provided progress of the investigation. The reply said it was unnecessary to provide sequential progress, because the same informant also had provided the suspect's name and description, and the information that panties had been found in his truck. Not only was the information that he had been looking at "pornographic sites" unnecessary, it did nothing to lessen its prejudice, the reply said. The state claimed the defense denied that the pornography reference was prejudicial, but the reply said this was wrong. While the defense conceded that the reference was not intentionally made, the reply said that it never made any concession about prejudice.

The state's contrary recollection is notably not supported by any citation to the record, and should be rejected, said the reply.

The question of reasonable doubt was addressed next, with the reply stating that the definition of "reasonable doubt" was a misplaced and misleading analogy and should be abandoned by the legal system.

The reply said that it was respectfully submitting that the court should take a fresh look at Nevada's instruction of reasonable doubt. Equating reasonable doubt to doubt that would govern or control a person in the more weighty affairs of life, the reply said, should be abandoned as a legal definition.

The reply continued, saying that the court should require that the Federal Judicial Center's reasonable doubt instruction should be given in its place, instead, in order to keep there from being any uncertainty or confusion in the jurors.

Addressing items at issue in the penalty phase of the trial, the reply said that the jury was, on two occasions, incorrectly instructed that it had to find the mitigating circumstances outweighed the aggravating circumstances "beyond a reasonable doubt." This was clear error, requiring that the death penalty imposed in the case be vacated, the reply said. It claimed that the jury had been improperly instructed that the death penalty was an eligible penalty if they could not find that the mitigating circumstances outweighed the aggravating circumstances beyond a reasonable doubt. That step, under that standard of proof, can never be part of a jury's death penalty calculus in Nevada, the reply stated. By making it so in this case, these instructions unnecessarily interfered with the jury's penalty deliberations. The reply said that this instructional error required either a new penalty hearing or an order vacating the death penalty, with instructions to impose a sentence of life without the possibility of parole.

* * *

The reply next dealt with the appellate attorneys' argument that the death penalty in the case was excessive, considering both the crime and the defendant.

According to the reply, the court should review a death penalty to determine whether the sentence of death was imposed under the influence of passion, prejudice, or any other arbitrary factor, and whether the sentence of death was excessive, considering both the crime and the defendant. In response, said the reply, the state contended only that the record did not support the notion that the verdict was the product of passion or prejudice.

The reply then claimed that the state had gone on to undermine its own position by its statement in the response, when it said the community avoided a serial killer only because law enforcement was able to catch the killer before his next graduation ceremony.

The reply said that the passion in that narrative was apparent, and operating under that premise, the jury had imposed the death penalty. Therefore, it said, the court should vacate the death penalty as being excessive. For the reasons set forth in the opening brief and in the reply, it said, the court should conclude that this case was one in which the jury's penalty decision was imposed under the influence of passion. The court should not review the record myopically, it said, and, therefore, the court should also conclude that the sentence of death imposed in this case was excessive, given the circumstances of the murder and Mr. Biela.

This was submitted on September 11, 2011.

* * *

Sadly, Judge Robert H. Perry did not live to see the Nevada Supreme Court issue its final ruling in the Biela case. On December 20, 2011, he lost a lengthy battle with heart disease and passed away at the age of sixty-eight.

Judge Perry was perhaps best known for presiding over the Biela trial, but prior to being appointed to the bench in 2005, he had worked for twenty-nine years as a successful plaintiff's attorney and was voted "Trial Lawyer of the Year" by Nevada in 2004.

Almost a year of orders, motions, notices, and updates followed, passing back and forth between the appellant, the respondent, and the court. On August 1, 2012, the Nevada Supreme Court filed an order of affirmance, upholding the death sentence that had been imposed on James Biela.

The order began with a recap of the case against Biela: the testimony and evidence involved, the results of the trial, the penalty phase, and the sentencing.

Biela raised claims related to severance, sufficiency of the evidence, guilt phase jury instructions, the alleged prejudicial impact of juror-initiated questions, and penalty phase weighing of aggravating and mitigating circumstances. *For the reasons explained below, we reject his claims and affirm the judgment of conviction,* the order said.

According to the order, Biela claimed that the district court erred in denying his pretrial motion to sever the counts related to each victim. He contended that the three crimes were not connected together, and did not consist of a common scheme or plan, and that the joint trial was prejudicial to him.

We disagree, the order said.

Biela claimed that because the crimes were committed in different places, at different times, and against different victims in different ways, there was no evidence of a plan. The district court, however, noted that the victims were all college-aged women and the crimes were committed within a mile of the UNR campus, within four hundred yards of each other, late at night or in the early morning. Each was a sexual assault with violence and threat of future violence, and each victim's underwear was taken. The district court agreed with the state that these facts were similarities, not differences, and showed escalation, and therefore of purposeful design.

The district court did not err, the order said.

Biela's next argument was that the crimes were not connected together, the order said. The test for connectedness recognized by the court said that cases could be connected if they were proven by clear and convincing evidence and shown to be relevant to prove motive, opportunity, intent, preparation, plan, knowledge, identity, or absence of mistake or accident.

The district court ruled that the similarities in the facts were sufficient to prove that the offenses were connected together:

We agree, and conclude that Biela failed to carry his "heavy burden" in showing that the district court abused its discretion in denying his motion to sever.

* * *

Biela's team next put forth the argument that the state committed reversible plain error by repeatedly violating the district court's order that prohibited the characterizing of certain evidence as pornographic. According to his previous submissions to the court, the state had violated that order on three occasions, but no objections had been mounted by the defense during the trial.

We are unable to review whether these occasions constituted a violation of the district court's order, the order said, adding they could not discern plain error where Biela failed to articulate convincingly how those putative violations prejudiced him and, thus, how his substantial rights were violated.

On the matter of juror-initiated questions, the order said that Biela claimed the district court committed reversible error when it allowed the jury to allow questions. Even if the district court did not err in permitting jury questions, Biela further claimed, the district court did err when it failed to weigh the risks of permitting such questions on the record, to restrain their number, or to instruct the jury that it should not put undue weight on these questions.

While he admittedly acquiesced to the allowance of jury questions and to the procedure by which they were asked and objected to, the order stated, Biela claimed that the errors were nevertheless plain and affected his substantial rights. He additionally claimed error as to the one jury question to which he did object, and said that it was also error for the juror questions to be allowed.

The supreme court stated that it had recognized that allowing juror-initiated questions did pose certain dangers, but it might also "significantly enhance" the "truth-seeking function" of the trial process and, therefore, had left the decision on whether to allow such questions to the "sound discretion" of the trial court. Beyond the bare and conclusory contention that the community's interest in the case posed the danger of an overly inquisitive jury, Biela did not point to any specific way in which his substantial rights were violated. Further, Biela could hardly complain of a procedure to which he had agreed.

For similar reasons, the order went on to say, the district court committed no error in failing to restrain the number of jury questions. The appellant claimed a count of ninety-nine juror questions, and said the "excessive" number proved evidence of a jury that had thoroughly abandoned its role as a neutral finder of facts.

Biela never objected to the number or alleged excessiveness of the jury questions, and the district court did not err in failing to object in his stead, the order determined.

Also on the matter of jury questions, Biela claimed that the district court should have stated on the record that it had weighed the risks of asking jury questions against the benefits and then giving its reasons for allowing the questions in his case.

We discern no plain error, the order countered, *and we also decline his invitation to adopt the disapproving stance of the federal courts on the practice of asking questions.*

Biela had also contended that the district court erred in failing to promptly instruct the jury not to place undue weight on the responses they received to their questions. This instruction was given on the fifth day of the trial and at the close of evidence.

The supreme court found that there was no error, as the district court twice gave the undue-weight admonition to the jury.

Additionally, Biela claimed that the district court erred when it denied his motion for a mistrial because one of the jury questions presupposed that he was guilty of assault with a deadly weapon.

The supreme court disagreed, pointing out that the district court held a hearing at which it asked the juror who authored the question whether it indicated that she had prematurely decided Biela's guilt as to count 1. The juror stated that it did not indicate that, and the parties declined to ask any followup questions. A fair reading of the juror's question supports the district court's determination that the juror was simply requestioning factual information and not revealing a premature opinion:

We therefore conclude that the district court did not abuse its discretion in determining that neither removal of the juror nor a mistrial was necessary.

The next area of argument concerned sufficiency of evidence, with Biela contending that reversal was required on count 1, the sexual assault of Amanda Collins. Her identification of Biela as her rapist, Biela had claimed, had occurred only after media reports named him as a suspect in the Brianna Denison case and Amanda had seen his photo on a newspaper's website. This allegedly had made her identification of him "suspect." This had been presented as a sufficiency-of-evidence claim, but Amanda testified at trial, identified Biela as her attacker, and maintained that he had sexually assaulted her.

Such testimony, standing alone, is sufficient to support his conviction on this count, stated the court, saying that they rejected his claim that certain facets of Amanda's testimony rendered it incredible as a matter of law.

Several contentions were raised concerning jury instructions in the guilt and penalty phases of the trial. Bicla claimed that the district court erred when it declined to give the federal-pattern jury instruction on reasonable doubt and gave Nevada's statutory instruction, instead, the order said.

This court has repeatedly held that [Nevada's] instruction is constitutional and that it will defer to the legislature for changes to that instruction. Therefore, the district court did not err in giving the statutory reasonable doubt instruction.

Biela's second argument had been that the district court had committed reversible error when it gave an instruction explaining the trial would occur in two phases and that, if the jury found Biela guilty of murder it would then be called on, in the second phase, to decide whether or not to impose the death penalty. Biela claimed that instruction was in error because it exceeded what was required and invited the jury to convict him of first-degree murder so that it could then get to the penalty phase.

The court ruled in its order that the jury instructions had conformed to the legal requirements; the defense had agreed to the instruction at trial; its failure to object precluded the court's consideration of his claim on appeal.

* * *

The next issue addressed in the court's order concerned Biela's argument that he should be given a new penalty hearing because the penalty phase instructions erroneously told the jury that it was required to find that the mitigating circumstances outweighed the aggravating circumstances beyond a reasonable doubt. The jurors in the case, the appellant claimed, had been given jury instructions for the penalty phase that frequently, but not uniformly, stated that in order for a juror to find Biela ineligible for the death penalty, the mitigating circumstances must have outweighed the aggravating circumstances beyond a reasonable doubt. The beyond-a-reasonable-doubt standard had been inserted into two weighing instructions at the request of the state, Biela claimed, with Biela's acquiescence.

The order stated that the instructions in this case correctly informed the jury that in order to find Biela death eligible, it must first find beyond a reasonable doubt that at least one aggravating circumstance existed. The relevant statutes only required that the jury must also find that any mitigating circumstances did not outweigh those in aggravation.

The order went on to say that no Nevada statute mentioned a burden of proof as it pertained to the weighing determination, and the court said that it had long rejected claims that the weighing of the mitigating and aggravating factors in a death penalty case was subject to the beyond-a-reasonable-doubt standard. The court had previously held that because the weighing determination was a moral issue and not a fact-finding exercise, it was not susceptible to a standard of proof. As a result, the order said that

while the existence of an aggravating or mitigating circumstance was a fact susceptible to proof under a reasonable doubt or preponderance standard, the *relative weight* was not. The two instructions given in this case thus misstate the law and similar instructions should not be used in the future.

According to the order, Biela did not object to these instructions and had failed to demonstrate that the beyond-a-reasonable-doubt language had been prejudicial to him:

But because Biela cannot demonstrate that the verdict was affected by the inaccurate language, or that he was otherwise prejudiced, any error in the two instructions does not rise to the level of plain error that would warrant reversal.

The order then addressed Biela's claim that the cumulative effect of the errors committed during his trial warranted reversal of his conviction and sentence.

Having found only one error that was not itself prejudicial, we conclude that Biela's claim of cumulative error lacks merit, the court said.

In the court's final statement of the order, its mandatory review, it said that the law required that the court review every death sentence and consider three points. First, whether sufficient evidence supported the aggravating circumstances found; second, whether the verdict was rendered under the influence of passion, prejudice, or any arbitrary factor; and third, whether the death sentence was excessive.

First, the four aggravating circumstances found by the jury were based on the four felonies of which Biela was convicted of in the guilt phase. Sufficient evidence existed to support these convictions, including the surviving victims' testimony, the evidence corroborating that testimony, and the extensive DNA and other forensic evidence presented, according to the order.

Second, the order said, there was nothing in the record demonstrating that the jury's verdict was the result of passion, prejudice, or any other arbitrary factor. Biela claimed that the extensive media attention this case received polluted the jury pool with fear that a violent sexual predator was on the prowl for months and that the evidence that the police released to the media further served to inflame members of the community, according to the order. To the contrary, the order concluded the jury's finding of twenty-three mitigating circumstances, and the ninety-nine questions it asked during trial, provided ample evidence that it was attentive, thoughtful, and did not rush to judgment in the determination of either guilt or penalty.

Finally the order stated that it found that the death penalty was not excessive in this case. Despite his evidence in mitigation, the presented evidence quite persuasively showed that Biela entered someone else's home early in the morning, pressed a pillow to a sleeping woman's face until she choked, and abducted her. He then raped her, strangled her with the strap of her best friend's thong underwear, and left her body in a field. This crime followed his stalking and sexual assault of two other young women.

The order said that those crimes and this defendant were *of the class or kind that warrants the imposition of death.* Having considered Biela's contentions and conducted the review required by NRS 177.055(2), the supreme court concluded that no relief was warranted:

We therefore ORDER the judgment of conviction AFFIRMED.

That decision generated another flurry of orders and motions, and on August 23, 2012, Biela's attorneys filed a petition for rehearing. The petition asked for the rehearing because, it said, the court misapprehended facts in the record concerning Biela's objection to the giving of two penalty phase instructions, overlooked or misapplied controlling authority to Biela's detriment, and misapprehended facts demonstrated prejudice.

In his opening and replying briefs, the petition said, Biela had held that the district court had erred when it instructed the jury that in weighing the aggravating and mitigating circumstances, it had to find beyond a reasonable doubt that the mitigating circumstances outweighed the aggravating circumstances. The supreme court, it said, had agreed with Biela, noting that the two instructions *given in this case . . . misstate law, and similar instructions should not be used in the future.*

The petition also said that the "beyond a reasonable doubt" standard had been inserted in the two weighing standards at the request of the state, with the defense's acquiescence. The word "acquiescence," it said, was defined as "passive assent" or "agreement without protest." The record demonstrated not acquiescence, it said, but, rather, defense objections to the proposed insertion of the language into the instructions on different grounds.

The petition claimed that the record also demonstrated that an objection would have been futile.

The petition then relayed most of the record concerning the meeting held on Thursday, May 27, 2010, that pertained to the previously referenced defense objections and "acquiescence." In attendance at that 2010 meeting were Judge Perry, Deputy District Attorneys Elliott Sattler and Chris Hicks, Gary Hatlestad and Terry McCarthy from his office; Maizie Pusich, Jay Slocum, and James Leslie from the Washoe County Public Defender's Office; and the defendant, James Biela, as well.

The purpose of the meeting was to settle penalty jury instructions: *depending on what the jury does in Phase One.* McCarthy asked at one point during the meeting if he and the rest of the prosecution representatives could be excused for a short time to "finish discussing something." After they returned, and Judge Perry resumed settling the jury instructions, the state suggested "a small change" to the instructions, which later became an issue in Biela's appeal. The defense objected to the small changes, but on a different basis; the defense felt that the jury might be misled to conclude that it must find mitigating circumstances beyond a reasonable doubt. Mr. McCarthy contended that the proposed language "should only go to weighing."

Hicks:	Yeah, that line qualifies the weighing process, not the mitigating—not finding of the mitigating circumstances.
Perry:	Yeah, I think if you're talking about the weighing process, I think it is

> beyond a reasonable doubt, but not the mitigating circumstances.

Pusich: Your Honor, I just don't want [the jury] to end up thinking that the qualifier applies to the mitigating circumstances, because it absolutely does not.

McCarthy suggested alternate wordings, and both Judge Perry and the public defender Pusich accepted one of his suggestions.

Pusich: Although, honestly, I'm still concerned that [the jury] is going to think they have to find mitigating circumstances beyond a reasonable doubt. I think if they want to modify weighing, they may have to actually put their qualifier somewhere they're talking about the weighing process.

Judge Perry said he felt that her latter point was "something that can be pointed out at argument."

McCarthy: The jury is told they need not be unanimous about mitigators, and I think that pretty much tells them that they can use any standard of proof they want.

Pusich: We've told them quite clearly that beyond a reasonable doubt applies to the aggravating circumstances. Now, if we add that into section two, which is discussing mitigating, it appears to impose a burden on the jury that they do not have.

Terry McCarthy then suggested that the instruction read, "The jurors need not find the existence of mitigating circumstances unanimously or beyond a reasonable doubt." Maizie Pusich agreed to that language.

The petition claimed that it was clear that Pusich's objection to the first proposed language was because of her desire that the jury not be confused as to its freedom to find mitigating circumstances on any basis. Her acquiescence, the petition said, was to the state's second suggestion, which was a correct statement of law.

Accordingly, the petition said, *the court's use of the word "acquiesce" to characterize Biela's stance on these improper jury instructions in the district court misapprehends facts in the record, and rehearing should be granted.*

The petition stated that because jurors are presumed to follow jury instructions, the court should equally presume that the inserted language did affect the jury's weighing process, to Biela's detriment. The jury was twice improperly instructed that the mitigators had to outweigh the aggravators beyond a reasonable doubt. The error did not benefit Biela, but prejudice to him did occur. Additionally, the petition said, although the instructional error in the case was prejudicial to him, at the same time it actually benefited the state by placing an undue burden of proof on Biela. The state should not be allowed to benefit from instructional error of its own making, stated the petition, therefore rehearing on the penalty instruction issue should be granted.

The conclusion of Biela's petition for rehearing claimed that the instructional error complained of in the appeal was so fundamental to notions of due process and fairness that it could be considered harmless. The instructional error in this case, it claimed, resulted in a clear misstatement of the law. So clear, in fact, that the court had instructed: *Similar instructions should not be used in the future.* The court should not just look to correct future error, said the petition. The two weighing instructions should not have been used in this case, and this court must, on rehearing, reverse the jury's sentence:

Respectfully, the improper penalty jury instructions used in this case warrant relief on direct appeal, not in some future collateral proceeding.

For the reasons set forth, it is respectfully requested that this court grant a rehearing on the penalty instructions at issue in this appeal.

This was submitted in August 2012.

Chapter 32

On October 15, 2012, Tracie Lindeman, the court clerk of the Nevada Supreme Court, filed a clerk's certificate that certified that the following judgment was full, true, and correct:

The court being fully advised in the premises and the law, it is now ordered, adjudged and decreed, as follows:

ORDER the judgment of the conviction AFFIRMED.

The court being fully advised in the premises and the law, it is now ordered, adjudged and decreed, as follows:

Rehearing DENIED.

Judgment, as quoted above, entered this 15th day of October, 2012.

James Michael Biela's first round of appeals in the Nevada Supreme Court had come to an end.

Chapter 33

Now that James Biela's first round of appeals to the state supreme court had been denied, the next move to be made by his attorneys on his behalf would be the filing of a petition in federal court. His appeal to that court would contain all the same issues that he had claimed in his first state appeal round, very likely with several other issues added, which could include any number of other complaints. It was also to be expected, thanks to some controversial legislation, that the petition would include the allegations that both his trial and appeal lawyers had failed to do their jobs satisfactorily, thus his loss of the cases and the initial series of appeals.

In 1991, a bill had been passed that gave death row inmates the right to have lawyers to assist with the preparation of appeals. Six years later, the Nevada Supreme Court ruled that those lawyers must be capable if the legislature was going to make the right to legal help for death row inmates a mandatory requirement. Because of this law making the right to legal counsel a requirement, many prosecutors and judicial officials claimed that the time for appeals had inadvertently been extended for as long as another decade. Death row inmates could claim ineffective representation by their first postconviction attorney when they made their second postconviction appeal, and those claims stretched out the process interminably.

The federal court would then send the case back to the state court to review the inmate's new claims, which would include the claims of ineffective counsel, and the state would review the case once again. The claims of ineffective counsel could cycle back and forth between the state and federal courts for years, delaying the execution date again and again.

The delays that had come into being since the passage of the laws had caused a great deal of debate in the Nevada Legislature, with some of the assemblymen supporting the removal of that extra layer of appeals.

"I think the appeals process should be limited to one at the state level and one at the federal level," said Assemblyman Don Gustavson, R-Sparks, who added that he thought that his fellow legislators should be willing to consider changing the law. He said that he believed it "takes forever and is way too costly," adding that sometimes the inmates died of old age before they exhausted all their appeals and were scheduled to be executed.

Legislators who were opposed to changing the appeal laws claimed that the extra precautions and the high cost of the appeals were ultimately worth it. Assemblywoman Sheila Leslie, D-Reno, said that she didn't see much interest in the legislature to take the issue up again.

"You can't put a price tag on a person's life," she said.

The ACLU also weighed in about its own disagreement with the proposal to eliminate the mandatory representation requirement. They stated there was no room for error when the courts were dealing with life-and-death issues.

"When the state makes the decision to put someone to death, never is there a more crucial time to ensure that their lawyers are zealously and effectively representing their defendants charged with a capital crime," said Lee Rowland, staff lawyer for Nevada's ACLU chapter.

"The decision to put someone to death can't include a margin of error for incompetent counsel."

Because most death row inmates were indigent, public defenders were being appointed to represent them, and they were often overworked with caseloads that were much too high, Rowland said. She said that while the system allowed for a thorough review of an attorney's competence during the appeals process, there was a severe limitation on what defendants could do in order to prove their lawyer ineffective, citing as an example one case where a lawyer was not pronounced ineffective, even though he had slept through what was referred to as "noncritical" parts of a legal proceeding.

"We as a society need to ensure when we provide lawyers to poor defendants charged with death, that those lawyers do everything they can to ensure there are no factual or legal errors made in those cases," she said.

On the other side of the debate, there was a great deal of criticism among those who felt that the long delays caused by seemingly endless appeals were unfair to the families of victims, to law enforcement, and to the entire justice system.

Wayne Teglia, a former Reno police officer who had investigated many death penalty cases during his career, said that the legislature was "being careful to the point of absurdity. You can't get the death penalty carried out. How do you think the families feel?"

The only way that the state would see Biela executed, Teglia said, was if Biela decided to drop his appeals process and voluntarily choose execution. Washoe County DA Richard Gammick said that it benefited everyone when a death row inmate stopped his appeals. But ACLU attorney Lee Rowland pointed out that out of the twelve inmates executed in Nevada since 1976, eleven of them had voluntarily given up their appeals and had chosen to die. Rowland said that was disturbingly similar to state-sponsored suicide.

Richard Dieter, of the Death Penalty Information Center, said that a death sentence usually amounted to around twenty years of solitary confinement, with most inmates on death row eventually dying, but from natural causes rather than from execution. The question had been raised in the U.S. Supreme Court as to whether such long death row stays should be considered cruel and unusual punishment; and whether that, in turn, was in violation of inmates' Eighth Amendment rights.

Dieter said that the court had not thus far accepted a death penalty challenge that was based on the length of time an inmate had spent on death row, but two of the Supreme Court justices had disagreed with the court's refusals that had been made on that basis, claiming that suffering occurred when time spent waiting for execution was prolonged. Another justice said that it was "incongruous" to allow the inmates a roster of constitutional claims that extended their wait—then, at the same time, to complain about the delay in execution. But one of the first two justices said that the delays could not be blamed on the inmates, but on the states, for failing to comply with the U.S. Constitution's requirements in the first place.

The average length of time inmates spend waiting on death row in the United States has substantially increased over the years. The national average waiting time in the 1970s and 1980s was around four years from sentencing to execution, increasing to around thirteen years by 2008. By the time Biela went to the Condemned Men's Unit at Ely State Prison to join the other eighty inmates on Nevada's death row, the average time there was a wait of seventeen years, and one prisoner had been there for over thirty years.

Before his retirement from office, one Nevada assemblyman said that because of the astronomical cost of the appeals process to the state, Nevada needed to take a thorough look at the system and decide whether convicting a murderer to death, instead of giving him a life sentence, was worth the extreme price tag.

Assemblyman Bernie Anderson, of Sparks, sponsored a bill prior to his retirement that would temporarily suspend the death penalty while the state studied its true cost. The bill had not yet passed when Biela was convicted, but Anderson said that capital cases and the appeals that followed them were costing taxpayers millions . . . per individual case.

"The death penalty absolutely costs more money [than life-in-prison sentences]," Anderson said.

"In fact, the DA's office, the public defender's office, everyone agrees it's much more costly than incarceration."

Anderson said that those offices needed to help make the public aware of the real costs of death penalty prosecution and conviction, and whether that cost was beneficial to the state or if it would be better spent on education or other more constructive matters.

"We're going to have tough economic times ahead of us in the next three or four years," Anderson said, "and every dollar counts."

Anderson said that since he was retiring before his bill was due to be considered, he did not know if anyone else would take up sponsorship of it and if it, or any version of it, would ever pass the legislature. He believed, however, that it did have some support. That support might have eventually come from some of his colleagues in the legislature. However, when it came to James Biela and his appeals process, the citizens of Reno had a very different set of opinions.

Chapter 34

When Biela's first round of appeals began, reports of the claims being made in his opening brief were widely reported in the media and promptly began to generate outrage. Readers of the *Reno Gazette-Journal* were furious, and the letters, e-mail comments, and website postings began to pour in to the newspaper and its online forum.

This creep has been convicted fairly and is seeking reversal of those convictions based solely on technicalities, not because of innocence, said the first reader to comment, adding that Biela needed to remain on death row until his sentence was carried out.

Prayers with all the families, it concluded.

The next person to weigh in was listed as a "top commenter," and he had evidently read a detailed account of the content of the opening brief. This reader was disturbed by the phrasing of one item in particular. His well-written, thoughtful online post stated: *There is nothing "ordinary" or "run-of-the-mill" when it comes to first-degree murder. If we, as a society, have become so inured to violence that we can accept that concept, then our own demise is not far behind.*

Biela might somehow manage to escape the death penalty, the writer continued, but to overturn his conviction would be unconscionable.

Another commenter said that she thought Biela was a murderer of the absolute worst kind, and she expressed the hope that the court would not let him continue to pollute the air that she breathed.

A UNR student commented, *We are fortunate this thug is off the streets. Whether he rots in the Ely prison or is executed is irrelevant to me, though I think a lifetime behind bars is the harsher punishment.* What was important, the writer said, was that the community was rid of Biela.

Now he wants a new trial, not because he isn't guilty, but because he said he should be tried separately for each crime. What difference does it make if you are found guilty five times in five trials or five times in one trial, except it would cost the taxpayers more? Stick a needle in his arm and be done with it, another Reno resident shared.

There was great interest in Biela's appeal process far beyond the Reno area, too, with one comment from a Montana reader, who said Biela should be given no more compassion than he gave his victims: *Needle or rot in prison, either or. Just as long as he never gets out to hurt anyone else. Keep in mind, he raped more than one person. Unfortunately, he took the life of his last victim! Thoughts and prayers to the victims and their families.*

A student at Truckee Meadows Community College (TMCC) in Reno agreed: *That was not a one-time deal. He is a recidivist and should be considered a danger to society and to women in particular.*

Another top commenter posed the theory that

Biela had evidently decided prison wasn't all that bad: *He's segregated, so he doesn't have to live in fear, eats good, gets medical care, and pretty much will spend the rest of his life laying on his ass watching TV . . . but this appeal shows he's terrified of the needle.*

The TMCC student posted again, asking why the public was still wasting money on Biela: *He wants a new trial? What chance did he give Brianna? I don't want my tax money going to feed him, clothe him and giving him medical treatment.*

She went on to say that she was working two jobs, still couldn't afford medical insurance, and Biela was getting everything for free. Regarding his execution, she wrote, *Get it done and over with, a   stop wasting taxpayers' money.*

While the community expressed its o   on on Biela's first round of appeals, the Bring B   stice Foundation had been using every possible o   rtunity to address legislators and other group   d organizations about the DNA testing they felt w   essential for all those arrested for felonies, not just those who were convicted. Foundation members spoke to lawmakers at committee meetings, forums, and every other gathering they could attend, giving detailed information and statistics on DNA—and especially on the crimes that could have been prevented if Biela's DNA had been in the system after his assault charges involving Angi Carlomagno and her neighbor.

A preliminary law that the foundation had researched and was referring to as Brianna's Law was drawn up and presented to legislators. It read as follows:

> *Adapted from Assembly Bill 234 of the 2009 Nevada Legislature and SB09-241 of the Colorado State Legislature:*
>
> *This law would require that a biological specimen be obtained if a person is arrested for a felony. It would provide that if the person is convicted of the felony, the specimen must be kept. If it is determined tha*... *...person already has a specimen on file with the ...... repository for Nevada Records of Criminal History, another specimen does not need to be obtained. If the person is acquitted or the criminal charges against him are dismissed, the forensic laboratory testing the biological specimen, the law enforcement agency collecting the biological specimen and the central repository for Nevada Records of Criminal History shall destroy the specimen and all records related thereto, including those held with the federal combined DNA index system, only upon the specific written request of the person the specimen was taken from.*
>
> *Funding for this law will come from several, as of yet undetermined, mechanisms that may include: additional fees for violation of public safety laws, increases in "sin" taxes or other applicable taxes, federal grants, and private donations. Once a secure and recurring funding source has been identified, said funds will be deposited in the "Genetic Marker testing fund" and specifically used to counteract the funding needs of this law.*

There was support building among lawmakers for DNA testing following arrests, and the foundation's efforts were consistently met with sincere consideration and appreciation for the dedication of the organization. Hopefully, the passage of Brianna's Law, or an equally workable version of it, would be a reality in Nevada, as well as in other states in the near future.

Chapter 35

The Bring Bri Justice Foundation was primarily focused on its work regarding DNA testing, but it was also doing a great deal more than lobbying legislators for the passage of Brianna's Law, following Biela's conviction and sentencing. While his appeal attorneys were busy filing motions and writing his opening brief, the foundation had been hard at work on a great many other projects: fund-raisers, assisting in missing persons searches, and donations to other organizations with similar goals and objectives.

On behalf of the foundation, a motorcycle run and women's safety fair was held at Reno Harley-Davidson, which sponsored the event, with the help of the Crusaders Motorcycle Club and Miller Brewing. Thanks to the cosponsors and their loyal following, and the many supporters of the foundation, the event drew a large crowd and was very successful.

Summit Racing hosted a raffle for a large toolbox, with all the proceeds from the $5 tickets going to the foundation. The well-planned advertising for the raffle offered this invitation to the public: *Stop by and*

*make sure you don't miss out on your opportunity to help
out this great charity and maybe win yourself an amazing
toolbox!*

Clearly, there was outstanding support for the
foundation from all aspects of the community: citizens, businesses, law enforcement, and educational
institutions. All worked to make the foundation's
efforts a success and to keep Brianna's memory
alive.

Onc of the finest achievements of the foundation,
aside from its unending efforts to bring about the
passage of a version of Brianna's Law, was its contri-
bution to the purchase of three new passenger vans
for the Associated Students of the University of
Nevada (ASUN) Campus Escort Service, in collabo-
ration with the University Parents Fund, the Stern
Family Fund, and Carson Dodge Chrysler Jeep. Additional support was provided by ASUN and the
Graduate Student Association.

The vans were a part of a free service that provided prompt safety escorts and rides to more than
thirty thousand students, faculty, staff, and visitors
each year. During semesters the escort service was offered seven days a week, from 7:00 P.M. to 1:00 A.M.,
with the service closed during school breaks and
holidays. Rides were offered within a two-mile radius
of campus, and either the starting point or ending
point of the ride had to be a property or recognized
unit of the university, including its fraternity and
sorority houses.

Brianna's aunt Lauren said that the Bring Bri Justice Foundation had become involved in the program
because it coincided so well with the foundation's
commitment to the safety of all women and children
in Nevada.

"The fact that you can call and be escorted to your car ensures your chances of getting to your vehicle safely," Lauren told the media. "We thought it was a very worthy program."

The utilization of such an escort service could have conceivably made a difference in preventing the assaults on Amanda Collins and Virgie Chin.

One of the most worthwhile efforts of the foundation came with its dedication to aiding in the search for missing persons and in publicizing those searches to engage the volunteer efforts and financial support of the community.

One good example of this service to missing persons and their families came when the foundation received approval from the Reno Police Department to organize a series of community searches for a young girl, sixteen-year-old Karamjit Kaur, of Stead, Nevada. The foundation immediately launched a call for volunteers to participate in the searches; and for those who were not able to take part in the searches physically, the foundation asked for donations of water, granola bars, and other snacks for the searchers.

This was only one of many such search efforts aided by the foundation, and many other people from other parts of the country contacted them for the information packets the foundation put together on how to organize, search, publicize, and work with law enforcement and the media in the event of a missing persons situation.

Through the efforts of Brianna's family, friends, and scores of total strangers who had come to love "Reno's Daughter," her legacy was growing stronger every day.

Chapter 36

Several touching tributes to Brianna Denison were included on the Bring Bri Justice Foundation's website. Links were posted to two songs that had been written about Brianna: One composition was by Louis Bonaldi, who played piano on the recording of the song. Vocals were provided by Tim Snider, Rodney Branigan, and Trevor Gilmer. The song was recorded at Tanglewood Productions in Reno. The song's title was "Bring Back Bri," and it was played often at events sponsored by the foundation.

The other song, "Not Time to Say Good-bye," was written and produced as a touching tribute by Brianna's brother, Brighton Denison, with his collaborator, close family friend Danielle DeTomaso. Along with the link to download the song is their statement, *They want the world to hear it!*

Also on the foundation's website is an obituary tribute to Brianna. It tells of her outgoing nature and compassion, her love for traveling, and her ability to connect with people from all walks of life. The merits of being a loving, spiritual, respectful, and trusting human being had been instilled in her at an early age by her family and friends, the tribute said, and she had been raised in the tradition of honoring children as our most precious possessions. When Brianna and Brighton had been born, their parents had considered them to be the greatest gifts of their lives.

Brianna was survived by her mother, Bridgette Zunino-Denison; her brother, Brighton Denison; her maternal grandparents, Bob and Barbara Zunino, of Mendocino; her maternal uncle John Zunino; and her cousin Ashley Zunino.

She also left behind her paternal grandmother, Carol "Fifi" Pierce; her aunts Lauren Denison and Rena Denison Terry; her uncles Mark Denison and Steve Terry, along with thirteen cousins and many other extended family members throughout Nevada and California.

There were also hundreds of thousands of others who had come to love Brianna and think of her as their own; the law enforcement and judicial communities throughout Reno, the state of Nevada, and countless numbers of other people throughout the nation and in other countries who had heard Brianna's story and had seen her beautiful, smiling face in newspapers and magazines, on television, and on the Internet. After her death, Brianna had brought people from all walks of life together, just as she had in life.

On the website of the Bring Bri Justice Foundation, one of the pages, Safety Tips for Women, offers some excellent advice for self-protection. Much of it can be found on other similar sites, but in this case, the tips are geared toward young women and to arm them with the information they need to provide protection specifically against the kind of attacks Biela's victims were subjected to. The advice is well worth presenting here, in the hope that it might prevent an assault or even save a life.

Women are advised, first and foremost, to trust their instincts and if something or someone doesn't strike them as being safe, they should leave the situation as quickly as possible or get help immediately.

Be aware of your surroundings, the site says, telling women not to talk on their cell phones or use their iPods while they are walking, particularly at night. *Know where you are going and what's going on around you.*

Clothing is also a major safety consideration, and women are advised not to wear provocative clothing or, at least, to cover up revealing outfits. Hoodies or other similar shirts or jackets with hoods are also a no-no; they can be pulled over a victim's eyes and face during an attack. Also to be avoided are high heels, or any other type of shoes that could slow a fleeing victim down. Being able to run could mean the difference in being snatched or getting away safely.

The site recommends using confident body language: head up, arms swinging, and walking briskly with an air of being in command. But despite the display of confident bearing:

Lock your doors. Have your keys ready in your hand when walking to your car. Once you get into your car, lock the doors immediately and drive away. When you get home, make sure your doors are locked once you get inside.

It's important to have a plan in case of attack, the site advises. Women should know in the back of their minds what they would do if they were attacked.

If the attacker wanted his victim's purse, the site states, *Don't hand it to him, throw it to the side and run.*

Another point of advice given on the site is for women not to be in the wrong place at the wrong time. Wrong places include parking garages when alone, alleyways, and isolated streets; wrong times are any time when the areas are dimly lit, or at night. When walking, the site advises, walk in groups, and don't drive alone when traveling into bad neighborhoods or in unfamiliar areas.

One of the best deterrents against attack is noise; scream as loudly as possible for help, and run away screaming for help if you are able to flee.

The most important item on the list is this: If you are the victim of an attack, don't be afraid to come forward. By doing so, you might save another woman's life.

The Brianna Denison Foundation is to be commended for producing the list of safety tips as a part of the vast amounts of materials and resources they have made available to the public. Their goal in establishing the foundation, according to Lauren Denison, was to find a way to carry Brianna's name forward and not let her die in vain.

With all the good that Brianna's family and friends have already done, and that they will undoubtedly continue to do, they have made the most effective and lasting tribute to their beloved Bri that they could have possibly accomplished.

Special bonus for true-crime fans . . .

Turn the page for a compelling excerpt from

BLOOD AMBUSH
By Sheila Johnson

Available from Pinnacle Books,
an imprint of Kensington Publishing Corp.

Chapter 1

Early evenings in April are a treat for the senses in almost any part of the country, but even more so in rural northeast Alabama. Pastures and fields are bright green with new growth, dogwood trees and fruit orchards stand covered in fragrant pastel blossoms, and the smell of freshly tilled soil carries for miles on the breeze. And sometimes, when the wind is right, the workers plowing the fields can catch the equally pleasant scent of the great lake that covers a large percentage of the area that makes up Cherokee County, Alabama.

Cherokee County adjoins the Georgia state line and is best known as the location of Weiss Lake, one of the finest fishing and recreational areas in the southeastern United States. Countless professional fishing tournaments are held year-round, drawing entrants from all over the country, and the hundreds of miles of shoreline have become lined in recent years with lakefront homes, docks, campgrounds, and boathouses.

The lake, which covers forty-five square miles, is a result of the Coosa River being dammed in the 1950s by the Tennessee Valley Authority (TVA) in order to provide hydroelectric power for a large portion of northeast Alabama. Construction of the dams caused the extensive flooding of hundreds of acres of farmlands on all sides of the river. The huge lake that resulted is surrounded on almost all sides by the fertile fields and pastures of the county.

Darlene Roberts left her job in Rome, Georgia, on the afternoon of Thursday, April 6, 2006, on her way home to Cherokee County, Alabama. It was a fairly short commute, and she and her husband, Vernon, enjoyed living out in the country. They had been married for four years, and had met where they both worked, at Temple-Inland Paperboard and Packaging, Inc., near Rome, where Darlene worked in personnel management and Vernon was a supervisor.

Vernon had gone for a doctor's appointment that morning, and had been told by his physician that he would have to start taking medication to lower his high blood sugar levels. He got back to work in time to meet Darlene and some friends for lunch, and told them about his diagnosis. Darlene immediately began planning ways that she could change their diet in order to help get Vernon's blood sugar levels down, and she assured him that they'd make it just fine with the changes that she had in mind.

Vernon left work a little early that afternoon to do some painting and plumbing work around the house; he expected his brother to come for a visit over the weekend, and Vernon wanted to get things finished up before his guest arrived. He went home and started work, fixing a sink and painting the upstairs hallway, planning to have the jobs completed by the time his wife came home.

After she left work, Darlene gave her daughter, Heidi Langford, a ride to Heidi's home. Darlene often gave Heidi rides to and from work; it gave them a chance to spend time together, and sometimes they went shopping together. After she dropped Heidi off, Darlene stopped by Walmart in Rome to shop for some of the foods that would work well with the dietary changes she had talked about with Vernon and their friends during lunch. Her shopping list included lots of fresh vegetables, flour tortillas, pinto beans, and other ingredients for a nice dinner of fajitas. She also picked up some chicken fingers, corn dogs, and a few of Vernon's other favorites that he could still enjoy while keeping his blood sugar level lowered. Before Darlene went into the store, she called Vernon on her cell phone. She told her husband where she was, and asked him if there was anything else that he needed her to pick up for him while she was shopping. They both ended the call as they almost always did, telling each other, "I love you."

Charles Edward Young Sr. and his wife and stepson, Ryan Kyle Tippens, enjoyed spending time on Weiss Lake, and they had a weekend house on the lake in the Wildwood Acres area in Alabama, where they kept their boat and often went fishing. Despite the pleasant weather on the afternoon of Thursday, April 6, 2006, clouds were beginning to gather rather quickly, and severe thunderstorms had been predicted for the coming evening. The Youngs and Tippens decided to move their boat from the lake house to a nearby campground with a boat launch they regularly used.

At around 5:30 P.M., Young and his wife were on their way to meet Tippens at the lake house, where he planned to take the boat out onto the lake and meet his stepfather at the dock at the campground to load the boat back onto its trailer. As the Youngs drove down Cherokee County Road 941 toward the lake, they saw an unfamiliar black Dodge pickup truck with a hard bed cover backed in at the double gates beside the entrance to a pasture and farm pond that adjoined the road. A few minutes later, Tippens drove past and also noticed the truck sitting beside the gate. He saw two people there—a large gray-haired man and a shorter woman. Tippens didn't think anything seemed particularly strange or out of the ordinary; people from the neighborhood often fished in the pond. He continued on his way to the lake house, got into the boat, and took it around the lake to the campground to meet the Youngs.

After the boat was pulled out of the water and secured onto its trailer, the Youngs started back down County Road 941. Around an hour had passed, and there was now a late-model white sports-utility vehicle (SUV) sitting a short distance down in the high grass and willow saplings of the pasture. The black truck was still in sight, but it had moved down to the end of the road at the intersection with County Road 182. Young Sr. noticed that the same two people who had been with the black truck earlier were still there, but now the hard cover of the truck bed had been raised.

A short time later, Tippens drove past, pulling the boat and its trailer. He, too, saw the same black

Dodge pickup he had noticed earlier on his way to the campground. The truck was sitting beside the road, but it began to pull away as Tippens got closer. It looked to him like the truck was being driven by the same gray-haired man he had seen earlier.

Jose Luis Richiez was leaving for his home in nearby Summerville, Georgia, after a day on the job at Wildwood Acres Farms. Richiez had heard the local weather reports calling for possible severe weather moving into the area overnight, but he looked forward to the ride back to Summerville. On such a nice spring day, even with a few clouds beginning to gather in the west, it was going to be a pleasant trip.

Just before reaching the intersection of County Roads 941 and 182, Richiez saw a black Dodge Dakota pickup stopped on the side of the road with its hard bed cover raised. Thinking the truck might have broken down, Richiez was intending to stop and ask if he could help. As he got closer, he saw a man and woman fighting on the roadside beside the truck. The man was big, gray-haired, with a mustache, and the woman was smaller, wearing a light-colored shirt and jeans. Richiez was shocked when he saw the man hit the woman in the face and throw her back into the passenger side of the truck.

When the man hurriedly took off his shirt, tossed it into the back of the pickup, and jumped back into the cab, Richiez decided his safest move might be to mind his own business and continue on his way without stopping. As he passed the black truck, it pulled out onto the road behind him and closely followed him to a stop sign at the intersection. Richiez began to get uneasy; the gray-haired man had looked very big. When he pulled away from the intersection out of sight of the black truck, it didn't follow him any farther, much to his relief. Richiez didn't see the truck again, but he kept a close lookout in his rearview mirror all the way home, just in case.

While Richiez was being followed down the road by the black Dodge truck, another member of the Young family, Charles Edward Young Jr., was going toward his home on County Road 941 and noticed the white SUV sitting down in the pasture, near the pond. It looked to him like it might be stuck, so he stopped and called out to see if anyone was around that needed his help. No one answered, and no one was in sight at the vehicle or nearby in the pasture. Young Jr. started to walk down into the pasture and check on the condition of the vehicle, but he was wearing a pair of sandals and decided he'd better not try to push through the tall grass and into the field without having on a sturdier pair of shoes. He didn't notice anything else unusual in the pasture near the SUV, and thought that if anyone had needed help, the motorist had probably already left the pasture, so Young Jr. went on his way.

Chapter 2

Jason Alan Sammons and his friend Ellis McNeill Williams were enjoying the spring afternoon. The two were at Sammons's house on County Road 182, having a beer out in the yard while they talked and put away some tools Sammons had been using on the job that day. Both young men worked hard, and they liked to relax after work and spend a little time together enjoying a "cold one."

When they heard a gunshot that seemed to come from the pastures down the road, they didn't pay much attention. In such a rural area, an occasional gunshot was nothing unusual. The vast majority of people who lived in the area were hunters, and still more people fished regularly, either at the lake or in the many ponds. And those who fished were likely to take a gun along on their fishing trips; snakes were very fond of the water, especially the farm ponds, where there were plenty of frogs and big tadpoles to attract them. When the two young men heard a couple more shots a short time later, they were still unconcerned.

About half an hour passed, and after the tools had

all been cleaned and stored back in place, ready for the next day's work, the two friends decided to take Sammons's John Deere Gator all-terrain vehicle (ATV) and ride around the neighborhood for a while. Sammons grabbed Williams a beer out of the cooler and they started up the Gator and rode around over Sammons's farm; then they went across the highway and turned onto County Road 941.

When the two men saw a late-model white SUV sitting partially hidden in some willow bushes in the pasture beside the road, their first thought was that it might have been stolen or wrecked, so they rode down into the pasture to check it out. Car thieves often abandoned stolen vehicles off the road after they had been stripped. But this SUV seemed not to have been tampered with, so the men looked to see if its driver was in the pasture. When they found that no one seemed to be around, they pulled back out of the pasture and continued with their ride.

When Sammons and Williams turned around and started back down the road a short time later, they were still curious about the nice late-model abandoned vehicle sitting out in the pasture. They drove the Gator through the field down to the SUV again to have another look. This time they looked more closely and saw that there was, after all, some damage to the underside of the front of the vehicle, and it looked as though it might have been driven down and gotten stuck in the field. It just didn't look like the type of car someone would take down into a rough pasture like that, too nice and new to be driving around through the high grass and over the rough ground. Besides, it was sitting there with several bags of groceries in the back. They might need to call somebody, they decided, and report it, just in case there had been some kind of problem.

As they started to leave the pasture, Sammons glanced over toward the small pond a short distance away and noticed that something at the water's edge didn't look quite right.

"Man, what's that down there in the pond?" he asked Williams. "Do you see it?"

Sammons steered the Gator down toward the pond to a place where he could get a better look at what he saw floating in the shallow water. He started driving slowly, but slammed on the brakes, his heart pounding, when he saw what looked like a body lying at the edge of the pond. As he and Williams pulled up, got off the Gator, and carefully stepped a few feet closer, they could see that it was the corpse of a woman, floating facedown in the brackish water. From a short distance, it looked like she had suffered some horrific injuries to the head and back, and there could be absolutely no question that the woman was dead.

As the two men stood there, hardly believing they had stumbled onto such a nightmarish scene, Sammons noticed that some shotgun shells were lying nearby on the ground, two blue and one red, looking fresh and clean, as if they hadn't been lying there very long. He recalled hearing several gunshots while he and his friend were standing outside at his home, and he realized that what he and Williams had heard was more than likely the firing of the shots that had killed the woman in the pond.

Chapter 3

At first, Sammons and Williams stood and stared, frozen in place, horrified by their discovery. Then they realized that they had to snap out of it, get moving quickly and call someone for help as soon as possible. Sammons couldn't get service on his cell phone in the low-lying area around the pond, and he knew that he was going to have to go back up to the road before he could make a call. The men backed away from the pond, jumped back onto the Gator, and carefully moved it away from the area so they wouldn't damage any evidence or disturb the scene. They were anxious to get some officers there as quickly as they could, but they took pains not to disturb a few patches of grass and weeds that looked as if they might have been recently walked through and flattened.

As they were hurrying out of the pasture, shaken by what they had found at the pond, a gold extended-cab Chevy pickup drove by the pasture on the dirt road at a higher-than-normal rate of speed, headed for the main highway. By the time Sammons and Williams got the Gator back onto the road, the speeding pickup had already disappeared out of sight down County Road 941.

Sammons pulled the Gator to a point on the road that was slightly higher uphill, to a place where he could get cell phone service, and he hurriedly called Cherokee County 911. After he told the dispatcher what he and his friend had found in the pond and gave the operator directions to the scene, the two men drove the Gator back to the pasture gate to wait beside the road for the authorities to arrive. It would be getting dark soon, and the coming storm was making the evening air unseasonably warm and muggy. It was not cold at all, but Sammons and Williams were shivering.

Todd Waits and his wife were going out that evening to the nearby town of Cedar Bluff, Alabama. They left home at 5:30 P.M., and as they returned home at around 7:00 P.M., they met a tan Chevrolet Stepside pickup truck going out toward the main road at a fairly high speed. Minutes later, after they turned onto County Road 941, they saw two men standing beside the road next to a John Deere Gator. The men, whom Waits recognized as Jason Sammons and Ellis Williams, began frantically waving for him to stop.

"Man, there's a woman down there, dead in the pond," Sammons shouted at Waits as he pulled up beside them. "I just called 911," he continued, "and they ought to get here pretty quick."

Waits could see that the two men were shaken, visibly upset by what they had discovered. He decided quickly what he should do.

"I'll take my wife on to the house, then I'll come right back down here," Waits told them.

When he had dropped his wife off safely at their home, Waits hurried back down the road to the pasture gate to wait with his frightened neighbors until the authorities began to arrive.

The three men didn't have a long wait; within a few minutes, the flashing blue lights of emergency vehicles lit up the darkening skies as law enforcement officers began coming up County Road 941 to the blue metal gate at the entrance of the pasture, and the cars of county deputies and investigators soon lined both sides of the road that stretched alongside the pasture.

Chapter 4

When Cherokee County investigator Michael B. "Bo" Jolly was dispatched to the pond off County Road 941, he was one of a group of several officers who were the first to arrive at the scene. A 911 caller had reported finding a woman's body floating in a farm pond, apparently shot and killed. This was a very uncommon occurrence in rural Cherokee County, Alabama. When such calls went out on the scanner, they quickly drew responses from every officer and agency in the vicinity.

At that time, Jolly had been an investigator for the sheriff's office for three years, and had spent a total of seven years in law enforcement. He had served as the lead investigator on countless cases during that time, but this case would prove to be the main focus of his career for many months to come.

The 911 call had come in to the dispatcher just before seven o'clock, and by 7:10 P.M., Jolly and Deputies Kirk Blankenship and Kneely Pack had begun gathering at the scene, along with Drug Task Force officers Charles Clifton and Scott McGinnis. Clifton, commander of the task force, had arrived first, and had already started securing the scene. He had also identified the witnesses who had placed the initial 911 call, Sammons and Williams, and had gotten them and Waits started on writing their statements with details about how they had come to be at the pond that evening, and what they had found there.

When he arrived at the pasture, Jolly walked with Clifton down to the pond and looked at the body floating, facedown, not very far out in the murky water along the edge of the pond. It appeared to be the body of a Caucasian woman, probably in her mid-thirties, who had been shot several times at very close range, causing extensive damage to her head, back, and arms. The wounds appeared to Jolly to be consistent to those made with a shotgun. The victim was fully clothed in tan pants and a tan blouse, but a piece of light green plastic stretch wrap had been looped around her neck.

A short distance away from the pond, a late-model white Nissan Murano SUV had been driven into a clump of bushes in what looked to the officers like an attempt to conceal it from passersby on the road. The vehicle had not been wrecked, but there was damage to the lower front end, where it had been driven from the gate into the pasture, then through the mud and high weeds. When the Alabama license tag bearing the number *13BO341* was run, the SUV had not been reported stolen, and the name and address of its registered owner was determined. The address, the information revealed, was only a couple of miles farther down the road from the pasture. When they received that information, the officers knew that there was a strong likelihood that the driver of the SUV was, in all probability, the woman whose horribly mutilated body was now floating in the pond.

A short time later, Investigators Mark Hicks and Jimmy DeBerry and Cherokee County sheriff Larry Wilson arrived and joined Jolly and Clifton at the edge of the pond. Sheriff Wilson quickly decided that his department needed to call and request immediate assistance from the Alabama Bureau of Investigation (ABI), and the Alabama Department of Forensic Sciences (ADFS) was also notified that they would need to be en route. In the meantime, the daylight was rapidly beginning to fade, so the investigators began placing evidence markers and photographing the scene while they waited for the ABI agents and forensics personnel to arrive.

Chapter 5

Vernon Roberts couldn't understand why his wife, Darlene, was not answering his repeated calls to her cell phone. She had called him earlier, around 4:45 P.M., to tell him she had just arrived at Walmart in Rome, Georgia, to shop for groceries on her way home. She asked him if there was anything that he needed her to pick up for him, and said she'd be home soon. After they hung up, Vernon went back to the work he'd started as soon as he had gotten home, painting the upstairs hallway. When he finished, he worked on the faucet in the upstairs bathroom, then cleaned the bathroom in preparation for his brother's arrival for a visit. His work done, Vernon took a shower, expecting his wife to be home before he was finished, but she still wasn't there when he got out of the shower. He began to get concerned, and he called her to see if everything was okay.

There was no answer on her cell phone. Vernon called Darlene's daughter, Heidi, to see what time her mother had dropped her off at home after work. He told Heidi he couldn't get in contact with Darlene, and after trying unsuccessfully to call her mother's cell phone, Heidi called Vernon back and told him she hadn't been able to contact her mother, either.

Vernon told Heidi he was going to go out looking for Darlene, thinking that she might have had car trouble or a flat tire in an area where there wasn't a good cell phone signal. He got into his pickup truck and hurried down County Road 941, and as he drove, he tried again several times to call as he headed toward Rome. The calls continued to be unanswered; he still could only get Darlene's voice mail.

Vernon drove all the way to Walmart and rode up and down all the rows in the parking lot looking for Darlene's vehicle. When he didn't find it, he turned around and started back toward home, expecting that they could easily have missed each other en route. He hoped that Darlene would be at the house waiting for him when he arrived.

Vernon was talking to Heidi again, telling her he was nearly home and would let her know if her mother was there, when he saw a large crowd of emergency vehicles at the pasture entrance and down at the pond, with their flashing lights, blue and red, lighting up the dusk. He told Heidi what he could see up ahead, only a couple of miles from their house, and he told her, "I think Darlene's been hurt."

He didn't have time to give Heidi any further information; when the officers saw Vernon's pickup coming up the road, they stopped him and checked his identification. They immediately knew that he was the husband of the victim in the pond, and they detained him, loaded him into a patrol car, and transported him to the Cherokee County Narcotics Office on the other side of the county, in Leesburg, Alabama, for questioning. They did not give him any information other than to tell him that his wife had been hurt and they needed him to come with them so they could talk.

Chapter 6

At around 10:00 P.M., ABI agents Jason W. Brown, Brent Thomas, and Wayne Green arrived at the crime scene where the Cherokee County officials waited for them. They all immediately began collecting evidence and taking additional photographs with the help of ADFS investigator Mark Hopwood. Cherokee County coroner Bobby Don Rogers pronounced Martha Darlene Roberts dead at the scene, and her body was transported to Cherokee Medical Center, to remain until it could be turned over to the Alabama Department of Forensic Sciences for autopsy.

Severe weather was on the way for the overnight hours, and the officers tried to work as quickly as possible before the coming storms moved into the area. There would be much additional work to do during daylight hours on the following day if weather permitted at all, but the scene would need to be carefully preserved during the night. It was decided that several officers would spend the night at the pasture to keep the crime scene secure, and the work of searching for evidence would resume as early as possible, on the next morning. In the meantime, Vernon Roberts was being held a distance away, in law enforcement offices in the Leesburg City Hall, being questioned by two deputies, who had not yet told him exactly what had happened to Darlene. Vernon was not at all pleased at being detained, and he was getting more and more disturbed at being held without an explanation and interrogated. However, the officers were determined to uncover any inconsistencies there might be in his account of his whereabouts during the time before his wife's body was discovered.

Lieutenant Jimmy DeBerry and Cherokee County Drug Task Force commander Charles Clifton knew, like all law enforcement personnel, that the spouse is almost always the first person who falls under suspicion when a husband or wife has been murdered. They left no doubt that they expected not only cooperation, but a complete and detailed account of Vernon's activities for the entire day.

The handwritten statement, given by Vernon Roberts at 8:45 P.M., said that he and Darlene had gotten up that morning at six o'clock as usual, and Darlene left around 7:00 A.M. to pick up Heidi and give her a ride to work. Vernon left home around 7:10 A.M. on the way to Temple-Inland Paperboard and Packaging, Inc., in Rome, Georgia, where he and Darlene both worked in the same building and were scheduled on the same shift.

Vernon said that he left his office around 10:00 A.M. for a doctor's appointment and returned at noon in time to have lunch at the mill with Darlene and their friends Leesa Norton, Danny Alexander, and Lynn Willoughby. Vernon said that he returned to his office around twelve-thirty, and Darlene called him at four-thirty to let him know she was leaving work and planned to pick up Heidi, give her a ride back to her home, and then stop to get some groceries at Walmart on the way.

Vernon said that he went home from work and started the chores he had planned to get completed on that afternoon before his brother arrived for the weekend, and he said that Darlene called him to see if he needed anything from Walmart while she was there. After finishing his work and taking a shower, Vernon said, he was surprised that Darlene hadn't come home yet, and he grew concerned that Darlene didn't answer her cell phone. He called Heidi to see exactly what time her mother had dropped her off at home. He claimed that he told Heidi he was getting worried because he couldn't contact Darlene after repeatedly calling her, and he said that Heidi also had tried to call her mother and had no luck, either.

Vernon stated that he told Heidi he was going to look for Darlene; then he went to Walmart, didn't find her there or anywhere else on the way back from Rome, and headed home, only to be stopped on the road, detained by the officers, and brought to the Leesburg office for questioning.

Vernon then signed a waiver of rights, and the interrogation began in earnest.

Chapter 7

After confirming that his wife's name was Martha Darlene Roberts, Vernon answered the officers' questions with mostly the same information he had already given in his written statement. A few additional things came to light as he recalled details, such as a white convertible that came past his house while he was working on his chores, sometime between 6:00 and 7:00 P.M., turning around in the driveway of a house up the road, then driving back past the house, and a couple of shots he'd heard coming from the direction of the pond while he was outside the house, working on the pool. He believed, he said, that he'd possibly heard the shots after Darlene had called him for the last time, from Walmart.

"I didn't give it a thought," he said of the gunshots. "That area is just covered up with deer and turkey, and she wasn't late yet, so I didn't think anything about it."

Vernon also remembered seeing Williams and Sammons on the Gator.

"I saw the two guys on the Gator, and I thought

they were down there weedeating around the pond so people could fish better," he said, adding that Darlene's son, Benji, had talked about doing that same thing on one occasion, because the grass and weeds were very tall around parts of the pond.

"That's what I thought those guys were doing. I didn't care if they fished in that pond. It's not mine, so go ahead."

Vernon said that when he was stopped by the officers on his way home, "I knew there was something bad, wrong.

"Heidi called, and I said, 'Something's wrong, there [are] police cars all over, the ambulance . . .'

"Heidi is going to panic," Vernon said. "She was very nervous about her mother, when she wasn't able to get in touch with her. I went home thinking she'd probably be there already, but I got stopped. You said she'd been injured, but what happened? Did somebody shoot her?"

One of the officers said later that he had found it very odd that Vernon had not been more upset. He had not, at that point, been told whether or not his wife was dead, injured, or just exactly what it was that had happened to her, or why he was being interrogated.

"I just said to him that all I knew was that she was hurt bad," the officer said.

Heidi called Vernon's cell phone during the interview, and Vernon handed the phone to the deputy, who told her that she needed to come on over from Georgia, and the officers who would be there at her mother's home would explain to her what had happened when she arrived.

During the course of the questioning, Vernon had been becoming increasingly agitated, and as the questions grew more personal, tempers began to flare.

"What about another woman in your life?"

"Never!" Vernon answered emphatically. *"Never!"*

"Have you ever been in any trouble, or hit an ex-wife or anything?"

Vernon said the only trouble he'd ever been in was a charge of driving under the influence years earlier in Texas, and he'd never hit any of his wives. He had earlier reported his first wife as being Janice Dunaway, the mother of his two daughters, and his second wife was Barbara Ann Comeaux, who lived near Atlanta, he said. He and Darlene had been married for about four years.

"Who's mad at your wife?" Lieutenant DeBerry asked.

"Nobody," Vernon replied.

"Who's mad at your wife?" DeBerry shouted.

"Nobody!" Vernon shouted back.

"Somebody was mad at her and knocked her in the head! Did you knock her in the head?"

"No!" Vernon shouted. "I would never, ever hurt her, I cherished her with all my heart. We adored each other!"

Vernon claimed he would never be unfaithful to Darlene, no matter what.

"That's what makes me think that something's wrong," Clifton said. "Something might have happened today between you and her that might have caused you so much anguish. . . . There's no way, if you hurt this woman, that we're not going to find out."

"I told you on the way over here," Vernon said, "I worshiped that woman." He told the officers to have his hands tested for gunshot residue for having shot a gun that day. He and the officers then argued at length about whether he would get jealous if somebody hugged his wife, with DeBerry asking repeatedly if it would make him mad if a coworker or friend hugged his wife in front of him.

Vernon yelled, "My wife is injured and I'm sitting here listening to *this*? *This is crap!* I love my wife!"

Vernon was then asked if he'd found his wife with somebody else. He replied that Darlene had been taking antibiotics for a serious yeast infection.

"Do you think she'd try to be with anybody else like that?" he asked the officers, infuriated by their questions.

"There's no two people on God's earth that gets along all the time, never has a disagreement, never gets pissed with each other—it don't happen," DeBerry said. Vernon immediately disagreed, and said he and Darlene always got along.

"Now, if she's going to be okay and I ask her, will she say you never disagreed over anything? If there's something you need to tell us, tonight's the night. Extenuating circumstances could cause a man to do something he'd never do otherwise in a million years. We're offering you a chance to tell us now. Right now the district attorney will take everything into consideration—tomorrow'll be different. Right now, whoever hurt your wife is behind the event. They need to be out front of it."

Vernon talked again about his last call from Darlene when she called to see if he needed anything from Walmart.

"The last thing I told her was that I loved her," he said.

"Is that what you said right before you shot her, looked her in the eye and told her you loved her?

You told me you never let her out of your sight, that's what you said. Jealousy will eat you up. Now's the time to help yourself—"

"I told her that on the phone!" Vernon interrupted. "Look at the phone records! She called me on her cell phone from the Walmart parking lot! I'm not worried about Darlene being unfaithful. I love my wife. I didn't have to worry about not trusting her because we genuinely loved each other, not because I was jealous of her! You did say she was injured, didn't you?"

"I'm going to say she was hurt bad," the officer said, repeating his earlier statement.

Vernon showed Clifton and DeBerry how to bring up the last numbers on his cell phone to verify the calls he'd sent and received that day. Then, as tensions eased a bit, he said that he and Darlene had a good life, living out in the country.

"My second wife hated it and couldn't handle it," he said, "and she moved back to Texas."

Vernon was asked if he'd noticed a hard-cover black Dodge pickup in the area that day, or if he knew anyone who owned one, and he said no. Then he was asked if he owned a shotgun. His wife's son, Benji, had left one at their house when he moved out after living with them for a time, he said. Benji had taken the shotgun, which had belonged to Darlene's father, and he'd had the barrel sawed off. Darlene took it away from him and hid it somewhere in the house, Vernon said, but he did not know where it was.

When he was asked if he and Darlene had ever had any trouble with Benji, he said Benji and his mother had argued over his continuing use of drugs, calling it a "knock-down, drag-out fight," after which

Benji had moved out of their house and gone to live with his girlfriend in Rockmart, Georgia.

When asked if Darlene had any problems with her ex-husbands, Vernon said she did not. He made several disparaging comments about the character of one ex-husband, but he went on to say that she had never had "an ounce of trouble" from him. Her other ex-husband was the father of her two children, Benji and Heidi. There were no current problems with him, either, according to Vernon.

When the questioning concluded, Vernon agreed to his home being searched, and he was returned to the scene. A thorough search of the house, however, turned up nothing that could help with the investigation. So far, Vernon Roberts had an airtight alibi.

Chapter 8

Investigators spent a late night at work at the pond off County Road 941, with Investigator Mark Hicks, Lieutenant Jimmy DeBerry, and Chief Deputy Tim Hays staying overnight in the rain to protect the scene. The following morning, Jolly and his team, along with a large number of other officers, reported to the pasture at first light to begin searching the area for evidence again, starting to comb through the tall weeds looking for anything they had not been able to see earlier. Quite a few items had been collected the previous night, before it grew too dark to do a detailed search, but the deep, stamped-down layer of grass surrounding the pond could be hiding many crucial pieces of evidence, which would be more easily uncovered in the light of day.

Among the first and most obvious items that had already been recovered at the scene the previous evening were three shotgun shell casings, two blue and one red, and their wadding, found lying in the mud at the edge of the pond. Each piece was carefully bagged and labeled, to be tested for evidence in the event that the murder weapon was recovered. Some long strips of white cotton gauze had also been found and collected, one lying near the side of the Murano and one farther away, out in the field.

Most of the green plastic stretch film had remained looped around Darlene's neck when her body was removed from the pond, but a couple of additional smaller pieces were found floating in the water; those had rough, jagged edges and looked as if they could have been ripped away from the main piece of green film by the shotgun blasts. They were all recovered and bagged.

The Nissan Murano was processed for evidence at its impound location, Larry's Tire & Towing, in Centre, Alabama, by Investigator Jolly on the morning of April 7, along with Vernon Roberts's brown GMC 1500 pickup truck, which had also been impounded until it could be thoroughly checked for evidence. There was nothing inside the pickup other than some personal items, which included an umbrella, a jacket, and some papers. A couple of redbrown stains on the headliner and passenger-side doorpost proved to be inconsequential.

The Nissan Murano, however, yielded much more pertinent evidence, including Darlene's bags of groceries in the rear cargo area containing a receipt from Walmart in Rome, Georgia, dated 6:22 P.M. on April 6, 2006. There was also a recoil pad for the butt stock of a shotgun lying on the floorboard on the driver's side of the vehicle. A hair was adhered to the recoil pad, and it was carefully collected along with the pad.

There were several red-brown stains inside the Murano, and swabs were taken for analysis. They were located on the headliner, the door and steering wheel, and the passenger-side doorpost. Jolly also processed the Murano for latent prints, but none were recovered. Extensive photos were taken of both vehicles.

While Jolly photographed and collected evidence from the vehicles, the other officers continued to search the scene and found quite a few more items. Approximately ten feet from where Darlene's body was found, a chewed piece of gum lay on the bank of the pond. The back of a watch was also found lying nearby, and a broken bracelet—silver with pink stones—was found near the gate at the pasture entrance. Several other items, which would later prove to be unrelated to the case, were found at the pond, likely dropped there by some of the many people who had come there regularly to fish. There were also many footprints in the mud at the edge of the pond, but the water content of the soil was so high after the rain that the prints had very little definition, and photographs of the prints show them very blurred and containing standing water.

Two other items, which investigators believed would prove to be evidence in the case, had been found thrown out on the side of the road near the scene. Two traffic barriers marked *Floyd Co* with highway signs attached, one reading BE PREPARED TO STOP and the other MEN WORKING, were obviously the property of the road department in Floyd County, Georgia, and had very likely been picked up off the highway and transported over the state line into Alabama by someone other than Floyd County Road Department employees. They were tested for latent prints, but the Department of Forensic Sciences was unable to recover anything from them.

News of the murder of Darlene Roberts spread

quickly, both in Cherokee County and in Rome, Georgia, with the news media reporting in detail about the discovery of her body in the farm pond. Her coworkers at Temple-Inland were shocked to learn that Darlene had been killed only a short time after they had last seen her leaving work for the evening. Ralph Stagner, the Temple-Inland plant manager, told *Rome News-Tribune* and *Cherokee County Herald* staff writer Kathy Roe that Darlene had been liked and respected by both management and employees at the plant.

"She was a true professional," he said. "We are all deeply saddened by this, and we will miss her. Our thoughts and prayers go out to the family."

Cherokee County sheriff Larry Wilson gave the press as many details about the slaying as he was able to disclose at that point in the investigation, saying that his officers knew the type of weapon used, but they had not recovered it.

"We'll see if we can come up with a motive and a suspect," he said. "We want to talk to anyone, neighbors, anyone who may have seen something." Wilson said autopsy results were not expected for several days, and he was concerned that the heavy rain and severe weather, which was expected, might destroy crucial evidence.

On April 7 and 8, officers fanned out around the community, going house to house to talk with any of the area's residents who might have information. Several had already come forward to report seeing a black pickup truck with a hard bed cover in the area at the time, and others reported having heard shots. Most of those who saw the black truck had been able to give a description of its occupants, a large gray-haired man and a smaller woman with brown hair.

Some reported the two seemed to be fighting, and had seen the man hit the woman. Others reported that it looked as though the woman's face was red and she was crying.

Three of the officers conducted a roadblock on the morning of April 8 at the intersection of County Road 182 and County Road 941 in an effort to contact more possible witnesses. While there, one of the men, David Storey, noticed a garbage collection can sitting nearby with a bag protruding from it. Storey saw a paper sticking out of the bag with the name *Roberts* on it, and he and the other officers decided to check the bag in case it contained more evidence. A stained brown straw purse was inside, along with a pair of blue jeans and some paper towels that appeared to be bloodstained. They also found some blue masking tape with tan paint and what they believed to be bloodstains on it, with some hair stuck to it.

Those items, as it turned out, had no value to the investigation, since they had come from Vernon Roberts's home improvement projects on the day of the murder, but another item inside the bag did prove to be useful. It was the hangtag from a brown Rosetti viscose tote, a new purse Darlene had recently bought and had been carrying on the day of her murder. The straw purse found in the garbage can had evidently been discarded in favor of the new one that Darlene had bought during a shopping trip with Heidi a few days previously. Since the new Rosetti purse had not been recovered at the scene, officers now had a good description of exactly what kind of purse they needed to be looking for.

Later on the morning of April 8, the investigators at the scene decided to try to search for the murder weapon in the murky pond. They thought it might have been thrown in there after the shooting. It would require some special equipment, which was requested and was soon en route. While the officers waited for it to arrive, a partial pair of eyeglasses was spotted, almost completely hidden in the weeds and grass. The left arm, lens, and nosepiece of the glasses were collected by Investigator Mark Hicks and were turned over to the ABI for testing. This would soon prove to be the most important piece of evidence that would be found at the scene, and it provided the investigators with the break they needed to move forward very quickly with the case from that point. But until the analysis of the glasses was completed, there were still very many interviews to conduct and statements to be given.

Sheriff Wilson told the press that there were "some possibilities" for suspects in the murder, but he did not disclose any further details. The owner of the broken eyeglasses would soon be identified he knew, and then much more information on the suspects would be made public, and arrests in the case would soon follow.